"Simply brilliant. This book is a masterclass in creating the life you've always wanted. The true genius of it, though, is the way Lisa has distilled a lifetime of substantial spiritual teachings into 12 digestible keys. In the most approachable, playful, and practical ways imaginable, Lisa delivers on her promise to give you all the tools you need to step into a life of sustained joy and happiness. If you trust her, your life will be transformed, and how you see and interact with the world, yourself, and the people around you will be changed forever."

—THOMAS LLOYD QUALLS, award-winning author of *Happiness Is an Imaginary Line in the Sand* and *Painted Oxen*

"Lisa McCourt's newest instruction manual for living a life of joy is simply incredible. It is so rich with meaningful content and actionable steps! The depth of work presented here is clearly going to change lives, mine included. Lisa's wisdom is so heartfelt and accessible as she takes readers into a very deep dive into living what I could only imagine was God's ultimate plan for human beings. I know it was a labor of love that must have cost her on many levels, and I'm so grateful for her dedication to elevating love and joy in the world!"

—PAUL BOYNTON, bestselling author of *Begin with Yes* and other transformational books and teachings

"*Free Your Joy* has a clear message: joy is our natural state. This book is like a complete workshop that clearly explains how to remove all the clouds that stand between you and the sun of your natural state. However, it isn't just philosophy; the book is filled from beginning to end with exercises because, as Lisa puts it, learning joy is a path of doing. What stands out the most is the kindness on each page, as the author is such a genuine and understanding guide. It would be impossible not to change your energy and get closer to who you truly are after reading this."

—**CHRIS NIEBAUER,** author of *No Self No Problem: How Neurobiology Is Catching Up to Buddhism*

"Happy people don't just happen. They often struggle, suffer, and experience loss and defeat before they find their way out of the darkness and despair and back into the light. Then they can become a living, loving light for others who have lost their way. For millions of people across the world, Lisa McCourt is that light, and this book is that way . . ."

—**ROBERT MACK,** positive psychology expert, celebrity happiness coach, and author of *Happiness From the Inside Out*

"From time to time in her book *Free Your Joy,* Lisa will introduce an essential bit of wisdom with the words, "And to you, my darling reader . . ." and every time I read them, I felt as if she were placing a perceptive hand on my shoulder and gently asking me to pay attention. In those synchronistic moments, I received a wisdom offering that felt timely and needed. I know that as you read her brilliance, you will receive the perfect gifts for your heart as well."

—**DAVID AULT,** spiritual teacher and author

"Lisa McCourt has produced a clearly written guideline for anyone called to experience more consistent and greater joy in their lives . . . Simple, straightforward, and captivating . . ."

—**DR. STEVEN FARMER,** author of *Animal Spirit Guides, Messages from Your Animal Spirit Guides* oracle cards, *Earth Magic,* and *Earth Magic* oracle cards

"Thank goodness there is actually a manual for how to live a joyful life! There was a time in my life when I did not think it was possible to be joyful. I thought I was relegated to feeling blue all the time; in fact, I did not know I was low-key unhappy until I started feeling real joy. It was such a relief to realize this was something that I could change, and do, and learn. Lisa McCourt has given us the keys to the kingdom of joy. Hallelujah!"

—**LISA CAMPION**, author of *Awakening Your Psychic Ability* and other books

"Lisa has a gift for making the attainment of constant inner joy feel both doable and possible. The 12 Keys she explores reach deep inside and help reveal not only where your inner joy is hiding, but how to live day-to-day to nurture and nourish it in your life. Best of all, *Free Your Joy* makes you feel joyful, hopeful, and positive while even just reading it!"

—**SUMMER MCSTRAVICK**, author of *Stuff Nobody Taught You* and *Flowdreaming*

" . . . Dive into the pages of this transformative book and unlock the secrets to a joy-filled life . . . Say goodbye to stress and embrace a life of true fulfillment. Happiness is within reach, and this book will be your guide!"

—**ELDON TAYLOR, PHD, FAPA**, *New York Times* bestselling author

"Are we all looking for more joy in our lives but are so overwhelmed with the state of the world that we don't know where to find it? Then open this book and find your answers with the wisdom, humor, and contagious joy that Lisa McCourt can offer to you! Your soul and heart will thank you!"

—**KAREN DRUCKER**, musician, author, spiritual teacher

"Lisa carries the archetypal spirit of the mother, who is sincere in her quest to love everyone she meets into the fullness of their being. And she does this in the most innocent and tender of ways. Her teachings are always from the heart. Readers starved of affection and warmth from their own species will no longer be so when they read this book and allow themselves to receive Lisa's love."

—**a.h. walker,** mystic, poet, yogi

"Having worked closely with Lisa for nearly two years now, I can attest that her methods are solid, her joy practices are extremely effective, and she has made them as accessible in this book as any teacher ever could. She's a genuinely joyful being with an authentic desire to guide you to become one as well. I've watched her grow her intuitive gifts, which are immense, and which have made her group facilitation even more powerful than it already was. It is a privilege to teach with her and walk this path with her. If you follow the steps she's laid out for you here, there is a very good chance you'll transform your life."

—**VICTORIA SHAW, PHD, NCC,** author, spiritual teacher

"*Free Your Joy* is a truly wonderful roadmap for bringing your own innate joy to the surface. It is full of practical tools and insights that help you cultivate the experience and expression of the joy of life that sometimes mysteriously eludes us. And Lisa is the perfect facilitator to bring this material to us. Having owned a bookstore for many years, I interacted with numerous teachers and writers. Few of them embodied their message as Lisa does. When it comes to her, I would say that joy is her native language. It's who she is, and her passion is to help others find their joy."

—**DAVID CRONIN,** former owner of Changing Times Books and Gifts

Lisa McCourt

Bestselling Author and Founder of Joy School

FREE YOUR *joy*

The 12 Keys to Sustainable Happiness

Foreword by S.C Lourie

Health Communications, Inc.
Boca Raton, Florida

Library of Congress Cataloging-in-Publication Data
is available through the Library of Congress

ISBN-13: 978-07573-2452-9 (Paperback)
ISBN-10: 07573-2452-5 (Paperback)
ISBN-13: 978-07573- 2453-6 (ePub)
ISBN-10: 07573-2453-3 (ePub)

Publisher: Health Communications, Inc.
301 Crawford Blvd., Suite 200
Boca Raton, FL 33432-1653

Cover, interior design, and formatting by Larissa Hise Henoch

To my joy anchors—

Katy, Thalia, and David

Contents

• • •

ix

Foreword

...

As one who initially felt resistance to the hype around ideas of vibration and manifestation, I must admit that after reading *Free Your Joy* I am coming away with a completely different feeling about these universal laws. Lisa is a genuine advocate for joy, and after reading her book and getting to know her, I would in fact suggest she is a walking and talking embodiment of it and all she teaches. She is so loved and esteemed for all the light she brings to the world. From the first time I met her, I was quietly enraptured in her bright energy and just simply struck by the buoyant ambience she so effortlessly exudes. I went away from our first meeting so impacted by her presence that I wondered two things: Was she too good to be true? And if she was the real thing, how did she do it? How did she embody with such vibrancy something I am always looking for more of? Through our budding friendship I have been entirely persuaded that she is indeed the real thing, and by reading her book I now know how she has done it!

As Lisa so poignantly writes in the first key, "you can only heal you by loving you better." All her keys exude this truth that it is the only way to truly locate your joy, your potential, your magic, and your wellbeing. Lisa became the force of joy that she is through her commitment to these keys and to learning how to love herself better. And she will help you to do the same.

Lisa's reflections and comprehensive framework for manifesting joy in your heart, mind, and life comprise a wonderful and meticulous voyage into what I believe is the very fabric of the universe: love. It is all love. The joy-seeking, the practicing, the "kerklunks" (I love that word!), the observing, the insightful referencing and shout-outs to other writers and thinkers, the skill-developing, the manifesting, the flowing, the embracing, the vertical living. All of it! You might read through some of the pages and question whether what Lisa is suggesting is too good to be true as well. And in the same breath I can verify Lisa and the sustained sparkle in her eyes is all genuine and true, so, too, is her map for sustainable happiness. It's real.

The life you so deeply want is available to you, and the way toward it is through joy—the kind of sturdy and practical joy and self-love that shines through all the instructions in this book. Lisa answers all the how-to questions that might crop up as you read with logical, thorough, and inspired explanations. I agree wholeheartedly with her suggestion that you work at these ideas over the same generous period of time that you would give to any skill you want to develop. But it's almost like she's in your mind, ready for any questions or resistance that might emerge as you take her hand as your guide. She writes like she is walking right by your side, gently whispering that you can do this for your life, that you are worthy of the joy of your deepest dreams, that you are going to surprise yourself and will eventually make the good stuff happen.

Having been on my own self-love path of sorts for over ten years and having been on the lookout for any opportunity to garner more joy in recent ones, I have finished this book reminded of why I love this journey of homecoming so much, and with new perspectives on concepts that are also fundamental in my own life and work.

I never thought I would connect the dots like Lisa's words have guided me to do. I never thought I would ever read about one's vibration described in such a loving and integrative manner. But I'm now ready for joy to come alive for me in a new way. If you have picked this book up, then I imagine you are ready for that too.

—S.C Lourie, *The Power of Mess*

Acknowledgments

• • •

I owe a tremendous debt of gratitude to the teachers I've had throughout the many spirals of my journey, both the official and unofficial ones. Many are in these pages, and many more are written into the pages of my heart. Thanks to my created family of heart-sisters and heart-brothers cheering me on, I've found the courage to pull all the weird-seeming little threads that have led me right here.

I'm also mightily grateful to Christine Belleris and all the other talented HCI people who had a hand in bringing this offering to life, as well as to my much-loved Joy Schoolers who helped shape its contents and from whom I continue to learn every day.

I was able to write this book from the coziest happy place I could ever imagine writing from because I'm blessed beyond measure by my huge-hearted husband, David, and my remarkable daughters, Thalia and Katy. They provide, simply with their presence, my joy sanctuary of creativity and bliss.

And finally, I thank my cherished helpers from the other side, Polly Hogan and Bettye McCourt for their generous and ongoing guidance and love.

Preface

• • •

*I*f you're taking the time to read this preface (many readers habitually skip right to the meatier sections), then you and I are already simpatico. I would never skip the preface either. To me, it offers a tiny opportunity to know the author more deeply and knowing someone deeply is about my favorite thing ever. We are embarking on an adventure together, so I appreciate that you'd want to have this early chance to forge our connection.

I wrote this book because I couldn't *not*. I've been blessed with some extraordinary understandings, and I'm so bursting with these blessings that it physically hurts me to *not* share them. For several decades now, my existence has been organized around teaching the spiritual and energetic truths that transformed my life, because once your life has been transformed like this, there is simply no other use of your time that feels remotely meaningful.

Like many of us, I did not come from circumstances optimal for conditioning a human toward a joyful existence. I was born in a deep vibration of shame, internalized messages of worthlessness, and created an adult life anchored in those beliefs. I knew how to make it all look pretty on the surface, as many of us do, but there was no authenticity or depth, and no awareness that it could be any different.

I started glimpsing the truths I'm about to reveal to you several decades ago, but it took years to integrate and solidify them, and even more years to begin teaching them—first through workshops in schools and other venues and eventually through my live and online Joy School programs. I mention this because I've realized that a profound and lasting life transformation is not the kind of thing that happens in a weekend workshop, or from listening to that podcast, or reading that one book, or those twenty books for that matter. Each of these vehicles can provide valuable openings and frameworks, but as you'll see when we begin our journey, they are only pointers revealing what is possible. Learning a thing isn't living it, as convenient as that would be for us learning-lovers.

Learning joy is a path of *doing*. Walking a path means putting one foot in front of the other foot, again and again. I knew I must provide you with such a path because I've learned from experience that with the right guides and teachers, each step on that path moves you closer to a destination many barely believe is possible—an authentic, sustainable, joyful existence. The path ahead of you requires action on your part, and it is out of that action that your life will be transformed.

I've had countless cherished guides and teachers who have walked me down this path and you'll see them woven throughout these pages, often in their own words. I owe these teachers—many of whom have become my closest friends—everything. It's because they chose to devote themselves to raising awareness of these principles that I've been able to do the same. Thanks to their example and the generous sharing of their wisdom, I've created for myself a life of service that is joyful beyond anything I could have imagined. I encourage you to follow up with them via the Joy Kit available at LisaMcCourt.com. I created this online Joy Kit to give you easy access to all the light-bringers I mention in this book, as well as many other related resources.

You may have heard, "The path is not a straight line; it's a spiral." Becoming a deeply joyful human doesn't mean you won't have any more bad days, but once you learn to ride the consciousness spiral upward, you'll begin to appreciate even the challenging periods as ripe opportunities for exhilarating growth. Just in the past few years, I've faced devastating heartbreak with members of my family of origin, setbacks in helping my precious transgender daughter navigate her way in a world that is still horrifically cruel to ones as brave as she, and other difficulties that would seem to be thieves of joy.

Using the tools you're about to learn, I have transformed each of these challenges into invaluable opportunities for expansion and personal upleveling—to the extent that I'm truly, deeply thankful for them! I share this in case you're feeling like joy is the exclusive domain of those problem-free people out there. (Let me know if you find one!)

To be clear, joy is not a thing I'm going to help you create, chase, or manifest. It's already here. It is who you are, once you are free from all the obstructions that routinely block you from experiencing that truth. It's the step-by-step identification and gentle removal of these obstructions that I'm offering you in our upcoming time together.

As the obstructions are revealed and dismissed, your inner landscape is transformed, which then, in turn, transforms your outer landscape. In a recent meditation with my Joy Schoolers, lovely Sonya saw an image of a person encased in a suit of armor that resembled reptile scales, with the scales falling away, one by one, to reveal the tender, limitless human underneath. That's how this journey feels.

When I was pregnant with my first baby, I wrote a children's book called *I Love You, Stinky Face*. I wrote it because I was steeped in personal growth work at the time and starting to understand the crippling limitations inherent to unhealed trauma from buried beliefs of core unworthiness. I felt an overwhelming desire to save future precious beings from that egregiously common fate, so I wrote a book for parents to read to their offspring that I prayed would let these fresh humans feel, deep in their bones, how inherently lovable and valuable they are, no matter what. (The child in my belly when I wrote that book is my now-adult, beautiful and perfect transgender daughter. No coincidences in this wily Universe!)

Along with its nine sequels, it sold many millions of copies in the ensuing decades, and my fierce dedication to helping tender souls of all ages experience their wildly unlimited, joyful nature and inherent wonderfulness has only deepened since then. It's fueled many books like the one in your hands, and many iterations of my workshops, radio shows/podcasts, and Joy School trainings ever since.

I wrote this book because I know what it takes to create a life of peace and joy *despite it all*, and I desire that for you with every cell of my being. Darling adored reader, joy is nothing more than the comprehensive revelation of who you truly are.

Shall we get started?

Introduction

...

*"I never suspected that I would have to learn how to live—
that there were specific disciplines and ways of seeing the
world I had to master before I could awaken to a simple,
happy, uncomplicated life."*

—DAN MILLMAN

These are strange days. Our commitment to staying centered, loving, and peaceful is being challenged at every turn. Don't you wish you had a manual for not only surviving these challenging times, but transmuting them into fuel for exhilarating expansion and positive transformation?

Hey. Look at that. Now you do. (Well manifested! Good on you!)

We all want peace. We all want a life of joy and meaning. We want to feel blissfully comfortable in our own skin, moving through the world with grace and ease. But how many of us are actively taking the steps to create such a life? This is your opportunity to master these skills. You're embarking on an internal and external journey of shedding everything you're not, to uncover the joyful truth of who you are.

1

I've structured this journey with the intention that you'll spread it out over the course of a year. Naturally, I can't enforce this suggestion, so it will be up to you to set the pacing that's most effective for you. You'll be raising your personal vibration and improving your emotional health by practicing simple, pleasurable (mostly!) techniques that brighten your experience of each day. With every step in our journey, you'll feel more relaxed and positive, notice more balance and ease in your life, and manifest more of the things you desire. Whether you're starting from an all-time low point or just wanting to expand your already impressive capacity for living beautifully and meaningfully, these time-tested practices will quickly and consistently improve your ability to cultivate more aliveness, enthusiasm, and vitality in every area of your life.

Deep and lasting change is as simple as changing your vibrational address, and that's what we're about to do! Weekly suggestions and instructions for daily practices will transform your current default settings into constructive, beneficial new habits, with each step in the twelve-month journey building upon the previous step's foundation. These practices have been strategically designed to reinforce and solidify the most tried-and-true happiness principles found in ancient wisdom traditions as well as cutting-edge discoveries in the fields of psychology and science. Personal growth doesn't have to be monotonous, arduous work. It can—and should—be a gentle, self-loving, continual unfolding of your authentic essence.

Poet and philosopher Henry David Thoreau said, "As a single footstep will not make a path on the earth, so a single thought will not make a pathway in the mind. To make a deep physical path, we walk again and again. To make a deep mental path, we must think over and over the kind of thoughts we wish to dominate our lives."

This is the magic of the path you'll traverse! This is how the most profoundly effective life-upgrade principles become solidified as your default method for creating and experiencing your existence. You'll discover the powerful distinction between learning a life-changing concept or modality and mastering it.

Your life will be upgraded in two supremely valuable ways: First, you'll learn the art of genuine happiness (a rare skill most of us were never taught) and why it truly has little to do with your external circumstances. And second—because having desires and bringing them to fruition is a super fun thing we humans came here to do— you'll also learn how to get all those external circumstances you're after.

The combination of this internal and external journey is powerful beyond anything you're likely currently imagining. It is pure magic. I've used this magic to make my life amazing. I've used it to manifest love, money, beautiful surroundings, book sales in the millions, a deeply fulfilling career, a meaningful volunteer position contributing to my community, and countless other external realities I'm blessed to relish. But much more importantly, I wield these magic tools to shape and maintain my inner landscape. It's the inner landscape that determines the external one, darling reader. But only every time.

How did I build up this magic toolbox? First, through lots and lots of learning from pure, authentic masters of such things. But also, with tears—and blood and sweat (mostly the metaphorical kind, but no less gruesome). The culmination of all this is that I burst at the seams with desire to share the magic that has allowed me to recalibrate my setpoint for joy. Sharing this magic is what perpetuates my own joy, after all. And the good news is by now I've figured out how to skip most of the blood, sweat, and tears.

At Joy School, we define joy as living in full accordance with our true inner being. It's important to recognize that you are joy at your core. You came here as joy. The only reason you're not experiencing a deep sense of inner bliss and wellness in every moment is that you've got some stuff between your day-to-day you, and your true inner self—your inner being that is joy. We're going to clean all that up together. We're going to bring it up into the light, call it out for the flimsy nonsense it is, and let it go.

Joy is your birthright. And cultivating your own joy is the most unselfish, kind thing you can do for everyone around you, and for the world. So, if you've come here with any niggling little concerns about whether or not you even deserve to invest this bit of effort each week into raising your personal vibration, please, darling, let's set that aside. Your partner is tired of you looking to him/her/them for your joy. Your friends, your kids, your parents—none of them need the burden of contributing to your happiness. Happiness is 100 percent an inside job, and when you're taking care of yours, you have so much more to give to everyone around you. Everyone whose life you touch—from your inner circle to the kid making your deli sandwich—will have a better day when you are full from the inside, radiating that energy out around you, beaming it all over them. You're freaking sunshine, lighting up their lives. Sound good?

Our Feelings Aren't the Problem

Fluctuating emotions are unavoidable in this human adventure we've all opted to take, but they don't have to lead to suffering. Our suffering comes not from the emotions themselves, but from our resistance to them. Our feelings aren't the problem. It's the relationship we've established with our feelings that depletes our joy. And, to step it back even further, we think it's those things happening out there that create that bad feeling inside us—or that wonderful feeling, depending on what's happening out there. But the energetic truth is that what's going on *inside* you—what I like to call your inner landscape—is what's determining your *external* landscape. But only every time. Every single thing that's happening "Out There"—every bit of it originated "In Here." Okay, you can't see my hands, but I'm waving my hand out in front of me when I say, "Out There," and I'm pointing to my heart when I say, "In Here." See? Now it's like we're sitting here at my table having coffee together.

I know these are some big, kind of woo-woo statements. Maybe you're already of that ilk and that's how you found me. But if you're not, can you just hang in here with me for a bit? I promise there's a chance I can turn you. I don't have enough fingers and toes to count on them the skeptics who have come into my joy trainings with a far less-expanded viewpoint than the one they currently subscribe to. (And that comes with a huge uplevel to the joy.) There's real, hard-core science behind all of this, and I'll be sharing bits of it along our journey together.

I was talking about vibration with one of my podcast guests recently and she made a cool analogy about flying. You know how when the plane is flying at a lower altitude it's likely to be bumpy, with lots of turbulence? But when a plane's flying at a higher altitude it's smooth, stress-free, getting you where you want to go at top speed. Same for how we travel through life here. When our vibe is low—meaning we've got a lot of stress, anxiety, lethargy, or frustration pulling our personal vibration down—we'll get to our destination eventually, probably. But it'll be slow, uncomfortable, bumpy going, with a little juice splashed on our shirt. When we take the time and effort to elevate our vibration, it's smooth, pleasurable, and we get where we want to be much faster. This adventure will be about sustainably raising your vibration to fly at that higher altitude.

It's accomplished through commitment to installing new habits. Over time, these tiny daily decisions become full-blown, easy default patterns as the old falls away to make room for the new. The transformation shows up in all external areas—relationships, career, money—but most importantly, it shifts your inner landscape—the way you view and speak to yourself with that voice in your head.

Imagine you're making soup and you've heard about this best, most delicious soup recipe ever, and you're following the recipe, and you see that it insists you need to hold the spoon in your left hand to stir the soup. You think that's crazy, but the recipe says this is what makes all the difference, so you do it, even though it feels weird and you're rolling your eyes about it. Later, you eat the soup, and it is, indeed, the best soup you've ever had. You chuckle at the thought that stirring it with your left hand could have made any difference.

But the next morning you're getting your coffee and you playfully think, "I wonder what would happen if I stirred it with my left hand." So, you do, and the coffee does seem to taste extra amazing that morning.

Later that week you're making oatmeal, and you think briefly about stirring it with your left hand. But you're in a hurry, and as the thought passes through your mind you immediately dismiss it. You decide the soup had to have been that good because of the ingredients, the coffee the next day was probably just your imagination, and it was crazy to think the stirring hand had anything to do with it. And soon you're back to doing everything with your right hand because it just feels more natural and it was starting to take a lot of effort to notice and switch hands, and it probably was all hooey anyway.

This is human nature. This is what happens to most of us when we try to put some new, weird-feeling habit into our lives. How many times have you started a new practice like mindfulness, or healthful eating, or meditation, or personal boundary-setting, or fill-in-the-blank. Even when we recognize that we get good results, our default programming is so strong that most of us lapse back into our comfortable, familiar routines.

It's okay. We're human creatures, every one of us. Our habituated ways of doing things aren't even apparent to us; they've become the water we swim in. We hear people say we're "at choice," and we assume that on some level that must be true. But in the thick of things, it doesn't feel that way. It just feels *wrong* to stir soup with your left hand.

But guess what? People can change their hand dominance. It's been done millions of times by regular human beings. If you had a reason to, you could get just as proficient with your left hand as you are with your right hand. Or vice-versa if you're a leftie. All it would take is dedication and practice.

If you were going to attempt to change which hand is your dominant one, the first thing you'd need to do, throughout your day, is notice when you're using your right hand. All those tiny moments—opening a door, scratching your head—when you, without thinking, use your right hand to do something instead of your left. Noticing those moments, becoming the observer, would be the first step. It's the first step in changing your default thinking, too.

We're not going to change your hand dominance. We're going to change your thought-pattern dominance. You have default ways of thinking that are lowering your vibration and keeping you from living as the joyful creator you naturally are at your core, your true essence, your soul being. It's not an overnight process to go from one habituated thought pattern to another. But it also doesn't have to be unpleasant, exhausting work. It can even be joyful when we take our time and know how to hold the right kind of faith in the process. This is what we'll be doing together.

You'll change these habits by introducing "homeplay" into your life each week. "Homeplay" is my name for the *doing* suggestions that will go along with the theme of each of the 12 "keys" to sustainable happiness. It's up to you, of course, how much you decide to throw yourself into your homeplay, but it's important to understand that it's the *doing* of joy practices that elevates your vibration. Not the reading about them. Not the learning. Not going on that weekend retreat or taking that online workshop. Those are cool parts; those can give you a temporary lift and some glitzy "aha" moments, but it's the repetitive *doing*—right there in the thick of your regular life—that changes the sustained default setting on your energetic state. In Joy School we call this ongoing default setting your "Joy Setpoint." Every one of us has this setpoint, a spot of homeostasis where our joy comes to rest. We might get it bumped up here and there; we might feel it dip down here and there, but there's a level of overall, baseline happiness that feels natural to us, and that's where we're going to continue to level off until we learn the skills for sustainably elevating that setpoint. I cannot overstate how powerful these homeplay processes will be for you.

There are twelve keys to unlocking joy that you'll be exploring. Each is presented in its own chapter, with the intention that you spend a full month practicing each key before moving on to the next. (Of course, I have no way of enforcing this pacing; it is simply a suggestion to allow optimal integration.) Each chapter will introduce you to that month's vibration elevation focus, along with instructions for four different weeklong homeplay practices that go with the theme. Most months do not have precisely four weeks, so you're invited to be loosey-goosey and follow your own intuition when planning your month around these practices. One of the keys you'll be mastering is flexibility, so this is a chance to practice that! You'll use any extra days of that month as additional practice time for whichever homeplay suggestions felt most meaningful to you during the preceding weeks, or you might decide to combine them all! Please do not ever feel that the end of a week or a month means you should discontinue the practices you've been focused on. My hope is that every one of them will become a regular part of your life. When you see how powerful they are, I'm sure you'll want that, too!

Why a Year?

You might be anxious to get your joy on, and be wondering: why a year?

I've spent my entire adulthood learning deep spiritual truths that have the power to dramatically change lives, and then teaching those truths in myriad ways. I can't tell you what a passion and calling this is for me. I wake up every day feeling wildly blessed to have been able to structure a fine career around these passions. And here's the realization that has sunk in along the way: I used to think my foremost goal was to find ways to save you time and effort in your spiritual journey. I truly believed if I could just gather up all the pieces, and sift out the most amazing nuggets, and offer these nuggets up to you, all polished and artfully assembled—through my Joy School or through my podcast or my books—that I could save you the years of trial-and-error, one-step-forward/two-step-back frustrations that defined my own journey.

I was right. But only to an extent. Because this is just simply not fast work, sweet reader. Integration takes time, and there is nothing that can be done about that. I can promise you, beyond any doubt, that if you embark on the journey I'm laying out for you with sincerity, commitment, and a genuine desire to live more joyfully, these steps will result in a dramatically elevated Joy Setpoint one year from now. And you'll see beautiful, notable effects all along the way! But I don't advise trying to rush the process. If I could have authentically written a book promising a sustainably elevated Joy Setpoint in one month, I would have done it. But I've been in this field long enough to know what works, and I really want you to have what works. Changing long-held, deeply ingrained habits is completely doable, but only when a realistic timeframe is applied to that goal.

You'll be offered many tools as we move along together, and some will resonate more than others. There's a rule of thumb in personal growth work that says the suggestions to which you initially feel most resistant are usually the ones that will yield you the greatest results. There's truth to that, yet one of the things you'll be working on is developing a heightened connection and trust with your own intuitive guidance. Therefore, my bottom-line advice is to trust your own sense of what will be most meaningful for you (while keeping in mind that it might be the activities to which you feel the most resistance!) You'll be learning ways to discern the voice of your true inner knowing from the other voices in your head, but for now, whenever you feel resistance to something I'm suggesting, begin the practice of putting your hand to your heart and asking: "Is this resistance coming from my highest inner knowing?" Then, openly, honestly, sense the answer. It's a simple practice, but you'll be surprised at how reliable and powerful it can be when you've honed it for a while.

What I'm hinting at (without directly encouraging it!) is that it's okay to sidestep some of the homeplay suggestions I give you. Depending on where you are emotionally and energetically, some may feel more overwhelming to you than others. As you progress in your journey of elevating your Joy Setpoint, you'll simultaneously be upleveling your trust in your own beautiful intuitive knowing. Only you know what you're ready to take on, which is why no book (including this one) can ever prescribe exactly what's best for you at a given moment in time. Only your own precious soul has that intel, and that's why you'll have a wide array of tools and practices to try out and choose from as you go through this journey. (And there's always the next lap around the spiral for those practices that you might not be ready for right now.)

Here's an example: I was recently part of a small mastermind group where our shared intention was to elevate our consciousness in order to be even more effective leaders and teachers. The plan entailed a multipronged approach, and one of the strong suggestions was to raise the vibration of our physical bodies by consuming an all-organic, raw, plant-based diet. On paper, it made sense, and in many respects, I was attracted to the reasoning behind it.

But here's the thing: I'm not the meal planner or food preparer in my household. My beautiful husband is—among many other amazing things—a hobbyist chef and foodie. He takes great delight in feeding me in ever more creative and delectable ways. It's a big part of our daily joy together. We don't indulge much in empty food or anything that feels insulting to our physical health and vitality; we simply take great pleasure in enjoying a wide array of mostly healthy, nourishing, delicious foods. So, when I felt into what it would mean to limit his culinary canvas so significantly, I decided to ignore that particular aspect of the consciousness-raising program.

Would I have experienced even better results had I tried out the diet prescribed by that program? Probably. Maybe one day the time will be right for me to incorporate that practice into my consciousness-raising routine, and maybe I'll look back then and wonder whatever took me so long to be ready for that step. For now, I ended up exceedingly pleased with the overall experience in that group, and I did it while following my own soul's guidance. That's the kind of self-reliance I'm suggesting for you as we progress through this year-long journey. (And don't worry; I won't be messing with your food.)

Joy Is Already Here

There's a shift in perspective I want you to try on right now and hold in your heart to the extent you're able. Even though I'm promising you an elevated Joy Setpoint a year from now, it's important for you to know in your bones that your joy is already here. It's been here all along. What we'll be doing all year is not about manifesting or creating joy out of nothing, but simply about uncovering and revealing the boatloads of available joy that is already at your fingertips.

Take a moment right now to feel into this. What if there's nothing at all keeping you from the blissful existence that is your birthright other than some malleable habits we're about to shift? It's true, and this will become clearer as we move along together.

Paulo Coelho has famously said, "Life is a long pilgrimage from fear to love." But the pilgrimage is only one of perception. The love has always abundantly surrounded you, albeit eclipsed to varying degrees by the fear. You are love. You always have been. You can sub out "love" for "joy" here. Potato, potahto.

I'm going to ask that, before you move onto Key 1, you procure a beautiful journal and something you love to write with. Even if you think you're a terrible writer, or just don't think you want to participate to this extent in the upleveling of your joy, I'm humbly insisting you comply with this request. No one needs ever to see what you write, and there is zero expectation that it be grammatically correct, sense-making, or remotely literate. In many ways, it's even better if it's not! This journal will be a critical tool for connecting with a part of you that has likely been shut down for a long time. You might doodle in it. You might rip up some pages. You might lay down words, or you might scribble-scrabble a bunch of shapes and nothing-blobs. Just please make use of the tool. You'll soon see it as the invaluable communication device that it is.

Often, I'll ask you to read a prompt, drop into your heart, and then immediately spend some time writing down whatever impressions surface for you. When we do these exercises, please remove all expectations of yourself. Don't worry about capturing every little thing. Trust that the important things are the ones that come to you as you're writing. Do not wait to write until you know what you're going to write, that's the journaler's #1 rookie mistake. Just start writing something, anything, and that will open the valve for whatever wants to come through. Try not to stop. Don't correct anything or worry about spelling or grammar or making it pretty or spiritual. Just flow. Give yourself plenty of time.

At times, we'll be doing some visualizing. Please don't freak out about that. I know there are people who don't "see" in their mind's eye as clearly as others, and I don't want you to worry if you consider yourself to be one of those. There's a fancy name for it: "aphantasia," the inability to voluntarily visualize images in one's mind. When I ask you to imagine something, just tap into the feeling of that thing. However you experience that is perfect. There are only two rules:

1. Do not second-guess whatever first comes to you. It does not need to make sense to you. Don't push it aside to look for something better. Whatever occurs to you first, just go with it.

2. Understand that it will feel like you're making it up. That's fine. That's what intuition feels like, so you can go ahead and get used to that feeling. If you feel like you're getting "nothing," go ahead and *make it up*.

You Are the Microcosm Affecting the Macrocosm

Spiritual leaders have always told us the very best thing you can do to bring more light to the world is to turn up the light within yourself. I know that you already embrace this wisdom because you've found your way to this book and that means you're part of this global tribe in which we've made the decision to deliberately elevate our vibration together. Please know that you are joined in this intention by millions around the globe (with representation in dozens of countries on every continent except Antarctica via my *Do Joy!* podcast.)

Viewed through a certain lens, it could seem like a luxury to focus on joy during these turbulent times. I get that. I'd love for you to want it just for you—to love yourself that much—but I know a lot of us harbor conditioning that says it's selfish to think about our own happiness, especially when others are suffering. That's why I want you to additionally understand that your vibration affects every person you encounter throughout your day—in large ways and in miniscule ways. In person and online. Through everything from Zooms to texts to social media posts.

And you really have no way to measure how much impact your vibration is going to have on another person because the fact is we are all vibrationally sensitive to the energy of those we encounter to varying extents. We call those who are especially sensitive "empaths," but wherever you fall on that spectrum, you are absorbing frequencies from those around you all day long, and they're absorbing yours. To varying degrees, this is the case for your nearest and dearest; for the checkout clerk you interact with at the drug store, the guy who steps into the elevator you're on. Every person is an energetic entity, and energy affects energy. And then it just ripples out from there. Endlessly. This is what we scientifically know at this point in our human evolution.

That's why there is no clearer energetic truth than "If you want to change the world, you must start by changing you." As within, so without. You are the microcosm affecting the macrocosm. In every moment. In every way.

Your joy is needed on the planet right now. Perhaps more than ever.

KEY 1

Awaken the Observer

"*The privilege of a lifetime is to become who you truly are.*"
—CARL JUNG

There are some things you need to know right off the bat. Before I lay the joy banquet out upon the table for you, we need to clear the table, wipe it down, and artfully drape a pretty tablecloth on it. Since joy is our feast, let's talk about the definition of joy.

In interviews, I'm often asked about the difference between joy and happiness. You probably have a sense already that they're not the same thing. Happiness is a lovely state of being, but it's not likely that you will embody it at all times. It is possible, however, to maintain a baseline of joy. At Joy School, we embrace all of our emotions—even the ones that we don't readily think of as joyful. When we stop resisting emotions that are a perfectly normal and healthy part of being a human creature, they all have an undercurrent of joy in them. You can be sad, and not judge your sadness, or make it wrong, or feel embarrassed by it, or try to suppress it. You can be angry, or grieving, and feel a rightness and healthy release in those emotions. It's always our resistance to our natural feelings that causes us to suffer from them. When we don't make our emotions wrong, they have the opportunity to flow through us, and that's just what it means to be vibrantly alive.

Another foundational principle we work with in Joy School is this ancient truth: you, at your core—your essence, your soul—are supremely joyful, peaceful, and unlimited in your power to create. This is true when it comes to creating your art, your writing, your music, origami, pillow forts, whatever's your creative jam. And more importantly, it's true when it comes to creating your life. You create your relationships, your career, your home, your abundance, your spiritual evolution—every teeny, tiny aspect of your life is being created by you in every second that you're living it. So, when I talk about creativity, just know I'm talking about it primarily from this second perspective.

The Obstructions

Here's the glitch: even though it's true that you are wildly, unimaginably joyful and limitlessly creative at your core, it's equally true that you likely have some obstructions in the way of you consistently accessing and living from that core essence. From the Joy School perspective, "healing," "evolving," and "elevating consciousness" are all just other names for identifying and releasing these obstructions.

I've come across a few people who seem afraid of the word "healing" when used in the context of evolving and personal growth (as opposed to healing your physical body, which most everyone's cool with). I think that's because of some of the popular methods out there. I won't name names, but if you've ever enrolled in one of those full-immersion, tough-love weekend experiences, you know that it can be pretty terrifying! And word gets out about that. I'm sure those programs have been effective for lots of people—*and*—I also know firsthand that it doesn't have to be like that. I've gone the full distance with all of those, as well as many programs that are far more gentle and compassion-based. My experience is that the latter are much more effective and long-lasting than the former. You don't have to re-experience your trauma to heal it; you don't have to slay your inner demons head-on like a protagonist in an M-rated video game. There are much better ways to do it. And it takes some time, sure. But that's how it should be.

My point is that you can only ever heal you by loving you better. Starting with wherever you are with it right now, you work to uplevel that. Then you uplevel it again. And again. It feels so good, and becomes so easy, that you simply never want to stop. You are, in truth, never in need of healing anyway because you are already divine perfection. All that ever needs to be "healed" are the misconceptions that keep you from that recognition.

"Kerklunk" is the fancy term I use in Joy School for that gorgeous, sacred moment when an idea, a concept, some bit of knowledge you might have come across dozens of previous times, goes solidly *kerklunk* from your headspace down into your heart, your soul, your bones. Down into that place where you're *changed* by it because it's not just intellectual anymore. This is where it needs to be for it to shift your default patterns in how you think, how you respond, and what your body chemistry does with stimulation from the outside world. No intellectual understanding is going to do that until it *kerklunks* for you. Sometimes, it happens from hearing it in a new way or hearing how someone else has applied it to their life. That's what happens in my online groups all the time, so I'll be sharing the experiences of my Joy Schoolers with you throughout this journey together. Most kerklunks happen after repetitive exposure to the concept or idea, so we'll be hitting the biggies from a few different angles to ensure your kerklunks. The best part is, there's always a *next-level* kerklunk you can get to, which just keeps the whole never-ending process fun and spicy! In Joy School, we call it "spiraling," because an upward journey toward elevated consciousness typically involves looping through the same powerful principles again and again, each time from a greater level of awareness and integration. (You may have seen the term "spiraling" used in a negative way to indicate an out-of-control spiral toward *less* consciousness. For our purposes together, please know I use "spiral" to reference this point that we evolve our consciousness in upward spirals as opposed to linearly.)

I'm setting the intention right now that you'll get more kerklunks in the coming year than you could ever imagine. I want you to set that intention with me. That means even if I start talking about something you've heard before, I invite you to approach it with what Buddhists call "beginner's mind." It's so tempting and convenient to sort incoming information into those files we've already established in our minds instead of staying curious about what new insights might emerge. We want to see the world in black and white, but I promise you, it's a wild rainbow world with limitless hues to explore!

I have a little cheat-tool for getting into beginner's mind that I invite you to use. I call it the Etch A Sketch method. Remember using an Etch A Sketch when you were a kid? Call up an Etch A Sketch in your imagination right now and go crazy with

• • •

"In the beginner's mind there are many possibilities, but in the expert's there are few."
—SHUNRYU SUZUKI

those two dials so you have just a hodgepodge-y, wonky, line-filled screen. Those lines represent all the stuff you believe you *know.* Now imagine that line-filled screen, and then gently shake it until all the lines fade away into that weird silvery sand, and you're left with a blank, gray void. That's the space you want to be in for our processes during your joy journey. As you notice any thought arise that pulls you out of experiencing the moment with fresh eyes, just gently shake the Etch A Sketch and watch the old thought dissolve.

Intention-setting is one of the many tools that will become habit for you in the coming weeks and months. You are creating your life, in every moment, with the energy you send out. Another way to understand that is to understand that you create based primarily on your expectations. Whatever you expect, in essence, is going to be what you create as your reality.

It's not the easiest thing to authentically shift your expectations; that's why it's a skill to be practiced. I often say in Joy School, "Your subconscious isn't an idiot." You can't just declare, "I expect to have ten thousand additional dollars in my bank account one month from now," and have that happen, because if it's not what you authentically believe, then it's not the energy you're sending out, no matter what words or affirmations you're speaking, or how many times you say it. But with tools, with intention, with practice, you *can* authentically shift your expectations.

Let's practice the skill of intention-setting right now by setting an intention that your experience with this book is going to create powerful, potentially miraculous results in your life. A part of you already believes that or you wouldn't be reading this right now, so we're just giving some strength and support to that part of you, so it can be right.

Call up your Etch A Sketch, make all those crazy lines, and let that magical erasing sand do its thing. Then settle into a still, imaginative state. Take this moment to set an intention around whatever you hope to have shifted one year from now. You do this simply by using your imagination to create a vivid representation of this goal. Once you have that vision (or feeling) in your heart and mind, tap into the *emotion* it creates for you. Notice how your focus and attention creates the experience of the emotion itself. Deliberately crank up that emotion. You have the ability to do that, simply by imagining and/or recalling what that emotion feels like.

Whenever we have a desire, it's not the thing itself we're really after; it's the emotion we believe that thing will bring us. Notice how just by holding this vision you're able to feel that emotion's presence in your body. When you tap into the feeling state you've decided you want to experience more of in your life, you activate that frequency within your energetic self. That's how you attract and generate more of the feelings you want to have. We'll be using this tool all year.

That emotion exists within you. It's a part of you, as valid as any other part, and there's no reason for you not to choose to activate it. You're used to basing your feeling state on what is going on around you, but you're about to unlearn that inconvenient habit. I invite you to revisit that emotion via imagining the scenario of your joy expectation, as often as possible.

Your Cork Wants to Float

You are a vibrational being swimming through a vast field of vibration. You have a mix of negative and positive signals you've been sending out, which have seeded your world and resulted in your current reality, with all the yum and all the yuck that entails. If this energetic truth brings up any hint of self-blame or self-incrimination, you need to let that go, and please continue to do so throughout our journey. While it's true that you've undoubtedly created some unwanted circumstances in your past (and likely in your present), this is *never* a reason to blame or judge yourself. It's possible your soul knew exactly what it was doing when it created challenges for you because quite often, we can look back and see how our challenges were our greatest blessings, even when we didn't experience it that way at the time. Many spiritual masters teach that we even plan out the challenges we'll face as perfectly orchestrated opportunities to grow and evolve our souls. Please hold in your heart the truth that every one of us creates yuck alongside the yum; it's part and parcel of the human experience.

The good news is that the yum—the good, high vibration energy—represents your most natural state. Your cork wants to float. To quote Rumi, "Your task is not to seek for love, but merely to seek and find all the barriers within yourself that you have built against it." Again, you can sub out the word "love" for "joy" here—it's really all one and the same.

As I've mentioned, in Joy School we travel two parallel paths. The first path is about that inner landscape—learning the art of true, authentic peace and contentment and living vibrantly as your whole, precious self. Nobody's ever taught us that skill; that's just how it is at this point in our human evolution. So, that first path, that's the important one. But at the same time, we travel the parallel path of mastering manifestation. Not because checking off those accomplishments and getting all that stuff Out There is what's going to make us happy. It's not. All of that is just an ever-morphing, dangling carrot at the end of the stick.

We're not looking to uplevel our external circumstances because our happiness depends on it. (It doesn't.) We do it because deciding what we desire and bringing those desires into fruition is fun. It's juicy! It's what we humans came here to do, not just sit all enlightened on a mountaintop all day. We came here to *do* a human life, which means wanting stuff and getting it—wanting to create things and creating them.

I reference these two parallel paths because, conveniently, we make headway on both paths by pretty much the same process: the process of untangling and dismantling those obstructions between the day-to-day *you* that you experience yourself as, and that core, *truest* you that is pure joy and unlimited creative power.

You may be wondering, what will joy look like?

Whatever intention you set for yourself in that previous little imaginative exercise is giving you a pretty clear snapshot of what you believe your *external* joyful reality would look like. Romance and relationships, money and career success, leisure pursuits, accomplishments, homes, toys . . . these are the kinds of things we typically assume will make for a joyful life. Maybe you set an intention for some of those, and maybe you set an intention for more intangible qualities like more confidence, more inner peace. Maybe you had a mix. Whatever you chose was perfect. Your desires are reflections of where you are at this moment in time, so no desire should ever be discounted or judged by you.

And . . . I'm going to invite you to also consider a different kind of snapshot of your joyful life—one that is less externally visible, but far more lasting and potent. The following inner qualities are the ones you'll be cultivating throughout this coming year. They may not seem as exciting as what you came up with in your manifestation visualization, but I promise you they will do more to raise your Joy Setpoint than anything else. (And—spoiler—an elevated Joy Setpoint is what will bring in all those external things you want to manifest anyway.)

These are the inner qualities of an elevated Joy Setpoint and mastering them is what allows you to become the energetic magnet that will quite effortlessly pull in all of those external circumstances you'd like to create. Maybe that sounds a bit suspect to you right now. You'll see what I mean soon enough, when the magic starts showing up in your life. The synchronicities, the windfalls, the "chance encounters." You don't even have to believe in this magic for it to work for you.

HOMEPLAY FOR KEY 1, WEEK ONE

It's time to introduce your very first homeplay assignment!

Read over each of the qualities described below and spend this first week observing yourself in relationship to these characteristics. At any point in the week, when you feel you have a clear picture of where you stand in relationship to this trait, write the name of the trait in your Joy Journal and give yourself an honest rating to indicate where you are right now with this characteristic. It might fluctuate from day to day, so do your best to average it out and record where you stand overall at this point in your life.

Put some care and attention into your ratings this week; this is how we'll measure your progress later. In your Joy Journal, write the name of the trait and do some self-observation to give yourself a rating from 0–10 to describe where you fall. If you do not possess this capacity at all, you'd score a 0. If you possess it in spades, you'd rate a 10.

Here are the qualities that comprise an inner landscape of joy:

1. GROUNDED SERENITY

You might already associate joy with a deep sense of inner peace and tranquility. As we've discussed, this perfectly describes who you already are in your core essence. Perhaps you have moments throughout the week when you glimpse it. And perhaps there are many circumstances you encounter that seem to rob you of your peace.

Developing the capacity of grounded serenity entails building the muscle of authentic nonreactivity. It's not about struggling to keep your emotions in check or keeping a cool head. You won't find any recommendations here that entail denying or repressing your authentic feelings. It's about expanding your genuine trust that all is well and as it should be, no matter what situation arises. Even if it sounds like a fairy tale right now, I assure you it's a muscle that can be strengthened and a tremendous game-changer for your Joy Setpoint and your calmness of mind and heart.

Think about an average day for you. How often do little (or sometimes big) things pull you off your energetic center? Are you frequently frustrated? Annoyed? Agitated? Emotionally exhausted by people or circumstances that bug the hell out of you? All of this drains you of your precious energy, your chi, your life force. Whether this drain takes the form of angry outbursts or small emotional papercuts you try to hide, it's an unnecessary depletion of your valuable energy. Observe yourself throughout the week and decide where you rate on consistent grounded serenity. Record your rating in your Joy Journal.

2. PRESENT MOMENT IMMERSION

I'm sure you've been exposed to concepts of mindfulness and the art of being fully present to whatever the current moment is offering you. Eckhart Tolle has famously dubbed it "The Power of Now," and we'll be taking this concept to a juicy new level in the coming months together.

For now, just call to mind a typical day, and rate yourself on where you fall in terms of your capacity to be fully present throughout the day's various activities. In that interaction with your boring client or demanding child, for instance, does your attention go to the voice in your head, or stay fully focused on the person in front of you? Do you covertly scroll social media during tedious online meetings? Do you miss the scenery on the way to work because you're planning out the day in your mind? When in conversation with others, are you mentally rehearsing what you'll say next, or do you fully consider what the person is expressing in that moment? No judgment. We've all been there. Just see where you honestly stand on this and record your rating in your Joy Journal.

3. THE NAMASTE LENS

In my book *Juicy Joy*, I talked about installing the "Namaste Lens." Simply put, Namaste means "The divine in me recognizes and honors the divine in you." For those who have mastered this Eastern perspective, it's natural to love and honor all people with all their limitations. It's only our fears and protections that keep us from allowing ourselves to feel and extend that love.

You've probably heard the classic analogy about how holding resentment toward someone is like eating poison and expecting the other person to die, in that it harms the holder of the resentment far worse than the person being resented. In a similar vein, your soul-self wants to love everybody. It feels good to love. It doesn't feel good to judge and dislike people. Loving everyone doesn't mean you have to be in relationships with everyone. You can be honest with the people in your life regarding how much time you want to spend with them and what you want the nature of your relationship to be, while still loving every one of them.

I'm sure there are people in your life who make this practice easy, and there are probably a few who make it hard. On average, how well do you live the principle of Namaste and view those you encounter through the Namaste Lens? Give yourself a rating and record it in your Joy Journal.

4. UNWAVERING FAITH

Do you believe the Universe has your back? When things go wrong, do you rail against the situation, or deeply trust that every setback is an opportunity for something better to happen? Are you afraid of looking like a Pollyanna if you were to take that approach, or has life shown you that holding that perspective opens the portal to miracles?

Albert Einstein said that the most important question anyone can ask themselves is "Is it a friendly or unfriendly universe?" He knew that how you answer that question would determine everything you experienced. As we will be exploring together, we are always creating our next reality, based primarily on our deep-down expectations. People who expect to be disappointed, generally are. People who authentically expect to be delighted, generally are. You can't fake expectations, and that's why this work requires some dedication to new habits.

We'll get there. For now, just honestly look at how often you expect negative things to occur, as opposed to how often you truly expect wonderful miracles to unfold. In your Joy Journal, rate yourself from 0–10 on your level of Unwavering Faith.

5. LOVING THE QUESTIONS

"Perfect confidence is granted to the less talented as a consolation prize." —ROBERT HUGHES

In the words of my precious heart-brother Scott Stabile, "It's incredibly freeing to acknowledge my own ignorance, and to let go of the compulsion to be right at all costs. What a gift it is to be brave enough to say, 'I don't know,' and braver still to admit 'I was wrong.'" (You'll hear from Scott frequently on these pages because I adore how he expresses these truths.) Most of us like to be right. It's pretty much ingrained in us from early childhood. But this oh-so-human tendency is robbing you of tremendous joy! As you practice the suggestions in this book, you'll loosen up your desire for certainty and relax into the absolute thrill of uncertainty! Life is far more exciting when we're open to new knowledge, new opportunities, and experiences of novelty that our former selves would not have considered. Clinging steadfastly to your old beliefs and paradigms has created a false sense of safety for you, but you'll soon see that true humility and wide-open wonderment is far more conducive to a joyful life.

My talented wordsmith friend Thomas Lloyd Qualls says it like this: "We are supposed to question; it makes our faith authentic. Those who are afraid to question their beliefs tacitly admit the weakness of them. Those unwilling to acknowledge the possible validity of truths beyond their own, become rigid to the natural flows of life."

Right now, how easy is it for you to question your own beliefs and opinions? How likely are you to change your mind about important issues as you learn more about them? How comfortable do you feel in situations where you don't know the answer, or where your version of the answer is questioned? Rate yourself from 0–10 on how easy it is for you to be "wrong" or uncertain about something. Record your rating.

6. TRUSTING YOUR VIBES

Intuition. We all have it, but very few on the planet use it to the extent to which it's available. Trusting your vibes may sound similar to "being right," as described above, but it's actually the opposite. Many, many, many of the "beliefs" we subscribe to are not truly our own. We've inherited these understandings from our caregivers, our culture, and the societies we grew up in. We don't realize how arbitrary our belief system is because it's become the water we swim in.

Our conditioned mind wants to think we know what's what on this crazy planet at this crazy interval in time. But, as we'll soon be discussing in depth, we are just swimming through a sea of perceptions that are uniquely our own, based on the experiences we've had so far. Objective reality is a unicorn. None of us are experiencing it. Trusting your vibes means learning a new way to interpret the world around you. It's not an easy task to dramatically expand your habitual perception filter, but your joy depends upon it. Only when you are able to experience your life without the intrusion of this perception filter will consistent, daily joy reveal herself to you.

"Do not grow old, no matter how long you live. Never cease to stand like curious children before the Great Mystery into which we were born." —ALBERT EINSTEIN

As life unfolds, do you believe that your inner wisdom will always guide you (from the highest source of your knowing) about which direction to take or how to move forward in each circumstance? Right now, what is the extent to which you notice, trust, and act on your intuitive hunches and feelings, as opposed to the established "facts" you believe you know about something? Rate yourself in your journal.

7. IN THE FLOW

Many of us are planners. We like to have a sense of what's coming up next for us, and we especially like to be driving the bus that's taking us there. How comfortable are you when things don't go as you expected or planned? The rained-out picnic, the canceled meeting or date, the sick child—life is filled with unexpected turns and shifts in direction. Are you able to adapt and stay energetically centered and positive in these situations, or are you easily thrown off your game?

Rate yourself from 0–10 on how comfortable you are when plans/situations change unexpectedly or feel out of your control.

8. PROPENSITY FOR AWE

"A child's world is fresh and new and beautiful, full of wonder and excitement. It is unfortunate that for most of us that clear-eyed vision, that true instinct for what

is beautiful and awe-inspiring, is dimmed and even lost before we reach adulthood." —RACHEL CARSON

Rather than explaining this one further for you, I'll share some writing from one of my talented friends who demonstrates his capacity for awe through his delightful poetry.

The Earth and the Sky of It All
There are billions of leaves in the forest
And the light loves them all
But this one, being softly caressed, catches my eye
And I stop and marvel
Feeling the earth and the sky of the moment
The light, loving
Without possessing
I cannot begin to imagine
The joy light feels at
This simple, sacred touching
Is there anything more like Grace
Than light?
—DAVID CRONIN

What does awe mean to you? How do you rate on your capacity to derive a sense of awe and wonder from the situations and events you experience in your daily life? Record this rating in your journal.

We Handcuff the Universe

How did it feel to honestly observe yourself in those eight categories? Whatever your score on each one, you are doing fine. Please don't use this exercise to judge yourself. Releasing self-judgment is one of our first powerful steps together, so please don't make more tasks for yourself now! We're all works in progress, and the fact that you've embarked on this journey already makes you a self-growth superhero of impressive proportions! Your reward awaits. Not only at the end of the year, but at every single step along the way.

But I need to ask you an important question: are you sure you're worthy of all this joy you're wanting? Here's a hard truth: whatever degree of joy you're currently experiencing is the precise measure of the amount of joy you deep-down believe you're *worthy* of experiencing.

Read that sentence again.

You can *want* mountains of joy, but until you are rock solid in your certainty that you *deserve* mountains of joy, on every level, for every reason, in every respect, you have energetically handcuffed the Universe from cocreating it with you.

Joy so often comes down to one of its undeniable attributes: a foundation of self-love, self-acceptance, self-honoring. Self-love is one of those concepts we all think we understand. For some, just the sound of it is kind of cringy, like a self-indulgent pursuit for weaker-willed people than we like to admit ourselves to be. Many think they already have it. Others, who know they don't, secretly believe they aren't worthy of it anyway. It's tragic, because self-love is everything, yet it's so seldom understood. It's not about bubble baths and buying the shoes. It's entirely about what you're saying to you, in your mind, every single day, about every single thing. And it's more malleable than you'd think.

Darling reader, it's our nature to want happiness. All people across the world since the start of time have wanted this. We crave joy and inner peace because we know, deep down, it's our essence—the energetic charge that animates our form and gives us what we know as life. We crave a consistent experience of joy and love because we want that homecoming to *who we are.*

Yet, despite the fact that we've craved it since the beginning of time, most of us on the planet today are still far removed from that being our consistent experience. Why would that be? Particularly here in our advanced Western societies, where we have more conveniences, benefits, ease, abundance, than we've ever had? For the most part, thanks to scientific advancement and human ingenuity, our survival here gets easier with each generation.

Even culturally, from a norms-of-society standpoint, I'd argue that we've increased our capacity, overall, for acceptance and compassion and other higher-consciousness tendencies. (Yes, I do realize there's ample evidence today to the contrary, but from a big-picture, historical perspective, I stand by this assertion.)

So, why *haven't* we—on the whole—been getting happier and happier? I recently saw a statistic that said one out of four people in North America is on antidepressants. Think of all the people you know. One quarter of them feels the need to take a pill just to maintain a baseline satisfactory feeling to allow them to move forward with their lives. How can this be, despite all that we have going for us? Bringing your attention to that question is important for creating those openings that allow perceptual shifts to take place. There's clearly something *in the way* of our innate joy for most of us. The journey we're taking together will be one of clearing what's in the way.

So, how will we do it?

It comes down to this simple truth: where we're vibrating is all about our beliefs and our habits. We change our vibration by canceling our subscriptions to beliefs that don't serve our greatest good and highest joy and subscribing instead to better (truer!) beliefs. It sounds like an easy enough objective. It gets a bit trickier when you take into consideration that many of your habitual beliefs reside well beneath the level of your conscious awareness. Our work together, therefore, will be to bring them up into the light of consciousness where we can redesign them to your benefit.

Let's assume your rational mind is on board with what I'm saying. Your brain recognizes that you need to subscribe to new, better beliefs. This probably is not an entirely new concept to you, so what has kept you from subscribing to those better beliefs already? Aside from lack of awareness about many of your existing beliefs, the only other thing still pulling you toward the old, joy-thieving beliefs is habit.

Raise your hand if you talk to yourself in your mind. We do it all day long. Brain researchers tell us the average person has 70,000 thoughts per day. And the percentage of today's thoughts that are the same as yesterday's and the day before's thoughts is roughly 95 percent. Plus, for the average person, 80 percent of those are negative thoughts. We're going to be working with what psychologists call your *default mode network*. It's the habitual loops your brain defaults to when your mind is at rest. We all have a default mode network, and for most of us it's not designed for joy. (We'll be redesigning yours.)

Due to the automatic, outdated, ancient programming of our human brains, we are all subject to negativity bias and other inherent biases that hijack our minds. These biases developed, evolutionarily, to keep us safe. We no longer require them for our safety, but we haven't evolved as human animals enough yet for them to have disappeared. You may have noticed that most people's actions and choices are still motivated primarily by fear, and most fear is unwarranted. Out of all the thoughts we think, we tend to Velcro the negative ones, and let the positive ones slide right off us like Teflon.

Raising your vibration is a matter of turning this equation around. You'll be learning to intentionally Velcro the good thoughts—the thoughts of hope and solutions, and Teflon the totally unproductive, relentless thoughts of despair and fear and hopelessness. They're simply ineffective. We can't afford to wallow in them anymore.

Earlier in this chapter, you identified some external circumstances you'd like to manifest during our upcoming journey, so let's get you some kerklunks around manifestation. My colleagues and I joke sometimes about how, whenever you hold yourself up as a teacher of manifestation, someone's going to point to you and say, "Well, like why don't you have a private jet, if you're such a great manifestor? Why don't you have a chateau in the South of France?"

And I get it; I understand where it's coming from.

The answer is twofold. The first part, obviously, is that my deepest heart's desire is not going to necessarily match anyone else's deepest heart's desire. There are certain categories of things, like money and status, that generally we humans always think we want more and more of no matter where we currently stand with it. It's just what our culture perpetuates, exemplified by John Rockefeller, who, when asked how much money was enough, famously replied, "a bit more than I have." (Fear of scarcity is one of the features hardwired into that primitive brain that's no longer logical nor serving us.)

But one of the nuances to mastering manifestation is getting really clear on what our *inner* being longs for—what each of us deeply desires at a core, soul level, that often has nothing to do with what others are able to observe on an external level. This kind of clarity around what you truly want, as opposed to what you've been programmed to *think* you want, is a powerful manifestation accelerator! (Don't worry; it's on our to-do list.)

And the second thing, which I touched on earlier, is that manifestation can never outrun your core belief about your own deservingness. I'll unpack that a tiny bit now, and we'll be addressing it more fully in coming chapters. It's energetic law that you can never pull into your life more than you deep-down believe you deserve. Most of us who have dedicated our lives to this work—myself and my vast community of friends and colleagues—have overcome some pretty significant issues around our own worthiness. And, of course, there is always a next level to be reached on the spiral.

I know beyond any doubt that these tools I'm sharing with you work, because I've used them to create a life that is so far beyond what I used to create for myself. When I look back at who and where I was—emotionally, circumstantially—it feels like a whole other person's life. Today, I wake up every morning with tears of gratitude. I'm not kidding; that's my experience. I wake up beside the kindest, most emotionally generous, high-vibration partner I could ever imagine. I have deeply rewarding relationships with my two absolutely incredible daughters that make me so proud I could explode, plus other family and created-family relationships I cherish. I live in a gorgeous home, decorated precisely to my tastes and likings, with lots of nature, in a beautiful part of the country. I'm giddy-passionate about my ever-evolving career that lets me deliver my gifts in a way that feels purposeful and effective and like I'm making a difference in the world.

Does that mean I'm done manifesting? Heck no! The thing to understand is that manifestation flows through a *valve* for each of us, and it's a valve that we can continue to expand, bit by bit, with the practices I'm sharing here. The valve doesn't go from trickle to tidal wave; it opens gradually, over time. I've been working on opening my valve of deservingness for decades and it's been more rewarding than I could ever express. But it's still an ongoing process, as it is for every one of us who embarks on this journey. I'm loving every step along the way, so I don't ever wish that I could just wiggle my nose and get to the finish line. I'm happy there *is* no finish line.

I mention all of this simply to say the kerklunks you get with this work just continue to get kerklunk-ier. Manifesting all that external stuff Out There is just the natural evolution of upgrading what we've got going on In Here, so let's get back to our upgrading tools.

Week one of your homeplay for this first month of your joy journey was described above. It's the exercise of observing yourself and rating yourself in all of those categories that define a joyful internal landscape.

Here are your homeplay assignments for the remaining three weeks of this month. As I've previously explained, you are welcome to be loose with your adherence to these timeframe delineations. For instance, the first week's practice might spill over into the full month (building the skill of observing yourself is going to prove invaluable as we go forward!)

HOMEPLAY FOR KEY 1, WEEK TWO

It's going to sound ridiculously simple. I want you to begin by paying deliberate attention to your feelings. As often as possible throughout all the days of this week, go inward with a conscious compassion for yourself and just observe your feeling state.

With that voice in your head that talks to you all day long, ask yourself, "Darling, what are you feeling?" Why *shouldn't* you treat yourself with that level of tenderness and care and use terms of endearment with your precious self? Once you've observed your feeling state, notice if any judgment comes up. Do you roll your eyes at yourself for feeling how you're feeling? Do any thoughts come up that say you shouldn't be feeling that way? Or that your feeling isn't valid? Just notice what the voice in your head says and do your best to shift into an energy of compassion and curiosity toward your sweet self.

After letting your true inner being fully express its feelings to you while you work toward remaining nonjudgmental and embracing of them all, next, gently ask, "Darling, what do you need?" Again, you want to just try to stay open and receptive to whatever comes up. You may find that a simple way to provide for your needs and desires emerges from your intuitive self. Maybe you just need to open a window for some fresh air; maybe you need to close your eyes and be still and quiet for ten minutes. Maybe you need a cup of tea.

Until we take time to quiet our thoughts and go inward with this inquiry, we're likely to miss these obvious opportunities to nurture ourselves. But even if you get clarity around a much larger-scale need, or if your desire is not one that can be readily met, still, having switched your attention to what you want is an effective step toward working with universal forces to bring it to you. I first learned this practice from my friend and mentor Tej Steiner, author of *Heart Circles*. My sweet soul-brother Jacob Nordby makes it a journaling practice for the authors he coaches. (You can download a free guide to the related journaling practice at Jacob's website or link to it from the Joy Kit at mine.)

HOMEPLAY FOR KEY 1, WEEK THREE

Once you've had a bit of practice checking in with your feelings when it occurs to you to do so, add a third question to this practice. After determining what you're feeling and what you need, ask your precious self, "Darling, what would you *love?*"

Allow yourself to move into a dreamy state of consciousness as you focus on this third question. Whatever pops into your mind, whether it's about the hour ahead, the day ahead, or the decade ahead, intentionally build a little fantasy around it and indulge for a bit of time in this fantasy. Maybe something will pop into your awareness that you'll decide to grant yourself immediately; maybe what you'd love feels unobtainable at the moment. Either way, see if you can feel into this answer with some dreamy anticipation and joy.

This week you'll also crank up the three-question process a bit. One way to refine this practice is to schedule your feeling check-ins so you're sure to do them. Some of my Joy Schoolers even set their watches or phones to go off at certain intervals as a reminder. I suggest a minimum of three check-ins per day—more if you feel inspired!

Another way to make building your vibration-elevation skills a true priority is to record your check-in observations in your Joy Journal as you go through the week. (Journaling your observations is a powerful way to supercharge any of the practices we'll do here.) Another way is to share your new self-inquiry habit with someone you love, encouraging them to join you.

As we've discussed, becoming a skilled observer of yourself is a critical step in mastering the fine art of consistent joy. We're not used to looking at ourselves from the observer viewpoint, especially when it comes to being the observer of our own thoughts. Rather than observing that voice in our heads, most of us are in the habit of *identifying* with it, allowing it to inform us about how we're doing, and let's face it—we typically do not have the kindest soundtracks playing up there. It's okay. We've learned that habit, and we can unlearn it. You're on your way to a new and improved relationship with your thoughts.

HOMEPLAY FOR KEY 1, WEEK FOUR

Your fourth week of homeplay will be about observing that voice in your head and countering it with this practice I'll let my heart-brother Scott Stabile describe for you:

> We don't expect cars to fly us across the Atlantic, or to fly us anywhere. Cars drive. That's what they do. We don't condemn lions for eating gazelles. We might feel sad, sure, especially if we're watching it happen, but lions eat gazelles. It's what they do. I've never screamed at my oven to make me a smoothie or at my blender to bake me some bread. We are okay with things acting as they're designed to act, except when it comes to ourselves. To human beings.
>
> We humans are insane. We are envious, jealous, blameful, spiteful, unforgiving, vulgar beings. Sure, we're a lot of beautiful things too, but let's focus on the ugly so I can make my point. If we can learn to accept ourselves, the fullness of our humanity, all the beautiful and ugly bits, we are much more likely to generate love and create peace, with ourselves and with all the other hideous, gorgeous humans out there.
>
> Try this: Think of something you judge about yourself, something about which your mind can be relentlessly abusive. Now hold your hands over your heart, close your eyes and say out loud, the way you might to a child who just spilled his cup of milk, It's okay, honey; you're human. Say it again, maybe whisper it, and really feel it this time. It's okay, honey; you're human. Doesn't that feel good? Gentle? Honest? Forgiving? Accepting? Isn't

this how we want to be with ourselves? It's definitely how I want to be with myself. It beats the hell out of a typical mind-retort, something in the family of you're a worthless loser. Not even a honey in there. Our minds can be such assholes.

See why I adore Scott? Challenge yourself this week to see how many times you can give yourself an "It's okay, honey; you're human." Challenge yourself to mean it!

RECAP OF HOMEPLAY FOR KEY 1

To recap, here are the four homeplay assignments for this month. You'll spend a week focused on each of them. (And since most months are not precisely four weeks long, you'll have a few days when you'll follow your intuition regarding how to extend your practice.)

1. Observe yourself and rate yourself on the eight pillars of a joyful inner landscape as defined in this chapter.

2. Pause throughout the day to ask yourself, *Darling, what are you feeling? Darling, what do you need?* and observe the responses with compassion.

3. Add this question to your self-inquiry practice: *Darling, what would you love?* and allow yourself to indulge in some daydreaming about the answer to this question. You'll also crank up the practice this week by scheduling your check-ins, journaling about them, inviting a friend to join you, or all the above!

4. Throughout the final week of this month, every time you have a self-critical thought, tell yourself, *It's okay, honey; you're human.*

As simple as the homeplay for this month sounds, I assure you it will powerfully shift your energy in the direction of joy. It might not be perceptible at first, but for many Joy Schoolers even these first steps make a notable difference in their experience of life.

This book is a roadmap, but it's up to you to take the journey. It's only when you have a genuine and earnest desire to elevate your vibration that you'll be able to establish a new Joy Setpoint for yourself. Please keep in mind that even though I'm giving you a specific area of focus for each week (and each month), you will ideally want to make all these practices ongoing, soul-expanding fixtures in your life.

If you sincerely wished to play the clarinet in a renowned orchestra, you'd know the beginning steps would require you to practice the clarinet every day. You might not be awesome the first week you tried out the instrument. You might not even see consistent improvement right away. But to reach your goal, you'd hold the vision of you in that orchestra and you'd show up for practice, even when you didn't feel like it. Such is the path to a permanently elevated Joy Setpoint. Hold the vision, my darling reader, and here we go!

KEY 2

Know Thyself

"Love, peace, and happiness are inherent in the knowing of our own being. In fact, they are the knowing of being. They are simply other names for our self."
—RUPERT SPIRA

Welcome to the second month of your joy journey! I hope you came to some profound awareness last month about where you currently stand in terms of the qualities of a joyful inner landscape. And I hope you had a juicy month observing your feelings. I know it can feel weird at first, and even a little self-indulgent. How did it go with your practice of checking in with yourself and calling yourself "darling" and "honey"?

For many of my Joy Schoolers, using terms of endearment for oneself is difficult in the beginning. Sweet Joy Schooler Rachel said it brought tears to her eyes every time she did it. We'll be doing quite a bit to upgrade your authentic relationship with yourself so just keep doing the best you can for now, offering yourself every last drop of genuine compassion and love you can muster.

Maybe you came to some new realizations about what's real and true for you regarding your feeling states, and maybe you came to some realizations about the judgments you place on your feelings. No judgment if you found judgment! The last thing we want to do is layer more judgment on our judge-y, precious selves for being judge-y!

I've often named my workshops after the inscription at the Temple of Apollo in Delphi, Greece, which famously advises "Know thyself." This month, I invite you to know thyself in a way you may not have considered previously. It will lay excellent groundwork for this journey ahead.

In Joy School, the foundational piece to everything we do is recognizing and connecting ever more palpably with our non-physical selves. I like to use terminology I borrowed from Eckhart Tolle when I was immersed in his work over a decade ago. He taught that we all have a Horizontal Self and a Vertical Self. He hasn't used this lexicon much in recent years, but I've always loved how there's a clear correlative with these two terms, with each having its corresponding counterpart. More recently, I've heard Eckhart calling our non-physical aspect the "Deep I," and lots of teachers have used terminology like Higher Self, Soul, Spirit-Self, but none of those have a direct correlative for what to call that other part—the part that represents our non-spirit humanness.

This non-spirit aspect has historically been referred to as "ego" or "persona." Carl Jung called it the "conscious mind." Michael Singer says "psyche." I feel like those terms have other associations depending on where you first heard them, which is why I've always preferred the correlated relationship between having a Vertical Self (the part of us that represents our non-physical, energetic essence, our divinity, and alignment with source), and a Horizontal Self (our humanness—our name, our body, our job, our roles here in this time and place).

Many spiritual trainings begin with an exercise that asks you to make a list to describe who you are. Take a moment to do that now. Open your Joy Journal and quickly, off the top of your head, write all the words that describe who you are.

Done? Typically, many of the words we use to describe ourselves are labels like man/woman, parent, artist, entrepreneur—words to represent how we show up in the external world. These terms might include your job title, political or religious affiliation, or family positioning. Even more intangible descriptors like "free thinker," or "lover of life," are still labels we identify ourselves by. All of these are words we use to describe our Horizontal Selves. This aspect of us even includes our thoughts and feelings. (We'll dig around there more in a bit.)

The part that doesn't wear any of those labels is your Vertical Self. It's the *you* that is timeless, genderless, ageless, non-physical, joyful, and wise beyond comprehension. It's the most real part of you, as you'll soon discover. Your joy journey will be about bringing this part of you more into the forefront of your existence, while bringing the Horizontal Self a bit more into the background. Even a subtle shift in the direction of this repositioning creates tremendous ripple effects in your life. We're not looking to completely dis-identify with the Horizontal Self, and that would not even be possible if we wanted to; we're just looking to awaken the awareness and acknowledgment you give to this non-physical, often-neglected aspect of who you authentically are.

Albert Einstein said, "When you examine the lives of the most influential people who have ever walked among us, you discover one thread that winds through them all. They have been aligned first with their spiritual nature and only then with their physical selves."

Aligning with Your Spiritual Nature

The most tried-and-true, well-researched, and documented method for inching toward this repositioning is meditation. Maybe you're already a fan; maybe you've tried it and decided it's not for you; maybe you've never even given it a glance. I ask that you hear me out on this one, and even if you decide to pass on meditation in the traditional sense, please know you'll be given some alternatives, you're still cute as a button, and I love you right where you are.

I recently got to preview the latest book by my remarkable friend, *New York Times* bestselling author and researcher Eldon Taylor, *Questioning Spirituality*. In it, he shares multiple research studies confirming that the brains of meditators and daily prayer reciters are measurably different from the brains of the rest of us. Those who engage regularly with their Vertical Selves through these activities have brains that are thicker and demonstrate significantly more activity in the frontal lobes. This is measurable not just when the meditating or praying is happening, but all day long, and it just so happens that these attributes of the physical brain go hand-in-hand with a peaceful, joyful experience of life.

My favorite of the many reasons for meditating is deceptively simple: whatever you give attention to is what is going to grow in your experience. (If that hasn't solidly kerklunked for you yet, don't worry. It's not the last time I'll say it.) Giving attention to your Vertical Self through a regular practice of meditation or prayer changes your vibration, which goes on to change your actual physiology as well as what you attract into your experience. If you have any doubts about this, I invite you to do an internet search and read the plethora of studies revealing the myriad ways in which regular meditators' health has improved. Especially vast and impressive are the results that have been gathered on practitioners of Transcendental Meditation (TM.)

In the words of Caroline Myss, "The soul always knows what to do to heal itself. The challenge is to silence the mind." Silencing the mind (meditating) allows the Vertical Self to be felt to ever-greater extents over time. As Eldon points out, it's not that different from going to the gym for a while and then noticing a change in your muscular structure. In brain scans (fMRI), if a meditator is hooked up to the detecting equipment, scientists can see activation of the frontal lobe. Consistent activation of that part of the brain conditions it to a different level of activity that's been linked to higher rational functioning, better problem-solving, more resilience, and increased feelings of overall wellbeing.

It comes down to making the choice to deliberately set aside time for disengaging from your habitual thought patterns. Those well-worn loops of your habitual thinking are what typically get in the way of you connecting with the part of you that is your Vertical Self. That's why last month I asked you to begin the practice of being the observer of you. It takes effort and commitment to consciously observe yourself in your day-to-day life, but the more you do it, the closer it gets to being your default setting, an automatic reflex. Now that you've had a bit of practice observing you, I invite you to add this step going forward: When you observe your own thinking, keep asking yourself, "Who is doing this observing?" What you'll become more and more aware of is that it's your Vertical Self observing your Horizontal Self. This slight adjustment in perception is foundational to the miraculous work you're about to do!

Here's what Eckhart Tolle says about it: "The moment you start watching the thinker, a higher level of consciousness becomes activated. You then begin to realize that there is a vast realm of intelligence beyond thought, that thought is only a tiny aspect of that intelligence. You also realize that all the things that truly matter—beauty, love, creativity, joy, inner peace—arise from beyond the mind. You begin to awaken."

So, how about that meditation idea?

I've been meditating my entire adult life, and I can think of no other practice that comes close in terms of benefit-to-time-investment ratio. A part of you already *knows* you want to disengage from those thought loops. Anyone who enjoys a glass of wine, or other alcohol, or most recreational drugs, already knows. The reason we humans like those things is they turn down the volume on the uncomfortable but oh-so-addictive monkey mind. The problem with doing it via these substances is that it does nothing to train us in that skill, so as soon as the substance wears off, there's the monkey mind again.

Meditation, on the other hand, is a way to practice the *skill* of turning down the volume at will. Even if it feels like nothing is happening while you're meditating, that's okay. It's not about what goes on during meditation; it's about the skill you're acquiring that you'll be able to use during life *outside* meditation time. It's just like building any other skill. We're generally not good at anything when we first start doing it, but we understand we'll get better with practice. When you sharpen the skill of connection to your Vertical Self through daily meditation practice, it becomes infinitely easier to bring that talent into the rest of your life. Elevating your Joy Setpoint is largely a matter of mastering the ability to pull that skill out when you need it, right in that red-hot moment of whatever drama is unfolding.

You Are Not Your Thoughts

I often get a reaction from people that goes something like "You're always so happy; you're always smiling," the implication being, "What's wrong with you?" They think I must live some totally charmed life. And I do (because I've learned to create it that way.) But "bad" stuff happens to me, too. After nearly a challenge-free decade, some unexpected and heartbreaking situations have come up for me in the past few years. I'm not going to say there weren't any moments of deep sadness or sleepless nights (there were), but most of the time, I've stayed truly, sustainably, okay with it all, and I know that's entirely because of the tools I've used for several decades that let me deal with challenges in a graceful, fluid way. I know because when I look back at my life prior to learning these tools, "graceful" and "fluid" were certainly not words I could apply.

The biggest difference between then and now is that I used to identify with my thoughts. We humans tend to give a lot of weight to those thoughts in our heads. Whatever is troubling you today, worrying you, or making you feel bad, it's important to understand that a thought is causing that feeling. And every troubling thought you've ever had, has come from your Horizontal Self, not your Vertical Self. There are no problems over in the Vertical Self.

Your thoughts aren't your enemies; they're just not super reliable. They're much flimsier and more insignificant than it feels like they are when you're identified with them. When you can break out of full identification with your Horizontal Self, you can observe how malleable and illusory your thoughts really are, so we'll be building our toolbox for that during all the coming months.

It's not like the egoic mind of the Horizontal Self is bad, or something to get rid of. As I've mentioned, you couldn't even if you wanted to. We're here in this human body and it comes standard with the package. And when things are going great, there's not a lot of incentive to step out of identification with the Horizontal Self. I love letting my Horizontal Self run rampant when it's enjoyable to do so, because I know we're here for joy—including human joy, right here in the messy midst of our people-y experience! I love to revel in human stuff, the decadence, the pleasures of the flesh . . . and I profoundly appreciate having built up the muscle to be able to pick and choose between aligning with my Horizontal Self where all that juicy, earthy, human stuff happens, and my Vertical Self when a higher-consciousness perspective is called for. When things Out There are triggering you, or people break your heart, it's indescribably helpful to have the tools to be able to step out of the entanglement of the Horizontal Self and identify with the Vertical Self in those moments.

Becoming more clear about the Horizontal and Vertical aspects of you is the first way I'm inviting you to expand in "Knowing Thyself" this month. Here's the second way: I want you to practice remembering that you are not your thoughts. Your thoughts about any situation, thing, or person do not define you. The thoughts that cross your mind feel like clues to who you are, but we'll soon be exploring all the reasons that is simply inaccurate and why your thoughts are the least reliable indicator of the person you are at your core.

My literary hero Anne Lamott says, "Almost everything will work again if you unplug it for a few minutes. Including you." This month, we're working on ways to unplug you so that you can work better when we plug you back in. Meditation unplugs you. There's a Zen saying that goes something like, "You should meditate for at least half an hour a day. Unless you are too busy. Then you should meditate for an hour." In typical Zen subtlety, it makes the point that anyone who says they are too busy to meditate (too overly identified with the Horizontal Self) is someone who would greatly benefit from meditating.

I have a few options to suggest. If you've already got a meditation practice that's working for you, by all means, carry on! Maybe you'll see an opportunity in these suggestions to expand what you've been doing or add a new flavor into the mix. And if you don't have a committed, daily practice right now, let's see if we can find one that's right for you.

Say Hello to Your Vertical Self

I've always adored this Eckhart Tolle trick for getting familiar with sensing the existence of the Vertical Self. Once you've first accessed this sensation, it will come more easily the next time, so the following directions are to initially introduce you to this recognition of your energetic body: Hold up your right hand, outside your field of vision. Without touching anything, or moving your hand, or looking at it, is there any way you can know your right hand is still there? This exercise invites you to experience the inner feeling of the right hand. If you pay full attention, after a while you'll find the subtle sense of aliveness where your right hand is. Once you've done that, you've entered the energetic field of the body with your awareness.

You can lower your hand now. Sitting comfortably, see if you can feel that inner buzzing in the other hand, and in other parts of your body. Maybe you notice it in your feet, your thighs. It's almost like a mild, subtle version of what happens when we say a body part "falls asleep." This sensation you're feeling is your animating force, the thing that makes you alive, the Vertical Self within you. Spend a moment now cranking up this subtle feeling just by giving it all your attention and focus. I'll wait.

I hope you were able to really feel your animating force inside your body. Can you feel how your vibration is higher right now than it was before you did that little activity? Just by taking conscious control of where you were placing your focus and your attention, you were able to relieve yourself, for a moment, from looking *out* at the world around you. You were able to shift your awareness to something beautiful and meaningful inside of you instead. As we move forward, I want you to hold in your heart the realization of how easy it was for you to do that.

Now that you've accessed this entry point, and you have the sensation of activating this buzzing vitality within you, you might be able to go straight to feeling it next time you try. This is your energy field, your divine spark, the thing that differentiates your physical body from a corpse. Locating this part of you puts you into identification with your Vertical Self, the aspect of you that's always calm, resilient, compassionate, and wise, no matter what's going on around you. It's where your consistent joy resides, your creativity, and your highest expression of your authenticity. You can use this as a mini-meditation at any point in the day. It's wonderful to do as you fall asleep at night. Just feel the buzzing vitality throughout your reclining form. Putting your focus there helps divert your attention away from the endless stream of thoughts that want to keep you in full identification with your Horizontal Self.

I'm pretty sure this is the energy Franz Kafka was tapping into when he wrote, "You do not need to leave your room. Remain sitting at your table and listen. Don't even listen; simply wait. Don't even wait. The world will freely offer itself to you. To be unmasked, it has no choice. It will roll in ecstasy at your feet."

As a more formal meditation practice, I like to combine this technique with Transcendental Meditation. Most of us have minds that are enthusiastic multitaskers, so I've found that combining a few methods at once is even more powerful for silencing the monkey mind. Transcendental Meditation is the longest-studied form of meditation in the world, with the most science to back it up. It's extremely popular for its simplicity and effortlessness. Here's a very simplified explanation of TM, and how I combine it with awareness of your energy field. If you were to learn TM from a certified instructor, you'd be given a personalized mantra, a word that you'd repeat silently in your head throughout your meditation. For our modified purposes, I invite you to simply use the mantra "om."

It's recommended to meditate sitting comfortably in a chair. It's okay to sit on a bed with your feet up so long as your spine is pretty much vertical. This is just because when you lie down, you're signaling your body to go to sleep, and we want to keep this signaling different from that. So even in a reclining chair, you don't want to recline too far back.

Begin by sitting comfortably with your eyes closed for thirty seconds. Did thoughts rise up? See how that was effortless? Let your thought of the mantra be just as effortless. After thirty seconds, start repeating the mantra in your head. Don't try to force out all other thoughts. It's okay if other thoughts run in the background; just keep the mantra going, easily and effortlessly. You may find that thoughts fade away naturally, but they may not. If you notice that your attention has been pulled toward a thought, you don't need to try hard to banish it. Each time it happens, just remind yourself to focus a bit more on the mantra so that it's the primary thing in your head.

You'll naturally feel yourself becoming more peaceful. When that happens, begin paying attention to the inner body, as described above. Give your full attention to feeling the buzzing vitality that animates your form while still repeating the mantra in your head. The combination of these two points of focus will clear your mind to an extent that neither of them could accomplish on their own.

For the greatest benefits, you'll want to make this a daily practice, two times per day, twenty minutes per session. Don't set a timer for twenty minutes because you might be in a deep state and not want to be jarred out of it. Instead, just glance at a clock when you feel like it's been about twenty minutes. You'll naturally dip in and out of a meditative state during this time and when you think to glance at the clock it means you are naturally at a less deep place so it's fine to open your eyes then. If you see that it hasn't been twenty minutes yet, dip back into your buzzing energetic field and the repetition of your mantra.

Once you hit the twenty-minute mark (it's fine if you've gone beyond it), stop repeating the mantra but remain still with your eyes closed for another two minutes. Let your mind do whatever it naturally wants to do during this transition time back to full awareness. You might notice that your attention to the energetic body naturally fades during this transition time, but it's fine if it doesn't. Don't force it either way. This two-minute rest is important so that you don't come out of your meditation too abruptly. Not taking this transition time can result in headaches and anxiety so make sure you feel rested and refreshed before you fully open your eyes and continue your day. If you waited two minutes and still don't feel ready to get up, just wait a bit longer, keeping still with your eyes closed or softly focused.

You'll want to minimize distractions as much as you can during your meditation, but total silence is not required. It's okay to hear noises in the background if that's your only option. If you get interrupted, just take a few moments in silence again before you reintroduce your mantra. Except in the case of a real emergency, don't ever jump up from your meditation without taking a few minutes to gradually come out of it.

It's ideal if you can meditate in the morning and afternoon. For the morning meditation, it's best to get up and brush your teeth, shower, do some yoga stretches or whatever you normally do to start your day, and then meditate, ideally before breakfast or before you open your phone, computer, or work stuff. The afternoon meditation is ideally done mid-afternoon, and at least prior to dinner. I've known many people who go to their cars on a break from work to do their afternoon meditation. Some working parents, if they have young kids at home, will pull into a parking lot, find a spot away from other cars, and do their afternoon meditation there before they get home.

If you must wait until evening, that's okay, but try to avoid meditating right after dinner on a full stomach. It's always better not to have eaten heavily prior to meditating because your body is busy with digestion then and not as receptive to the state you want to achieve. It's best not to meditate right before bed, too, because after meditation your mind is typically alert and clear and not sleepy. But it's okay to break this rule if you're having a hard time sleeping because of anxiety or too many busy thoughts. You can get up and meditate in order to settle the thoughts, and then try going back to sleep.

Again, it's entirely possible that you won't feel anything noteworthy during your meditation. The goal of meditation is more about what you feel in your life than what you feel while you're meditating. Even if it seems like nothing's happening while you're in your meditation, in the hours afterward you will probably feel more calm, clear, and centered. Even if that is subtle, try to pay attention to how your overall day feels, or your week feels, after you have been meditating regularly for several days or weeks. The vast majority of

Joy Schoolers who embrace this practice report a much more calm, peaceful, higher-consciousness state of being after only a few weeks.

While I'm hoping you'll want to commit to the above meditation routine, I do understand that not everyone is keen to invest forty minutes per day in meditation. Even if you only do one twenty-minute session each day, you'll be giving yourself a tremendous gift. Maybe you simply can't imagine committing more than ten minutes. If that's what's true for you right now, do that. But stay open to the possibility that you'll want to do more in time.

And in case the whole TM structure I've outlined simply doesn't appeal to you, here's another of my favorite practices that only requires twelve minutes of daily commitment! (There are longer versions of this one, too. See how flexible I'm making this for you?)

I adore the Vedic practice of kirtan (singing meditation) in all its forms, and this particular version (also referenced in Eldon's book) has the added benefit of having earned recent validation from the scientific community. According to *Psych News Daily*, "Studies show ... that regular Kirtan Kriya meditation can improve mood, decrease anxiety, stress, blood pressure, heart rate, and cortisol levels, as well as decrease insomnia." To cement that point for you, I'm going to let Alzheimer's Research & Prevention Foundation tell you about it:

"Kirtan Kriya (which is pronounced *KEER-tun KREE-a*) is a type of meditation from the Kundalini yoga tradition, which has been practiced for thousands of years. This meditation is sometimes called a singing exercise, as it involves singing the sounds, Saa Taa Naa Maa along with repetitive finger movements, or mudras. This non-religious practice can be adapted to several lengths, but practicing it for just twelve minutes a day has been shown to reduce stress levels and increase activity in areas of the brain that are central to memory."

Eastern traditions have long relied on *kriyas* (the Sanskrit word for specific meditative movements) to enhance mind-body balance and healing, especially when combined with *kirtan* (the Sanskrit word for song.) The specific syllables in Kirtan Kriya come from a mantra for recognizing one's true essence (the Vertical Self).

Again, according to Alzheimer's Research & Prevention Foundation:

> From an Eastern perspective, it is believed that the placement of the tongue on the roof of the mouth while making these sounds stimulates eighty-four acupuncture points on the upper palate. This causes a beneficial biochemical transformation in the brain. In addition, Western research has revealed that utilizing the fingertip position in conjunction with the sounds enhances blood flow to particular areas in the motor-sensory part of the brain. Clinical research has shown that practicing Kirtan Kriya for just twelve minutes a day can improve cognition and activate parts of the brain that are central to memory. Replacing the Kirtan Kriya sounds with other sounds or replacing the meditation as a whole with other relaxing tasks, has not been shown to be effective.

Have I enticed you to give Kirtan Kriya a try? If you'd like to follow along with an audio, my favorite links for that can be found in the downloadable and ever-expanding Joy Kit at *LisaMcCourt.com.* For those of you with musical know-how, the notes are, A, G, F, G.

Here are the instructions:

1. Sit with your spine straight and repeat the sounds Sa Ta Na Ma while holding your hands in the mudras outlined below. With each syllable, imagine the flow of energy coming into the top of your head (crown chakra), making a 90-degree

turn, and flowing out through your forehead (third eye chakra).

2. For two minutes, sing the mantra in your normal voice.

3. For the next two minutes, sing it in a whisper.

4. For the next four minutes, say the sound silently in your head.

5. For the next two minutes, go back to whispering the mantra.

6. For the final two minutes, go back to singing out loud.

7. To end your session, inhale deeply, stretch your arms above your head, and then bring them down slowly in a sweeping motion as you exhale.

Instructions for the corresponding mudras (finger positions):

- Using both hands, on Sa, touch the index fingers of each hand to your thumbs.

- On Ta, touch your middle fingers to your thumbs.

- On Na, touch your ring fingers to your thumbs.

- On Ma, touch your pinky fingers to your thumbs.

Many of my Joy Schoolers have gotten hooked on this simple practice and continue it to this day. One thing I love about it is how it activates the energy body within you, generating that tingling feeling previously described. When I do Kirtan Kriya, I've noticed that tingle stays activated for hours after the short session.

Mindfulness Practice Suggestions

Kirtan Kriya allows you to move energy through you vocally, creating the vibration that leads to the buzzy feeling. This sung mantra/mudra combo has thousands of years of history and proven benefit (as well as recent research) to back it up, but you can move energy and create vibration through sound of any kind. With that in mind, let's add singing, humming, and chanting to your expanding mindfulness menu for those of you who, for whatever reason, are too resistant to "meditation" right now to give it a try.

Scientific studies have confirmed that singing releases endorphins and oxytocin. It's been documented to relieve stress and depression. It's a true workout for the lungs! Opening your diaphragm oxygenates your blood, creating more white blood cells and strengthening your whole body. Regular singing has been proven to increase your immune response. One of the beautiful enhancements to my life that I've manifested is being a part of Michael Beckwith's Agape Spiritual Center's Global Choir. Learning and practicing soulful, spiritual songs with my singing brothers and sisters every week never fails to crank up my vibration!

Even humming has been determined to relieve stress. I've always been an incessant hummer, and never realized until recently that research has documented "the humming effect," proving that humming is vibrationally and energetically good for you. According to legendary spiritual performer Deva Premal, "Humming creates a wonderful circuit of energy in your body, revitalizing its cells and charging its chakras." My whole life I thought I just had this annoying humming habit, when I've been charging my chakras all along! Some wise inner part of me must have known.

I believe we humans are meant to sing, and hum, and make noise. How many of us got through childhood without being told to be quiet? Probably no one. We get that message as kids, and we create this belief that being noisy is bad and people won't love us if we're loud. But our bodies crave it. I've seen recent indications that the scream therapy popularized by John Lennon and Yoko Ono back in the 70s is making a comeback!

I do breathwork regularly with my heart-brother Scott Stabile, and always, once the breath starts really doing its thing, I feel a sound moving through me and coming out of my mouth. It's not from my throat, and it doesn't feel like my voice. It's a primal sound from somewhere much deeper than that. And it's not pretty. But it feels fantastic moving through me, and especially moving *out* of me. Breathwork is a powerful healing modality I invite you to explore, and if you'd like to do online breathwork with Scott, you can find links for that at the Joy Kit at my website.

I want you to have options, so at the most minimal level, you can set an intention of mindfulness around almost any solo activity you enjoy—running, biking, cooking, knitting, dancing. If that's all you feel ready to commit to at this point, please at least commit wholeheartedly to giving this activity your pure, mindful attention for a specified amount of time each day.

Here's a mindfulness practice I find especially effective, inspired by my brilliant teacher and friend Holly Copeland. (There's a link to her meditation in your Joy Kit at *LisaMcCourt.com*.)

● ● ●

To begin, close your eyes and take a few long, slow belly breaths. Roll your shoulders, roll your head on your neck, do whatever your body wants to do to get still and comfortable. Bring your attention to this idea of the Vertical Self. Anything we give our attention to, we strengthen in our experience. Before anything, this Vertical Self is here, because it's consciousness itself, ever-present and available.

Start focusing on sounds you're hearing in your environment. Notice that sounds arrive in your awareness, pass, and go. Sounds appear in the awareness that is your Vertical Self. If you're listening for the sounds, you notice there's also space between the sounds. This space is consciousness. It's the consciousness from which the sounds are manifested.

Think about how it's the same with vision. Objects appear, arriving as light to your eyes, pass, and go. Seeing is your consciousness *receiving* sights. Feel into your body now and notice sensations. Notice the feeling of air on your skin, the weight of your body in your chair. Maybe there's some gurgling in your belly. All these sensations are arriving in this awareness that is your Vertical Self, changing and passing.

Everything is moving, and your Vertical Self is still. Maybe you notice some thoughts passing through your mind, even during this mindfulness practice. That happens. Maybe it's a memory crossing by. Maybe something on your to-do list. Notice that just like seeing, hearing, and feeling, thoughts arrive as information that your consciousness can observe, and then they pass and go.

Even emotions do this. Maybe you're noticing some emotion arise: impatience, self-judgment. Feelings, too—just like thoughts, hearing, and seeing—arrive as information. And they, too, will pass and go. So, we can understand that all of this—all of the thoughts, feelings, sensations, sights, and sounds—all falls under this category of information that we have the capacity to *witness* from this perspective of our Vertical Self. The Vertical Self *is* the witnessing consciousness, so it exists behind all of that. It's the field from which all of that arises. It doesn't come and go. It's timeless. Allow your attention to relax into this ultimate, deepest *you*, this vast, simple, awake presence.

While you're right there, take a moment to notice anything at all that you can sense about this presence. Does it have a form or any characteristics at all? It's often been said by spiritual leaders that it defies description, which is true, but it's also true that each of us will have a unique way we experience it, so see if that's something you can notice right now. Maybe a color, a feeling. Maybe a whole, fleshed-out visual representation. Maybe it has a sound or smell to it; maybe it's just light. Maybe it has a name or some defining characteristic you're just now noticing, however subtle.

And then, as you feel ready, gently reorient yourself back to the room just enough to record whatever impressions you may have been able to observe regarding how *you* uniquely experience your Vertical Self.

● ● ●

There's a famous phrase in Buddhism for describing the experience of consciousness itself: "the finger pointing to the moon." The idea is that the finger can point to the moon, but the finger is not the moon. That's what Buddhists say it's like to try to describe the experience of consciousness. So, don't beat yourself up if you couldn't find words or solid concepts to label your experience of your Vertical Self. Even if you just identified a feeling or some small shift within yourself, try to cement that into your memory. That'll make it more accessible the next time.

I've always experienced mine as a visual representation. From my first exposure to this awakening, I've "seen" it like a beam of light originating at my spine. Going there has a "falling back" feeling to it. The light extends infinitely both up and down, but it's kind of like a Gumby figure with stretchy arms that reach out in front to wrap around me lovingly. It's almost like my Vertical Self is giving a hug to my Horizontal Self. In front of me, I sense a small stage with a play going on, a bit like an aerial view of the movie *The Truman*

Show. All my life-stuffs are playing out on the little stage. I don't see it in a detailed way; it's more just a sense that what's going on there is Horizontal Me, doing life, but for the moment I've switched out of identification with that self. By energetically "falling back," I've moved into identification with the Gumby self (Vertical Me) that is so much bigger and richer than all of the silliness unfolding on the little stage. My Gumby self is holding it lovingly, just observing everything with compassion, and often with a bit of amusement. And it's like—*ahhhhh.*

I share that as an example, but it's unlikely you'd experience your Vertical Self in the same way as anyone else, and that's why I asked you to do your best to observe your own experience of it in the above meditation. It was to, firstly, bathe your Vertical Self in your attention because that's what will grow its presence in your life, and also to see if we could get some fingers pointing to the moon—some little details you might use as entry points as you build your skill of accessing and aligning with your Vertical Self.

HOMEPLAY FOR KEY 2—ALL FOUR WEEKS

You've probably figured out what your homeplay this month will be. You've read about several different options now for using meditation—or at the very least incorporating a mindfulness practice—as a way to build the skill of tuning into your Vertical Self, the most real and naturally joyful part of you.

For each week of this month, commit fully to at least one of the practices discussed in this chapter. Make it a month of experimentation so you can figure out what works best for you from this menu of practices. Of course, there are options outside of what I've suggested here as well. Many lovely guided meditations can be found on YouTube, and some beginning meditators find it helpful to have a soothing voice guiding them through the process. (I've gathered some excellent options for you in the Joy Kit at my site, including a transformational light language meditation channeled by my amazing friend Lynda Samphire!) I will say this, however: I encourage you, once it's comfortable to do so, to shift your meditation practice to a self-guided one for at least some of your meditation times. Your goal is to get accustomed to finding the still, quiet wisdom that resides within you, and that is best accomplished by not relying too heavily on someone else's voice to create your meditation experience.

It can be helpful to schedule your practice for a particular time (or two!) of day. Many Joy Schoolers use alarms on their phones to remind them of their meditation commitment. Even if you're only opting for a mindfulness practice, tying it to a built-in daily activity can help. For example, with a week-long practice of singing or humming for a set amount of time each day, you could make it the time you spend in the shower or your car. (That's where we all feel like we sound the best anyway!) Just be sure to pay attention to the feeling of the vibration in your body. Notice how long it lasts even after you've stopped singing or humming. One point of this experimentation is to show you how easily you can elevate your own vibration with a bit of commitment, so make sure you're noticing that elevation.

Additionally, I invite you to continue the practice you began last month of checking in with yourself—going inward to recognize and honor all your feelings with nonjudgmental compassion and looking for those small ways to nurture yourself. Hopefully by now it's become a habit you never want to break!

And no matter which of the new meditation/mindfulness practices you decide to focus on each week, I encourage you to additionally sprinkle in moments of experiencing your inner being, that electric pulse that courses through you. Initially you may find the easiest way in, is to repeat that trick you did with your hand, where you get still and centered and hold your hand up outside of your sightline and direct all your attention there. And then you feel it—that light, pleasant, buzzing. It's always there; you just don't notice it most of the time. Once you find it in your hand, it's easier to find it in other places throughout your body. The more you focus your attention on it, the more apparent it becomes. You could remind yourself every night that it's a really yummy, pleasant way to fall asleep. You could use it as a go-to calming technique when your day gets hectic.

Eckhart Tolle says, "Remind yourself to feel your inner body as often as you can. This alone, will help you to vibrate at ever higher vibrational frequencies, and therefore you will attract new circumstances that reflect these higher frequencies."

Please throw yourself into this month's homeplay! I've given you plenty of options to choose from, and each of them will help you lay the critical foundation for the work ahead. It is only by finding ways to disengage with the incessant chatter of your Horizontal Self that you can truly "know thyself" by developing a closer relationship with your long-ignored Vertical Self.

Understand Joy's Obstacles

"Life is a difficult assignment. We are fragile creatures, expected to function at high rates of speed, and asked to accomplish great and small things each day. These daily activities take enormous amounts of energy. Most things are out of our control. We are surrounded by danger, frustration, grief, and insanity as well as love, hope, ecstasy, and wonder. Being fully human is an exercise in humility, suffering, grace, and great humor. Things and people all around us die, get broken, or are lost. There is no safety or guarantees. The way to accomplish the assignment of truly living is to engage fully, richly, and deeply in the living of your dreams. We are made to dream and to live those dreams."

—SUSAN ARIEL RAINBOW KENNEDY (SARK)

I hope you had a beautiful month strengthening your connection with your own precious inner being—the energy field that powers you! I hope you're finding that practice as rich and yummy and elevating as I always have. It's all about commitment and being deliberate with some effective tools.

Whether it's going amazingly well for you, or it's frustrating you—whatever's happening there—just keep in mind it's a skill like anything else, and it gets easier and more rewarding the more you do it. Please continue doing it, either by experimenting with the options, or by maintaining a committed schedule with your identified favorite(s). If you're having any trouble adopting a meditation/mindfulness practice, or trouble being kind and compassionate with yourself, please don't add to the problem by judging yourself for that. Right where you are, right now, is precisely where you're meant to be, and I promise you can count on me to keep you moving in the right direction from here. Sound good?

I'm going to jump right in at the start of this month's reading with a journaling request of you. Complete it before you go any further, please. Take a few deep breaths, open your heart, and let your responses to the following prompts be quick and raw, with no filtering. This isn't the time to try to be spiritual or wise or evolved; this is just your human stuff we're gathering here.

Respond to these prompts one by one, pausing to write about each one in your journal before you move onto the next one. Taking that twenty-four-inch journey from your head down to your heart, write your most honest, automatic continuation of each sentence. Try to sidestep thinking if you can, letting your feeling dictate your response. Even if what pops up for you doesn't make sense, just let it come out through your pen onto the paper. Always, when you don't think you have an "answer" in your mind, just start writing anyway because that opens up the flow, the energetic pathway. Ready?

- What I'm most afraid of happening is:

- The worst thing about me is:

- What I'm most ashamed of is:

- I can't have what I most want to have because:

Since you're reading a book, and not physically at one of my work-shops right now, I can't ask you if you'd like to share your answers. But guess what would happen if you were at my workshop and people were sharing. Do you think there'd be a lot of judgment going on? Gasps of shock and horror? Nope. Never happens. We all have secret shames and fears we're harboring, precious reader. We typically avoid exposing ourselves to that extent with the people around us, and then we complain of feeling lonely and isolated, when the antidote to that is simply to expose more of ourselves. That's where we find our commonalities. That's where we see how we're all far more alike than different. As my international thought-leader friend Christian Pankhurst puts it, "Love is the experience of being felt by another." To experience love, then, we must be brave enough in our vulnerability to be correctly felt.

It is through the process of exposure and acceptance that we stop judging ourselves so harshly, and that naturally leads to us not judg-ing others as harshly. And all that hard, crusty, stuck energy of our judgments then gets freed up, and we feel lighter, and more liberated, and closer to that magical Vertical Self essence I keep referencing.

Our hidden, unacknowledged, unexpressed shame is one of the biggest offenders that's holding our joy and our creating potential at bay. Most of us have some shame that we're aware of, and most of us have a lot that we keep buried, even from ourselves. But it shapes our opinion and beliefs about ourselves. And energetically, we can never rise above our own self-assessment. You create all your external circumstances based on your internal assessment of who you are and what you deserve. Our manifestations simply cannot outrun our deep-down beliefs about our own deservingness. That's why it's so imperative to do this work. You can set your journal aside for now; we'll come back to this bit of writing later.

The Truth About Your "Reality"

Everything that exists in your current external landscape—the yum as well as the yuck—is the result of a unique framework you've established for creating and experiencing your life here in your physical human suit. So, this month we're going to look at how this personal framework for experiencing the world came to be. Chances are good you have no idea how truly, uniquely *personal* this framework is to you, and getting clear on that paves the way to a whole lot of joy you've been missing out on. Remember how I said you are pure joy at your core, but there are likely some obstructions in the way of that being your day-to-day experience? It's time for us to look at how those obstructions got there, because understanding that is the most critical piece to working with them.

Joy-pushers like me often end up talking about trauma. What's most important to understand about trauma is that we all have it to some degree, even if we didn't face down any of the biggies—the heartbreaking life events that we all recognize as trauma. I'm sure many of you reading this did experience that level of trauma; I've seen recent statistics indicating as many as 90 percent of us have!

But whether you consider yourself in that category or not, it's likely you formed some conclusions in your formative years about yourself and/or the world that are not serving your highest expression of joy right now. For our purposes here together, let's agree that "trauma" is simply whatever affected you negatively and caused you to form certain unbeneficial default patterns of thinking about yourself and the world. Trauma is caused not by specific events, but by the emotional response you had to those events. It's an important distinction.

I'll paint you a picture to show you how easily trauma can happen: Imagine a mom in the grocery store with a toddler. She's exhausted, just trying to get on with her day. The toddler runs away from the mom at checkout because he sees a shiny balloon display that fills his little heart with excitement. The display is not too far from the checkout area. Mom is watching the whole time, but also interacting with the checkout clerk, getting her groceries packed, paying her bill. It takes a while.

The toddler, meanwhile, as soon as he reaches the balloons, turns around to eagerly show Mom, and realizes Mom hasn't followed him. He doesn't see Mom anywhere. His eyes go from stranger to stranger and the panic rises in his heart, closing up his throat, stifling his voice. He's frozen in place, terrified now, convinced he's lost and abandoned at the grocery store forever.

From Mom's vantage point, it looks like he's just been standing there admiring the balloons, so she finishes her checkout and strolls over to him, ready to admonish him for running away from her. Maybe she even does start admonishing him, not noticing his terror at first. When he finally sees her, he breaks down and starts wailing in relief, just letting it all hang out. She's embarrassed and tells him to be quiet. She pulls him out of the store because he's making a huge scene. She thinks he's just wailing because he didn't get a balloon.

It's entirely likely that the child has just experienced an event that will leave a traumatic impact. Young children have a different sense of time than adults; to him it might have felt like he was alone and abandoned for hours. Unless Mom herself has reached a high level of consciousness and empathy, she'll probably want to minimize the whole thing, because she won't want to feel the guilt of letting anything bad happen to him.

In coming years, he might bring up the memory, saying, "Remember when you lost me in the grocery store," and she'd be likely to say, "I never lost you in the grocery store. You're such an exaggerator; nothing bad happened to you that day! I could see you the whole time." So, on top of his trauma, he feels gaslighted. She's telling him what he experienced isn't real or true. They each had a dramatically different experience of that same event, based on their unique *perception filters.*

Your perception filter is your personal framework for experiencing the world. It is truly unique to you, and we'll be working with it throughout your joy journey, so let's talk now about how this framework came to be for each of us.

When you came into the world as a fresh, new little human, you had a biological imperative to understand *how it is here* in this space and time. Right from the start, you were programmed to seek and store away knowledge about this wacky, overwhelming world and your place in it. As you grew, your parents, caregivers, school, and culture (maybe religion, too) all provided information for you so that you could *know* things. Since it was so deeply embedded in your human nature as a growing creature to want to make sense of this world you'd landed in, you eagerly gathered up these bits of knowledge coming at you.

It was a lot to take in, so, to categorize all this information, you set up mental "buckets" where you could file all these bits of data and definitions of things. This process started in infancy. Many experts believe it starts in the womb, even. It was important to you to know what each new thing you experienced meant, so you could have a frame of reference for moving forward. And these buckets that you set up as your filing system might have labels like, "I am this," "love means this," "money is this," "rules are this," "power is this," "my place in all of it is this," etc.

We all create this categorization system because life here is really overwhelming and we have a limit to how much information we can comfortably process. Our little human brains have only evolved to process a finite amount of the nearly infinite amount of information swirling around us. Creating these buckets is simply the only thing that makes it manageable for us. This goes on at a subconscious level.

Now, once you've set up a bucket, the easiest thing—the most natural thing—is to continue to fill it with *similar* bits of knowledge, rather than allowing for a contradicting bucket belief to develop. One powerful reason is that we all have a built-in confirmation bias. It's that natural tendency to subconsciously only seek out evidence for what we already believe and ignore evidence to the contrary. (We've seen plentiful examples of confirmation bias in our political and cultural climate in recent years, but that's a whole other discussion.)

Some of your buckets that you set up as a very new human probably cause you to look for, and find, gentle, beautiful things in the world. People who had the massive good fortune to set up mostly those kinds of buckets will continue to fill them with similar evidence as they move forward in creating and attracting their life circumstances. We all know these people who seem to live effortlessly blessed lives. But *most* of us have at least a few buckets set up that represent *unhappy* conclusions we came to in our earliest years—conclusions about ourselves, and conclusions about people and things out there in the world.

What Feeds the Buckets

Are parents responsible for most of our unnecessary limitations? Sure. Yes. No doubt. But parents are just operating from their own innate limitations. They couldn't help passing on their own crappy bucket beliefs; they thought that was how to love you and keep you safe. Because of that, and because of the way our culture tends to parent right now, always wanting to make our kids better, thinking that's helping them, it's likely that you established some bucket beliefs that aren't serving your highest joy and highest potential for creating your best life right now. There are many solid reasons why these negative bucket beliefs are so egregiously common, and we'll be looking at some of them as we work through these months together. For now, just understand that, in general, negative bucket beliefs, particularly about ourselves, are very much the norm.

We continue to feed these bucket beliefs not only because of our confirmation bias, but also due to the built-in negativity bias left over from caveman days. Back then, if you saw the tall grass moving, it could mean a rogue wind, or it could mean an approaching predator. Your negativity bias would cause you to assume the latter because it was important to your survival that you choose that assumption and start running. The red berries your prehistoric ancestor just discovered might be delicious and wholesome, but since you have a bucket belief about some red berries that once killed your cave-mate, your negativity bias is going to tell you to stay away from all red berries. This leftover negativity bias in our reptilian brains still tricks us into believing it's keeping us safe in the world, but it's more likely to be doing the opposite. As we've discussed, whatever we feed our attention to is going to grow in our experience, good or bad.

And that's the next unfortunate thing to understand. The way our buckets continue to be filled is bizarrely cyclical. Let's talk about perception. According to one of my favorite thought leaders whose work I teach through Joy School, the preeminent energy researcher Dr. Joe Dispenza, at any given moment, there are roughly 400 billion bits of information available to you to be processed. Out of those 400 billion, your brain can only register about 2,000 bits, and is only capable of fully processing about fifty bits of information coherently in any moment.

How does your mind decide which fifty bits to grab onto out of the 400 hundred billion available options? It's always going to be the ones that match those original buckets you set up. Remember, the buckets aren't obvious to you; they're not in your conscious awareness because you've spent your whole life filling them, so they've just become the water you swim in. Your definitions and rules about *how it is here* that you made up as a tiny child just continue to get reinforced because that's the way human awareness is programmed.

This is how your perception filter was formed. Every one of us has a perception filter that is uniquely our own—the product of our bucket beliefs. And that means every one of us is truly living in a unique world. There's no such thing as objective reality, because your reality isn't my reality or anyone else's reality, due to this tangly, thick web of beliefs that determines how each of us uniquely interprets the stimulus around us. As my heart-brother Jacob Nordby likes to point out, we're all just seeing reality through a keyhole. And none of our keyholes are lined up the same.

Remember, you're always propelled by that human need to make sense of the world and get smarter and smarter about what it means and how it operates. But as you can see, the conclusions you're likely to be drawing—even right to this day—are heavily influenced by factors that have no basis in objective reality!

This filter not only determines what you experience as reality, but it is extensively coloring your expectations. And you're always creating what you expect. The magic begins when you deeply comprehend that your whole framework for creating your life is based on *misconceptions* you absorbed as a tiny child.

In my workshops, I like to use an old Tony Robbins trick. I tell the participants, "Look around the room and make a mental list of everything that's red. Red, red, red—find all the red things, quick! Now close your eyes! And now, with your eyes closed, yell out one thing that's blue!"

After an awkward moment of no one yelling anything, I tell them to open their eyes and look around and find the blue things. Blue things were there the whole time; they just didn't see them because I'd programmed them to see the red things. It's a fun way to demonstrate that in any situation, what we find is what we're looking for. In that little game, the workshop participants do it consciously. But when we're not doing it consciously, we're doing it unconsciously, and that means letting our filters determine what we see, hear, and experience—*i.e.*, what constitutes our reality.

Most of us are observing "reality" *unconsciously* about 99 percent of the time. The part of your brain that decides what you notice and make "real" is called your *reticular activating system*, and you'll be learning some practices for taking deliberate control of yours.

• • •

"*Perhaps everything we believe is false.*" —DESCARTES

Your filter is always being reinforced. As you go through your life, your unconscious mind scans the horizon of possible bits of information to allow into your consciousness. It's like radar, and when it hits a bit of info that fits with one of your bucket beliefs—*ding, ding, ding!* You feel *that* must be what's true about the world because that feels familiar. That's how you make the unconscious decision to register this bit of information at the exclusion of other billions of bits. All this happens in a nanosecond. So, you pull in another piece of evidence for that bucket.

It's about to get really insidious, so buckle up. Not only does this system work to strengthen our early-formed beliefs to ever more fortified levels, but it also causes us to *create* more and more evidence that shores up these erroneous beliefs. This happens energetically, kind of like what we sometimes call "self-fulfilling prophecy." A child who's formed a bucket belief with some version of the story "I'm broken; I'm bad; I'm untalented; I'm not good enough just as I am," (which are especially common, easy beliefs to form) is going to create more evidence to substantiate that because it's what he deep down believes, and that means it's where he's vibrating. We're all creating our external reality based on our vibration. Maybe he'll perform poorly in school, or in sports, or make himself unattractive or unpopular in some way that confirms his unworthiness. Our outer world is always just a reflection of our inner landscape.

So, it's important to understand that we not only *experience* the world through this filter, but we *create* our world through it as well. It will seem like you can point to all this irrefutable evidence to support the truth of these negative beliefs about yourself, when the fact is, it's just that you've *selectively gathered* the evidence, based on where your keyhole's been lined up. And, based on your energetic output through this same filter, you've continued to attract and create new evidence to match it along the way. This is what I mean by "cyclical."

I'm going for a kerklunk here. Before we move into redesigning your filter, I want a serious lightbulb to flip on for you about why you *are* right where you are in your life. The good and the bad. The yum and the yuck. It isn't about blame or not taking responsibility. It's about "Oh, this situation where I feel stuck in my career, or where I'm not creating the meaningful relationships I want to be in, or I'm not creating the income stream . . ." All these things you can point to in your external world that aren't to your liking are only there as the natural, inevitable result of some misperceptions that you absorbed very early on and have continued to subconsciously feed, nurture, and curate your entire life until now. Everything you've created up until this very moment is the result of this process. Remember, we create what we expect, deep down.

This Is the Turning Point

But you've arrived at the turning point. Now—in this moment. Bringing this dynamic up into the light of your conscious awareness is precisely what needs to happen so that you can begin to start *authentically* questioning the negative thoughts that cross your mind, enough to form new bucket beliefs and start finding evidence for newer, fresh, more accurate facts about yourself and the world. The evidence to support these new facts has been there all along, in those 400 billion bits of information that you haven't been seeing. Just like the blue things in the room.

It doesn't happen overnight. I wish I could tell you it did. It starts as an intellectual understanding but as it grows as a felt, kerklunked understanding, it changes everything. So, that's the seed you'll work to solidly germinate in your consciousness this month through the homeplay I'll soon lay out for you. You'll know it's taken root when you feel that little, real spark of excitement about discovering what might be all around you, just outside your view from your keyhole. All the opportunities, synchronicities, connections that you've been blinded to—they've been patiently waiting for you to learn to line up your keyhole differently, or simply expand it.

Let's go back to our example of the kid in the grocery store.

Remember, as a small child, we don't see logic yet. We process events in terms of *feelings*. So, if you were that kid in the grocery store, you'd likely create a bucket belief about abandonment that you'd carry throughout your life. Another story you might form a bucket belief around might go like this:

> I see something wonderful that I want very much to be mine.
>
> I run toward it with all the happy, free-flowing enthusiasm and joy in my innocent, wide-open heart.
>
> Immediately (when I don't see Mom) I realize I've made a terrible mistake.
>
> I'm terrified, lost, abandoned, unloved, frozen in fear. My heart's racing; I think I'm going to die!
>
> Finally, after what feels like an eternity, Mom is there. Relief! I let my full emotions out.
>
> Mom gets super mad at me. I'm told to stifle my emotions. I'm scolded and pulled out of the store, and I didn't get that thing I wanted so bad, after all that.
>
> When I try to talk about it later, I get shut down. My experience is denied. There must be something really

wrong with me, and I should definitely avoid running
after what I want from here on out.

Once this narrative becomes a bucket belief, it's where your keyhole is lined up. You'll attract and find more evidence for it. Your
drive to understand how this world works, what the rules are, and to
make sure you're right about that, is so strong that you might even
subconsciously test this theory out a few more times by running away
from Mom when you see something fun and exciting out there. On
a subconscious level, you need to make sure your theory is correct.
And of course, Mom is naturally going to double down on the punish-
ments and discipline, so your subconscious goes, "Yep, that's a solid
bucket belief."

Then, as you go through life, without realizing it, this story is
where your keyhole is lined up, so even though there might be ample
evidence in the world around you that would tell a very different
story, your radar is going to scan the horizon and go *ding, ding, ding!*
every time you see someone out there going for something and failing, maybe ending up worse off than they were before. You'll be extra
aware of classmates being too playful in class and getting punished for
it, or later in life maybe you'll zero in on people who lose money in
a passion project. Maybe you're the one who gets punished in school
or loses the money. Again and again, you're wanting to be able to say,
"See? I knew it! It's not safe to go after what I want!"—not in your
conscious brain maybe, but in your subconscious, where you're programmed to find evidence to support your bucket beliefs.

This is how the early-formed story just gets stronger and stronger
for you, and it feels like the natural truth of the world, since it's all you
see because of the keyhole. This is what I mean when I say it becomes

the water you swim in. We're simply not wired to see what's beyond the keyhole until we take conscious control of the dynamic, like we're doing together here now.

This was just one example of how arbitrarily these stories that dictate our lives can be born, but you have hundreds of stories like this running you. We all do. This is how human beings *be*. Bringing these bucket beliefs up into the light of your awareness is the first step in releasing them so that you can write new stories from your now-mature, adult perspective. Now you have logic and emotional maturity. You didn't then.

And I need to clarify an important point: while I'm saying we need to unearth and discover these stories that have been running us, I only mean that we need to know *in essence* what the beliefs are about and what they're still creating in our lives. We can find that out by looking around at our current conditions. We don't need to tie it to a specific childhood memory to re-write the belief. If you were the kid in the grocery store, you wouldn't need to access the grocery store memory. You'd only need to recognize, by looking at your current and recent life situations, that you have a belief around going after what you want, and that belief has been creating unhappy situations for you. In some cases, it can be beneficial to access the memories and events that kicked off our bucket beliefs, and we have a protocol for doing that in Joy School, but it is generally not imperative to success-fully working with these old limitations.

For this month's purposes, the most important takeaway from this understanding—one that I hope is kerklunking solidly for you at this point—is, *You don't need to believe your negative thoughts about yourself or about the world because they're based in bullcrap.* Your thoughts come into your awareness through a totally unreliable filter you created when you were a baby and have continued to fortify ever since. Just because we have a thought, it doesn't mean we need to believe it! This can feel disconcerting if it's never occurred to you before, but it's ultimately super freeing, and it's the key in shifting a lot of energy in our lives.

It's true of every thought you've ever had, but when it comes to our thoughts about ourselves, our abilities, our potential—that's the most important area to shift up. We're going to have thoughts cross our minds all day, every day; that's what it means to be a human being. And many studies have shown that the vast majority of our daily thoughts are habitual—the same thoughts we had last week and last year and so on. That's going to continue to be the case until we start deliberately *noticing* and becoming the observer of our thought patterns and tendencies.

And then, once we're practiced at observing our thoughts, we can develop the skill of routinely questioning them. When we get clear that the negative thoughts we have about ourselves are bullcrap to begin with—are nothing more than the inevitable results of this faulty system that created our arbitrary filter—that's when we can authentically work to change them. You can tell a thought is false by its vibration. As my good friends and amazing coaches Andrea and Lee Vallely say, "*Your soul doesn't think you suck.*" Any thought that contains any message along those lines is not in alignment with the deep wisdom of your Vertical Self. As this realization kerklunks, it gets easier and easier to dismiss all those thoughts that are vibrationally handcuffing you from creating what you want to create.

When that "aha" firmly solidifies—that our negative default thinking patterns are simply inaccurate—that's when we're no longer trying to *trick* our subconscious mind with affirmations or positive-thinking gimmicks. Your subconscious isn't an idiot; it's not falling for that stuff. The gamechanger is when you see the truth that your current life was designed by a child, child-you. Even if it feels like you have evidence you can point to in your external circumstances that demonstrates that the negative beliefs about you are true, hopefully you now deeply understand that it was the faulty beliefs themselves that led you to create the evidence. New beliefs will create different evidence.

"Schema" is the word psychologists use for the repetitive behaviors and patterns we engage in. Every one of us has schemas running. It simplifies life to have default patterns for how we deal with things. It's possible to replace our harmful schemas with new ones through deliberate practice. And yes, you have to intentionally do it again and again to create a new schema. But I've helped people do it for decades so I know it can be done.

To tie this month's awareness into last month's, understanding your filter and how it operates is critical because that's what's between you—the everyday you that you experience yourself as (Horizontal Self), and your core essence, which is pure joy and unlimited creative power (Vertical Self). Once you change the relationship you have with your thoughts, you've begun a chain reaction that will upturn your entire existence.

I was born into an extreme vibration of shame. Shame smeared and distorted my perception filter for many, many dark years of living in a low-vibration state. I attracted and created my reality from that place, right up through my early adulthood. I've done rounds of clean-up on my filter many times in my life, and each and every time I've been able to bring myself up to a new level of estimation of my own authentic worthiness and deservingness (via alignment with my Vertical Self), it's been followed by a dramatic uplevel to my external circumstances. Same with all my Joy Schoolers over two decades. And it's never a one-and-done. We want to always keep working it.

Author and social scientist Malcolm Gladwell has popularized the idea that it takes 10,000 hours of practice to master whatever it is you want to master. It is my humble opinion that there is no more clearly advantageous skill to devote your hours to mastering than the skill of elevating your personal vibration to bring your Vertical Self into the foreground of your life. I know 10,000 sounds like a lot of hours, but however many hours it takes, there's no better way to spend them! (Don't worry. We'll make remarkable progress in far fewer hours, and you'll see benefits and results every step of the way.)

Revealing What's in Your Filter

So now, let's look back at the journaling you did when we were just getting started with this chapter. Whatever you wrote down in response to those prompts, I want you to now consider, *What does this say about me? Others? The world?* If I believe this thing, what am I believing about myself, other people, or the world at large? All of our underlying fears fall into one of these three categories. We fear that we ourselves are lacking in some way, or that others will respond to us or treat us negatively, or that the world itself is a frightening and unpredictable place. Take a moment to get some clarity around what your responses to the writing you did at the start of this chapter can reveal in terms of these three areas of fear.

Once you have some clarity around that, can you begin to see that these are simply some bucket beliefs you have about yourself, others, and/or the world? Choose one that represents a belief about yourself. If that applies to more than one, see which one stings the most. Which one stirs up the most energy when you bring it to mind?

Use your imagination now to consider this issue as if it were a whole stick within you, with opposite expressions of this trait at either end of the stick. I learned this metaphor from Esther Hicks and the group of non-physical entities she channels called Abraham. (Throughout this book I'll refer to them as "Abraham/Hicks.") The stick metaphor provides a brilliant way to recognize that no matter what trait or aspect of the human experience we're looking at, the truth is that we all have the full spectrum of that thing within us. The two ends of the stick represent the extremes, and every one of us has simply positioned ourselves somewhere on the stick with regard to that trait/quality/attribute.

See if you can recognize now that whatever you're believing about yourself is simply where you've lined up your perception keyhole on that stick with regard to your self-assessment. Recognizing that, can you question this belief? Maybe by recognizing it as a bucket belief you created out of the immature, faulty logic of a child, you can give yourself a bit of grace, love, and acceptance now with regard to this issue. Maybe that could come from recognizing that we're all human and none of us is knocking it out of the park on all counts at all times. That would be absurd.

Or, maybe by intentionally turning your attention to it, you can identify some evidence for where you *have,* in fact, been aligned with the preferred end of the stick. And maybe you'll begin to glimpse the evidence that was always there, just beyond your keyhole, that you already are enough, and lovable and admirable in regard to this issue. The whole stick is in you, just like it's in all of us. We've all just placed ourselves somewhere on that spectrum. If you've been giving your attention to examples of where you've aligned with an end of the stick you don't like, (because that's where your keyhole has been lined up thanks to your unreliable filter), and that makes you feel uncomfortable now, it just means you haven't been aligned with your true core nature. You adjust that alignment with your most powerful tool for reality creation: your attention. Your attention is the currency you use (mostly unconsciously) to create your ongoing reality.

In my book *Juicy Joy*, I talked about the stories we all harbor and how we use our attention to keep them alive. I wrote:

> It feels like our stories are created outside of us, by the things that occur in our lives. But as we've already discussed, our beliefs create our circumstances and everything that occurs is subject to many possible interpretations. So, our stories are actually created by our beliefs and perceptions, and then fed and strengthened by the attention we've chosen to funnel into them. Imagine right now that there's a faucet on your forehead, right at your third eye, with a garden-hose attachment on it. You send your attention out into the world through this hose. Everything that's in your life is a seed, the good and the bad. Whatever you're giving your attention to— those are the seeds you're watering. That's what's going to grow for you. Those are the seedlings that will sprout into stories if you water them enough.

> If you've got a problem and you put a lot of focus and attention on *resisting* that problem, you're watering the hell out of that seed. Even if you eventually struggle through this issue, hating every second of it, and somehow wrangle it under control, you've watered the seeds of the *essence* of the problem, so just like weeds around

it, more of the same kind of problem is going to keep popping up.

That's why people tend to keep repeating their stories by experiencing the same flavor of unhealthy relationship patterns, the same financial difficulties, the same health issues. Whenever you develop a strong negative feeling about a circumstance and put a lot of resistance into experiencing it (as opposed to welcoming any natural emotions that arise and looking for the lesson) you strengthen the seemingly magnetic force that brought it to you in the first place.   What if the only thing stopping you from creating your ideal reality is your failure to conjure up an ideal story-seed for yourself that you can believe in long enough to water it with the requisite amount of your attention?

The same goes for these fears and things you're judging in you. The only reason they've stayed alive in your experience is that you've fed them a continuous stream of your attention. You can decide now to place your attention on the end of the stick you prefer. The whole stick is within you.

Your Primary Lens

There's a theory in high-level consciousness work that author and thought leader Ken Wilber talks about, and Carl Jung talked about, and other of my favorite teachers have as well. It says that just as each of us has a unique perception filter, we each also have a *primary lens* on that filter that's unique to us, based on the culmination of our experiences, primarily the ones that involved strong emotions. It's emotion-based, and it drives all our decisions and actions to a much greater extent than the rational thinking mind. You know how you decide one thing with your brain and your smarts, and your pros and cons lists, and then you just find yourself doing a different thing? And you think, *that's weird, I had decided blah-blah, and now I'm doing the opposite.* That's this primary lens on your filter at work.

I'm telling you this because there's a good chance that you uncovered the primary negative lens on your filter earlier when you journaled your responses to those writing prompts I gave you. Look again now at your responses to those prompts. Do you see a connecting thread? Can these beliefs be boiled down to a common essence they share? It's okay if you don't see a connection, but for many of us, it's easy to spot a commonality in what surfaced. While it's true that you're always seeing the whole world, including yourself, through your distorted filter—there's often that especially focused spot in the filter that acts like a magnifying glass, pulling in even more unwanted evidence.

Because of that magnifying glass, you've given this belief a lot of energy. Throughout your life it's likely been there, sucking up the bulk of your chi, prana, life force. Even if it doesn't feel like it's getting much of your conscious attention, that could be a sign that you've successfully buried it, and the energy it takes to *keep* a belief like that buried is a lot. See if you can pull your answers into one negative statement about yourself, like "I am _____." If your answers don't easily pull together it's okay to do a few "I am" statements, but see if you can get it all to coalesce as one catch-all statement. Write this statement in your journal.

Next, put your hand over your heart and feel into the answer to this question: *What would the opposite of this statement be?* On that stick that represents the full spectrum of this trait or attribute, what's at the other end of the stick? What's the most positive flip for this trait? "Clumsy" becomes "graceful." "Stupid" becomes "brilliant." "Awkward" becomes "poised." Write the new, flipped statement in your journal.

Acknowledging that the original negative statement is just a bucket belief you formed as a baby and have continued to feed throughout your life because it's where your keyhole's been lined up, let yourself imagine, *Where do I have proof that this new, opposite belief is true?*

Call up your imagined Etch A Sketch. Fill it up with lines for all those things you think you know about yourself. Shake it all away. Look back over your life, or deep into your heart, and find the evidence that this new, flipped belief is just *as* true as the one you originally wrote. The evidence has always been there, outside your view from your keyhole. You have the power and understanding now to expand your keyhole to find this new list of evidence. Pretend you're a trial attorney gathering evidence for a case. Pause your reading now while you make this list of evidence as long and detailed as you can.

This is your new truth about yourself. If you don't quite believe it yet, don't worry; we're not done. But I'm hoping we've cracked something open. Once your filter's keyhole has been stretched out, it can never go back to its original form. You *know* now, on a meaningful level, that you are just as likely to *be* this new, flipped-belief version of you as the old version. If your thoughts are being pulled more toward the old belief, you have to understand that's just habit. Are habits easy to break? Nah. Not usually. But they *can* be broken with repetition and some commitment.

I want you to understand how huge this is. Every single thing in your life right now is there because of the vibration you've been emitting. Committing to breaking *this* one habit of thought, by installing your new, flipped belief in its place, will change the dial on the vibration you send out into the world. And the world *will* rearrange itself accordingly. It'll look like magic if you pay attention. I'm speaking from personal experience and the personal experiences of my many Joy Schoolers who have done this work.

You break a habit through repetition of the replacement habit. Recovering alcoholics become coffee junkies. Cigarette quitters take up gum. The more consistent and deliberate you are with installing this new habit—reminding yourself of this new truth about you—the faster you'll leave the old beliefs behind and start seeing the results of your elevated personal vibration.

Let's get you some homeplay around this! Here are your four homeplay assignments, one for each week of this month, in sequential order.

HOMEPLAY FOR KEY 3, WEEK ONE

Take that new belief you've discovered about yourself (the flipped version of the old, erroneous belief that was in your filter) and write it out in some way that's appealing to you. Make is as artsy and unique and attractive as you like. Maybe you'll even want to frame it, but at the very least, tack it up someplace where you'll see it. You're going to look at these words every day. You might want to additionally type them out in a document in your computer and make it your screen saver or make it the first thing you see when you open your phone each morning.

Work on your skill of self-observation by taking note of your response to these words each time you read them. What does the voice in your head say about them? Notice when it feeds you that same old bullcrap about your limitations and whatever it says about what's wrong with you. Remember, "Your soul doesn't think you suck." When you observe that flavor of messaging going on—which means any version of the story of you sucking in any way—replace the thought with the new truth about you. It's just as likely to be true. Just line up your keyhole better.

Remember my story about the soup? I'll tell you right now, it will start out feeling as weird as stirring soup with your left hand. That's why I told you the soup story—so maybe, when it feels weird, you'll remember about the soup and do it anyway. Your logical mind has now been shown why the new truth is every bit as valid as the old, faulty bucket belief. The only thing now tying you to the old belief is habit.

Spend one week committed to reminding yourself of the new truth, observing your inner dialog, and consciously replacing any thought connected with the old bucket belief with this newer, truer belief.

HOMEPLAY FOR KEY 3, WEEK TWO

For week two of your homeplay this month, you're going to practice the reverse engineering tool I shared with you in the Introduction. Every morning this week, as you're waking up, you're going to reverse engineer your day around this new truth you've decided on about yourself. You're going to look at your new truth and pretend it's the end of that day, your head's hitting the pillow, and you're reviewing your day in reverse. What kind of day did you have, living from this new truth about yourself? What were the little differences in your routine? How did you greet the people in your life? What did you eat for breakfast? What choices did you make about what you wore, which activities you took part in, how you took care of your needs and desires? You're going to pretend you're looking back on the day you just had (which is actually the day in front of you) and give sincere thanks for such a beautiful day.

You'll do this every morning, and as you then actually experience the day you reverse-engineered that morning, you'll use your powers of intentionality to focus all your attention on where this vision comes true for you. Celebrate every little confirmation that you successfully reverse engineered your day! If something pops up into your experience that seems more like evidence for the old belief, don't feed it any attention. If it's something that requires you to take some sort of action to take care of it, go ahead and take action, but do not feed it any level of heightened emotion or attention because that's what's been keeping these parts of your life that you don't like *alive*. Just take care of it. Whatever needs to be done. Take care of it with a deep understanding that it won't be in your experience much longer. Nothing in your reality can survive without your robust attention to it. You can literally starve it out of existence.

Your homeplay for this second week is to use those instructions to reverse engineer your day for at least seven days in a row. And you can add in specific, smaller time-frame intentions into your practice too, as needed. If you have a business meeting, or a promising date, or a difficult phone call to make, reverse engineer it before you get in there. Put yourself at the end of whatever event you're working with, and look "back" on it, seeing it all having unfolded superbly, and give thanks. The more you do this, noticing and celebrating the times and ways that it works like magic, and ignoring the times when it doesn't, the more you'll increase the percentage of it working. Truly. That's just how energy operates.

HOMEPLAY FOR KEY 3, WEEK THREE

You're going to expand on your reverse engineering skills this week, because practice makes perfect, and this is such an incredibly valuable skill to have if you'd like to manifest things in your external world. We decided that's something you'd like to do, right? Here's how you're going to do it!

Pretend it's a month from now. Pretend that you've been living in your new truth about yourself (the one you wrote out all fancy and look at every day) for the entire month. Imagine you've been rocking it. Coming from this truth, all the shifts you've been wanting to see in your external world have been happening. To the extent that it's feasible and believable for you, I want you to vividly imagine all the juicy improvements in your life that have come from living your new truth for one solid month. And in case you're having any trouble believing it, I will remind you that *these shifts are the natural, inevitable result of sending out a new vibration.*

Now pretend you and I bump into one another, and I ask, "Hey, how's the month been for you? What's been going on?" And you say, "Oh my gosh, Lisa, I am so thrilled about everything that's happened in this last month! Let me tell you about it." And you proceed to *recount* (because we're pretending it's a month out, remember?) all the absolutely wonderful things that have happened in this past month. Got it? Okay, here's the fun part.

Right now, I want you to take out your cell phone. Go to the voice recorder feature. Spend a moment in your imagined fantasy of what your life looks like a month from now, and then record the answer to the question, "How's the past month gone for you?"

Record it with as much feeling, excitement, and over-the-top enthusiasm as you can muster! Don't pre-plan it. Just allow yourself to embody the feelings you're wanting to have, then deliver a from-the-heart speech of gratitude about what an amazing month you've just experienced, living your highest truth about you. Include all the juicy details of your internal and external reality, letting the words just flow out as you record them.

Once you've completed that step, you want to treat this recording like the solid gold that it is. As part of your new replacement-habit practice, you're going to listen to this recording of you, in your own voice, in your own words, *at least* twice per day for this week. This is how you replace the beliefs in your filter and create a new external reality for yourself. As you listen, deliberately step into the emotion of what you're describing. You're going to be so blown away by the results you're going to want to make a new recording for each new month; I promise!

For all the days of this third week of homeplay, play the recording of your new truth while you're in your car, walking the dog, washing dishes, folding laundry. If you really want to supercharge its magic, listen to it while you gaze at your own gorgeous eyes in the mirror. Use your eyes to find that core essence, your Vertical Self. The eyes staring back at you are the exact same eyes that you came in with as a baby. Isn't that cool to contemplate? Everything else about you grows and changes and replenishes itself, but not your eyes. They truly are the windows to that part of you that is boundless, pure, unlimited joy and creative power. Don't ignore your precious eyes. Bathe them in your love. Use them to find and love the real you to an extent you've never reached before now.

HOMEPLAY FOR KEY 3, WEEK 4

You've taken most of this month to discover the powerful benefits of replacing your #1 negative (erroneous) belief with a better, just-as-true if not truer belief. Use the remainder of the month to practice this magic formula on another belief that's pulling down your vibration and limiting you! (One from your journaling at the start of this chapter or another one that you've recognized since then.) The idea is for this practice to become more natural to you, so repeat it even beyond this month with as many limiting beliefs as you can identify!

This is such a powerful practice for expanding your keyhole of perception! Any time a negative thought about you or the world crosses your mind, deliberately remember how unreliable these thoughts are. You've begun the practice of questioning your beliefs and replacing them. Even if you feel a bit clumsy and new at this skill, you are right where you're supposed to be.

As my brilliant friend, cognitive neuropsychologist Chris Niebauer puts it, "Humans make stuff up and then they believe it." Chris shares phenomenal insights through his books and YouTube videos to support your growing understanding that you are not your thoughts! You can find them through your Joy Kit or by searching for him online. The more kerklunked you get on this ancient spiritual truth, the closer you'll be to elevating your Joy Setpoint.

KEY 4

Feel to Heal

> *"What if my anger, my fear, my loneliness were never mistakes, but invitations? What if in skipping the pain, I was missing my lessons? Instead of running away from my pain, was I supposed to run toward it? Perhaps pain was not a hot potato after all, but a traveling professor. Maybe instead of slamming the door on pain, I needed to throw open the door wide and say, come in! Sit down with me. And don't leave until you've taught me what I need to know!"*
> —GLENNON DOYLE

Welcome to month four of your joy journey! I hope you've been getting more and more comfortable loving on your sweet self and living from your new, truer truth. Have you come to some realizations about that tangly web of erroneous conclusions that's clouding up your perception filter? Are you starting to pull back the curtain on some of your bucket beliefs? It's pretty eye-opening, isn't it?

From the moment you woke up today, to this delicious moment we're sharing right now, you've been swimming through a sea of perception. Me, too. It's true for every one of us, day in and day out. Each of us is perceiving reality through a keyhole, and none of our keyholes are lined up the same. A thing happens, and as it crosses the threshold of your unique perception filter, you assign it a meaning. Then a feeling springs from this thought, this meaning you've assigned it. Your default has been to assume the feeling is the result of the event, when it's always really been the result of this meaning you bestow. It's both unnerving and potentially exciting to embrace the truth of this, but I hope your homeplay practice last month has these concepts fairly kerklunked for you because we'll be building on them now!

We've established that you cannot believe your own thinking. Your thinking comes through an unreliable filter of your personal perception. And I know you probably think I'm going to say you can only believe your feelings, but, I'm sorry, dear reader; you can't believe your feelings either, because every feeling comes from a thought. Since the feeling is based on a thought that arose from a flawed perception filter, the feeling's message to you has no basis in anything real.

The feeling itself is real, and valid, of course, because you're feeling it. You might be thinking, *Why the heck has she had me paying all this attention to my feelings if they aren't even real?* That would be a fair question. It's not that the feelings themselves aren't real; it's just that you can't believe the messages that most of your bad feelings are trying to send you.

I'm going to break that down for you in this chapter, but the overview is this: your feelings are real things that create real chemical reactions in your body. But every feeling springs from a thought, and, left unchecked, the feeling will often then generate new, similar thoughts that pile onto the originating thought, generating even more intense, same-flavor feelings. Depending on what kind of thought it was, this cycle can be needlessly detrimental to your vibratory state, unnecessarily dragging down your joy, all because of a thought that was never true to begin with!

The reason most of your bad-feeling thoughts feel bad, is that they're in opposition to your soul's deep knowing. You, at your core, your Vertical Self with its pure essence of love and joy, are not in agreement with the thought that's causing the bad feeling, and that's why it feels bad. There are exceptions, of course—times when we feel genuine grief or sadness around a pure situation that's untainted by our faulty perception filter, or times when our intuition is alerting us to something we need to address. But for most of us, these situations account for a small percentage of the time we spend in low-vibration states.

You've been practicing honoring your feelings and accepting all of them with compassion for a very good reason. Your feelings are valuable, precious clues. They hold the key to gaining insight and clarity about what's in your filter. This is the broader perspective I've been talking about—the observer viewpoint we must master so that we can expand our perception filter and get it working for us instead of against us. Your feelings are not trustworthy in terms of the messaging they try to send you, but they are supremely valuable in gaining an understanding about the erroneous beliefs muddying up your filter.

This month, you're going to establish a new relationship with your thoughts and feelings. The reason this is tricky comes back to those hardwired biases I've described. Thanks to the confirmation bias, as well as the way our society is structured, we've spent our whole lives desperate to be right about things. Think back to your school days. If you have the right answer in school, you get rewards and praise and respect and gold stars. And if you get the wrong answer enough times, you get shame, punishment, and you're made to feel significantly "less than." These feelings still trigger our survival instinct because of that primitive fear of being ostracized from the tribe.

So, it's natural that we very much want to believe our thoughts are right, even when they make us unhappy! Even when they make us unhappy, the need to be right about our thoughts is stronger than our own desire for happiness! We humans are such bizarre creatures! But once we deeply understand that our thoughts are so terribly tainted by our filter, and we recognize that much of what's in our filter is working against us, it lets us open up to the realization that our thoughts are simply unreliable and defending their "rightness" is not doing us any favors.

Coming to clearly see that is the difference between the work we're doing together here, and traditional positive thinking. Positive thinking in itself is not very effective because when your conscious mind says, "I've got to think happy thoughts, happy thoughts, happy thoughts," it kind of begs the question, under what circumstances would someone set an intention like that? You would likely set an intention like that only when you know that deep down, you believe thoughts that are making you unhappy. Otherwise, you wouldn't even be trying to cover it with those positive affirmations in the first place, right? Well, your subconscious isn't an idiot. It knows when you're faking it. And your subconscious is responsible for the strongest energetic signal you send out that creates your reality. So, only when you deeply realize how your awareness system is set up to feed you bullcrap can you neutralize your identification with your negative bucket beliefs in a logical, authentic way.

I've told you we'd be working on two things: learning how to be happy, and also manifesting what you want (with the understanding that these two things are not connected in the way you've likely been led to believe.) The good news is that coincidentally, handily, you can work toward both objectives by deepening your practice with this one primary skill we're focusing so much on right now: getting you separate from your thoughts. Putting that space between you and your thoughts is what will allow you to create inner peace, joy, happiness, alignment with your Vertical Self. And, it's from that energy that you'll easily be able to create all the things you want in your external world. It's all about the vibration you're emitting every second of every day. It's from that vibration that you create every single bit of your experience.

That's why the last few months' homeplay has been so foundational. You've practiced being the observer of you, first by observing how you show up in relationship to the hallmarks of an inner landscape of joy, then by observing your feelings, then by adding in the practice of observing yourself as an energetic presence through various meditation techniques, and then by beginning to notice your own perception filter at work. Along the way, you've practiced treating yourself with compassion, which is critical to widening that deservingness valve that determines how much goodness you allow into your life.

As you've worked with these practices, you've probably noticed they have application for times when you're triggered. By "triggered," I mean any time you have an unpleasant feeling or reaction to something that happens. This month, you'll continue with your self-inquiry, while practicing showing yourself that compassion. But now that you understand how your filter works, you're going to add in a new skill for getting clarity on where those feelings you identify are actually coming from.

What Bugs You?

Before you go any further, take out your Joy Journal, and off the top of your head, make a list of everything that bugs you: the biggies and the smallies. Nothing is too insignificant for this list; make it as long and detailed as you can. Once you feel complete with the list for now, you can continue reading, but I welcome you to observe yourself throughout this month and add to the list as new things occur to you.

This list is showing you valuable information about what's in your perception filter. Let's break down how the filter operates a bit further now. We've established that every feeling you have comes from a thought. We humans tend to think that some external event causes the feeling, but there's an instantaneous, barely perceptible step in between those two things. It's a three-stage process that goes:

1. Event happens.

2. We have a thought about the event as it crosses the threshold of our unique filter.

3. And then we feel the feeling based on the thought, not the event itself.

Here's an example: Someone makes a rude remark about you. You feel that whoosh of shame, or indignation, or anger. It alters your body chemistry in a second. It *seems* like the feeling is a direct result of the event. But if you can push the slow-mo button in your mind, you see that no remark anyone ever makes has to affect you. It only affects you to the extent that you make meaning of it. So, when you go to that place of quiet inner reflection and ask, "Darling, what are you feeling?" the triggered part of you might answer, "I'm feeling hurt," or "I'm feeling frustrated that I can't win favor with this person." Or "I'm angry! That was so unfair! Who does she think she is?"

The next level you'll go to this month with your self-inquiry is: *What meaning did I assign this event? Beneath this reaction, what's the story I must be telling myself?* The deeper underlying question, of course, is: *What's the core belief that caused me to make this particular meaning from this event that just happened?* This takes some work, because even though the story behind it is what's causing your feelings, this all goes on in a snap, deep beneath the level of your awareness.

It will likely seem to you that whatever reaction you're having is the totally obvious reaction that anyone would have. But the truth is that whatever you feel from this incident isn't about the current incident itself; it's about whatever you've got stored in your bucket beliefs. Keeping that in mind, you might even get a glimpse of the bucket belief your feeling is springing from. This is extremely powerful work I'm throwing you right into, pretty early in our journey. This is how we gain clarity and awareness about what's in our filter, letting us glimpse where our keyhole has been lined up. We can't work with our perception filter or peek around it until we can plainly call it out for what it is.

To get back to our example, if you knew, beyond any doubt, that this remark was crazy and baseless, it wouldn't trigger you at all. If someone came up to you and said, "you're a rhinoceros," you wouldn't necessarily be offended. You know you're not a rhinoceros, so you might just laugh and think they're nuts. But if you happened to have a big nose, or a big butt that you're self-conscious about, you'd feel triggered and hurt. You'd automatically assume, based on your filter, that you knew what that remark meant. It's the meaning we make of anything that causes our feelings about it. For the remark to hurt you, there must be agreement somewhere inside you. Whatever story you've made up about yourself and stored in your bucket beliefs would have to jibe with your assumption about the remarker's intention.

For all you know, the person making the remark might have heard that calling someone a unicorn means they are a unique and magical creature, and then gotten the reference mixed up in their mind so that "rhinoceros" came out of their mouth instead of "unicorn." Of course, it's true that some comments are more unmistakably derogatory than the rhinoceros comment, but even in those cases, you're at choice to recognize that anything anyone says about you is only an outward demonstration of what's inside them and has very little to do with you. We'll do more with that in Key 6.

HOMEPLAY FOR KEY 4, WEEK ONE

Go back to the list of triggers you made in your journal and apply your understanding of the three-part response breakdown to each of these triggers you've identified. This can be so enlightening, particularly when patterns start to surface! Additionally, this week, when you feel triggered by anything in real time—big or small—you're going to practice applying this understanding in the moment the trigger is happening. For every trigger, you'll break it down into its three parts by asking yourself:

1. What is the event? (The thing you are experiencing or observing.)

2. What is the thought? (The meaning you're giving it; the story you're making up.)

3. What is the feeling? (Notice that the feeling is arising from the thought, not the event itself.)

As you do this, you'll keep in mind the truth that the event doesn't have any significance until you assign it a meaning on its way through your filter. For you to have any kind of negative emotional reaction to anything, there's a story underneath it. This week will be about noticing the difference between the event (the objective bones of the thing that happens), and the story where meaning is created. And I'll tell you a secret: for most of our triggers, it's the same story again and again, even if the external events seem different on the surface.

To clarify, when I say there's always a story behind it, I don't necessarily mean a real detailed story. There are about a dozen detrimental core bucket beliefs that most of us feed to varying extents. For many, many people, there's a bucket we keep filling that says simply, "I'm not good enough," or "I'm not lovable," or "People are mean," or "I don't deserve good things," or "I'm lacking, either personally or materially," or "I'm powerless." There are other common bucket beliefs, and there are more specific flavors of those, but those are some of the biggies.

I'm not going to stop reminding you of this: We create our lives vibrationally. We're creating every next moment, next hour, next day, based on where we're vibrating and what's prominent and activated in our perception filter. Until we change the makeup of our filter, we're not going to change our patterns of creation, and we're not going to be able to elevate our Joy Setpoint.

You are a reality-manufacturing machine. It's all you, my dear reader. As you travel through life, situation by situation, your mind is always asking, "How is it here?" and the answer to that question is not coming from objective reality. Maybe a sliver of it comes from objective reality, but the vast majority of your answer to "how is it here?"

is coming from whatever you're layering over that sliver of objective reality, according to the lens of your own unreliable perception filter. Then you create more unique reality for you to experience based on that energy. One of my favorite teachers, Alan Cohen, used to say, "Your world is your thoughts, pushed out." That's all it is.

HOMEPLAY FOR KEY 4, WEEK TWO

For this week's homeplay, you'll continue this same practice while adding to it. It takes repetition of this skill for it to become your new default setting, so don't give up when it starts feeling tiresome to do all this dissecting of your reactions. I want you to get excited every time you get triggered by anything! Get excited because it's an opportunity to build your muscle for this joy-revealing new skill! This week, now that you have a bit of practice under your belt, you'll start recording your observations in your Joy Journal. At least once per day (more is better!) write down the three parts you identify for every reaction to something that occurred that day.

Once you've recorded the three-part breakdown, focus on that second part—the meaning you ascribed to the event. Notice how the originating event is simply a thing that occurred, and notice how the feeling you experienced is all about the meaning you gave it. That's the primary skill we're working to kerklunk. With your advanced application of the skill this week, go ahead and see if you might be able to recognize a recurring core wound (bucket belief) related to this feeling and the meaning you ascribe to the events.

Once a probable core wound begins to surface in your awareness, you can look back on how you might have formed that bucket belief if you like, but it's not necessary. Just recognize that it's a bucket you've spent your life filling, based on a belief that was never true. Celebrate this recognition! It's only by making the unconscious conscious that we begin to heal!

Once you've identified a bucket, watch for all the places it shows up. See if you can try out making the choice to not believe your thoughts when they spring from that bucket. And don't expect this to come easily; if you find even just one clear application of this tool per day, you'll be doing fantastic with this practice! I'm throwing you right into the deep end with this month's homeplay. Even in my ongoing Joy School community where we support one another in this, it's commonly acknowledged that it's no piece of cake. The rewards though, once it starts to click into place, are lifechanging.

Keep in mind that even though you'll be coming to new understandings about the faulty thoughts that bring up certain feelings in you, the feelings themselves are real and are to be honored with compassion. It's the thoughts that are false. As that kerklunks to ever deeper levels, the feelings that come from these thoughts will begin to authentically shift on their own.

HOMEPLAY FOR KEY 4, WEEK THREE

I shared early in our journey that it's the resistance to our emotions that causes our suffering—not the emotions themselves—and I described how when you learn how to embrace them, every emotion can have an undercurrent of joy. That's the reward of a more clear, uncluttered filter, and that's what this third week's homeplay will begin to create for you.

Maybe you've heard Rumi's famous poem, "The Guest House":

This being human is a guest house.

Every morning a new arrival.

A joy, a depression, a meanness, some momentary awareness comes as an unexpected visitor.
Welcome and entertain them all!
Even if they are a crowd of sorrows, who violently sweep
your house empty of its furniture, still, treat each guest
honorably.
He may be clearing you out for some new delight.
The dark thought, the shame, the malice. Meet them at
the door laughing, and invite them in.
Be grateful for whatever comes, because each has been
sent as a guide from beyond.

Welcoming every emotion—opening our arms to Rumi's "crowd
of sorrows"—does not come naturally to most of us, because we've
been so conditioned to label everything Out There as good or bad,
wanted or unwanted. Doing the work of breaking our responses down
with this three-part-system will show you how automatic and ultimately arbitrary these labels can be.

Can you welcome the sadness, the meanness; whatever feeling is
there? That's this week's invitation. The distinction you'll make with
this week's homeplay is to make sure that you are fully honoring and
welcoming every emotion that comes up. There's a balance to be
struck here, so your work is to find the sweet spot. As you authentically begin to question the thoughts that cause you to create arbitrary
meanings of the events in your life, you will likely find your negative
feelings around these events begin to lessen. Whatever negative emotions remain, however, must be fully embraced with compassion.

It's important to keep in mind the cyclical nature of our filter that
loves to continually find more evidence to support whatever's in our

bucket beliefs. That's the energy that's pulling in all of your unwanted circumstances right now. The unhealed frequencies in your buckets are there because you did not have the ability to process those emotions when you first experienced them. Whenever you experienced something in your younger, impressionable years that you were not emotionally equipped to deal with, you stored this energy instead of allowing it to flow through you as it's meant to do.

The author Michael Singer calls these stored pockets of suppressed energy by their Vedic name: "samskaras." Eckhart Tolle collectively calls them the "pain body." We've been calling them your bucket beliefs. Gregg Braden and many other contemporary thought leaders describe, in anatomical terms, what happens within our physicality. Basically, every emotion creates a specific chemical cocktail in our bodies. When we haven't developed the emotional maturity to process the chemistry created by a traumatic event, this chemical formation gets stored in the form of neuropeptides that attach to cells in our tissues. It's measurable by modern medical technology. It's not within the scope of this book to go into all the well-documented science around this, but if it interests you, I encourage you to explore the fascinating work of Gregg Braden, Bruce Lipton, Candace Pert, Joe Dispenza, and Bessel van der Kolk, MD.

For our purposes together, it's about taking deliberate control of our mental dialog to create the internal emotional climate for healing to occur. In your mind, you want to start framing out your triggers something like this: "Okay, I'm feeling resistance to this thing that is happening. This probably means I have a bucket belief that matches the frequency of my current situation, and therefore some long-suppressed emotions are being reactivated. I'll let them surface and honor them with compassion, while also acknowledging that the thought that's led to this feeling probably sprang from a bucket belief I created long ago and have continued to feed ever since. This bucket belief is probably based in untruth that I misinterpreted when I was too young to process a feeling that was being created by some trauma I was experiencing. Even though this feeling is likely based in a thought that was never true anyway, I'll welcome the full expression of this feeling now, since all it needs in order to heal and release is my acknowledgment and compassion."

Of course, it's unlikely you'll go through all the nuances of that thought process right in the red-hot moment of your triggering! Read through that internal dialogue enough times that you feel its essence kerklunk in your heart. Once that happens, you can rely on a short-cut dialogue such as, "This feeling is probably not about what's currently happening. I honor and process this feeling by loving myself and having compassion for myself. This expansion of my keyhole of perception will allow me to be more effective in dealing with this situation."

For clarity, you might want to look back at the example of the toddler in the grocery store. Because the emotions of his situation were too strong for him to process, they got chemically stored away as the untrue conclusion: "It's dangerous for me to go after things I want." Unchallenged (by the kind of work we're doing together now), a bucket belief like that could very well run a person's life. There could have been many other baseless beliefs that additionally got stored from that one event, including abandonment issues or even uncomfortable feelings in grocery stores or around balloons! Most of us are walking around with dozens of preferences and avoidances that are the results of long-ago situations we have no conscious memory of.

Taking yourself through the above mental dialogue (and even the condensed version) right in the midst of your human-y existence requires some serious dedication. So, this third week's homeplay is to practice the application of this understanding by setting aside time to journal around it. Every day this week, look back on something that triggered you, and write, stream-of-consciousness style, about everything you were feeling in that moment. With all the love and self-acceptance you can muster, focus more on the feeling than any thoughts you might have about it. Encourage the feeling to expand within you (this is probably the opposite of what you normally do) so that it can all pour out onto the page. When you do this, you release more than just the feeling of that specific event; you unlock the storage system so that any energies you've stored that match the frequency of the recent trigger can be released as well. Eckhart Tolle calls it "digesting the pain body." It's about *not* running away from a challenging feeling, but lovingly sitting with it instead, honoring it by allowing it to fully unfold.

I adore the way my talented friend Thomas Lloyd Qualls talks about it:

"You don't have to wallow and roll around in your grief. But you must learn to turn around and look the monster in the face. Stop running from it. Stop pretending it isn't there. When we drag these monsters out into the light, when we use our words to expose them, they lose most of their powers. We see them clearly for what they are: parlor tricks, illusions, games that are rigged."

> "To stay with a broken heart, with a rumbling stomach, with the feeling of hopelessness and wanting to get revenge—that is the path of true awakening." —PEMA CHÖDRÖN

One of my favorite benefits of regularly inviting these long-stored negative emotions to surface is that you'll notice an increased capacity for savoring the naturally occurring *beautiful* moments in your life. It sounds contradictory, but inviting your challenging feelings into their full expression unlocks the gates within you that have been holding back your deeply *joyful* emotions as well. Think of it like a pendulum that can only swing in one direction to the extent it also swings in the other. When you've been blocking the full experience of your sadness, you're disallowing the pendulum to swing in the direction of the full experience of your joy. Many of us, in our attempts to avoid painful feelings, fall into the trap of relegating our pendulum to swing in tiny, controlled sweeps. Once we invite it to swing more fully (in both directions) we'll experience a depth of awe and wonder we've inadvertently been disallowing.

A sunrise or sunset, a puppy's wagging tail, the tender hug of your beloved, a rainbow, a fresh peach—with regular use of this practice you'll no longer take these sensory treasures for granted. A weird little snippet of nature that has always inspired awe for me personally is watching wind blow through the tops of trees just where they meet the sky. What inspires awe for you? This week, start training yourself to pause and invite these moments to take root in your soul. Researchers tell us it takes just twenty seconds of full attention on a good feeling for it to create new neural pathways in the brain and for the body to produce serotonin. Just twenty seconds! Yet so many of us let these moments slip by without deliberately holding them for that long. If you're having trouble coming across such moments, close your eyes and vividly *imagine* such a moment for twenty seconds. Research shows that works just as well!

At Joy School, we've had representatives from Heart Math Institute share their famous findings confirming that emotions are integral to the state of our bodily health. They've learned that staying in a state of frustration or anger for five minutes will suppress your immune system for up to six hours. But staying in a state of appreciation and love for five minutes will measurably strengthen your immune system for up to six hours! At Heart Math Institute, they call this beneficial state "heart/mind synchrony." Here's a quick and easy technique they teach for creating heart/mind synchrony that they call the "inner ease technique."

1. Close your eyes. Put your hand on your heart. Just this step alone will start the flow of oxytocin, the natural body chemical that creates a sense of love and wellbeing.

2. Next, imagine breathing in and out through the center of your heart. Use the power of your imagination to maintain this focus, breathing deeply into your heart and out through your heart.

3. Next, imagine that you are breathing in love, appreciation, ease. To help you hold the feelings of love, appreciation, and ease, you might want to imagine someone or something that evokes these feelings in you, like a cherished partner, pet, family member, or favorite place.

4. With every inhale, breathe in more of the good feeling, and you'll start to notice a difference in how your body feels.

This beautiful and simple Heart Math technique can be used to access and fuel your good feeling states, as described above, but it's also a wonderful tool for processing your challenging feelings. Bringing them up for healing within this container is a way to turn typically vibe-lowering emotions into poignant, vibe-elevating ones instead! Your challenging emotions are only lowering your vibration when you try to block or suppress them. Inviting them into this compassionate container is the opposite of that.

When you are alone and have centered yourself to do some healing work, go through the steps to create a loving container by breathing through your heart. Then call to mind whatever has recently triggered you with the intention of simply bearing compassionate witness to the feelings. Keep your hand on your heart and invite the feelings up while engaged in this simple form of mindfulness. Make love and understanding for yourself the priority. If tears come, wonderful. They may need to come many times, but with each round you'll be clearing the energetic space for more and more lightness, peace, and joy to flood into your experience.

To recap, this third week of homeplay entails welcoming your challenging emotions by journaling them and using the above Heart Math technique. Also notice where you've freed your pendulum to swing in the direction of a deeper experience of joy and awe, and practice holding those beautiful feelings for a minimum of twenty seconds!

● ● ●

"Walk with your grief and you will find it doesn't break you.
It breaks the walls around your heart that you always thought
were you but really, they have just been fencing you in. Walk
with grief and it will strip everything back and soften
the ground that the seeds of your dreams have been laid in.
It reaches right into your center to make your heart and soul
wholly accessible so that the light can get in and out freely
without so many obstacles." —S.C LOURIE

HOMEPLAY FOR KEY 4, WEEK FOUR

You'll extend your feel-to-heal work this week with some more dedicated practices for inviting your stored-away feelings to the surface where you can gently love them into release. We can fall into the trap of ruminating on these stored traumas instead of feeling them, so this week's assignments will be to help you sidestep that trap. It's an important distinction because perseverating on these issues feeds them energy and keeps them alive. Feeling them without resistance is the key to releasing them. It's what my dear heart-brother and teaching partner of decades, Robert Mack, calls "bearing witness with a loving heart." Here's a method he suggests, using the example of shame stored in the body:

> Scan your body to find where the emotion is stored. It might feel like a pain, a tightness, a stuck-ness. Go to where you feel the shame in your body. What temperature is it? What texture, color, consistency? This is how to give the shame your attention, without doing it with judgment. If you find yourself going back to your brain to think about it, redirect your attention back to your body. Bathe this area in your love and compassion.

> Then ask, what is it that is aware of this pain? What is noticing this shame? That's how you become the witness of it. The witness is not identified with it. It becomes clear to you that you have emotions and feelings, but you are not your emotions and feelings.

> Practice identification with the presence of that which needs no healing because there is no real problem.

(He's talking about your Vertical Self.)

And here is another technique for you to incorporate this week, from my podcast guest and friend Ian Haycroft. Among many things, Ian teaches the Buddhist principle of being in "right relationship" with the various aspects of our lives. He says the "usual suspects" we might want to investigate our relationships to include our parents, partners, children, roles we play, gender, work, money, and ourselves. Ian says:

> In the Buddhist tradition the concept of being in the right relationship with something is very important. Ask yourself, contemplate, is there a relationship with someone or something in my life that perhaps is not "right?"... distorted in any way? ... that has unresolved issues in it? Choose just one for now ... Remember, what we are trying to do here is release whatever story you have associated with someone or something. The story does not define you. Releasing the story is the goal, so as not to repeat it ...

- Sit in a quiet place where you can remain uninterrupted for some time.

- Allow yourself to calm down using whatever technique works for you.

- There is a place within you, a quiet place, where there are no problems to solve. Take your time. Go to that place. (For just a few minutes, decide that any of the problems and issues you are dealing with in life can wait.)

- When you are in that place, bring the relationship you want to heal within yourself to mind.

- Place it on the table (altar) in front of you in your mind's eye. Without judgment of you or anyone else, notice what emotions arise.

- Understanding that these emotions do not define you, notice them, face them. You are not required to "solve them," "fix them," or "figure them out." Just notice them.

- If tears, heat, pain, or chills arise, notice that too.

- Watch, listen, observe, feel. Take your time.

- There is a Wisdom Within you that knows what to do. Trust that part of you and just observe, notice.

- When it feels right for you, you can "say" (actual words not important) "I release you. I no longer need to hold on to this (choose the emotion). I release you from every cell, from the energy that gives life to my cells, and from every time in my life."

- Sit some more and quietly, in your own time, come back to being aware of this present moment.

I hope you make liberal use of these two powerful techniques this final week for this key, darling joy-adventurer! Setting aside a specified time each day for this emotional clearing will help you to commit to it. It's understandable to feel resistance to this kind of work; we've all gotten so good at avoiding uncomfortable feelings. If you can coax yourself into doing it just a few times, I think you'll find that the release and lightness and freedom on the other side of each session will more than motivate you to keep going. I hope you'll find this so liberating that you'll want to continue it well into the upcoming months.

The lightness is your goal! You can't vibrate at a higher frequency when your energy body is bogged down with all those stored-away traumas. Digesting them for release may feel like a bottomless task in the beginning, but everyone I've steered through this practice has eventually begun encountering the inevitable lightness that gradually ensues. Be kind and patient with your precious self. You are doing powerful, powerful work this month.

The rewards of developing this new relationship with your authentic feelings will astound you, not only because you'll be more peaceful and centered in your daily life, but also because it paves the way for manifesting all those external things you've been wanting with unprecedented ease and speed! The elevation in your personal vibration turns you into the magnet that draws to you everything vibrating similarly. It's energetic law.

• • •

"I am better off healed than I ever was unbroken."
—BETH MOORE

I want you to get more and more comfortable with the idea that we're just pushing pieces around a game board. I don't say this to minimize what you're going through; I hope it doesn't sound that way. I want to put my metaphorical arms around you and hug you while you full-on welcome every single feeling and frustration that's alive for you right now. Every bit of it is valid. And at the same time, I want you to open to the possibility that none of it is nearly as important as it feels, no decision is as critical as we think it is, and all that stress, and pressure, and anxiety that we layer over our life stuffs is the very energy that *brings* us all these things we deem our "unwanted circumstances." That's the bait that draws it all to us—all the yuck. And it doesn't have to be there. It's just energy. We can play with it. We can loosen it up. It's all just the inevitable result of identifying too closely with the Horizontal Self and losing sight of the Vertical Self.

Your Vertical Self doesn't sweat the small stuff. It's certain of your divinity and ability to do anything. Resting into its ever-welcoming embrace empowers you in boundless ways because knowing thyself means knowing that you are limitless, and your solid belief in your own limitless nature creates an energetic signature for attracting unprecedented miracles into your experience!

This is an energetic Universe, darling reader, and we're all living inside-out. Our inner landscape is continually creating our outer landscape; that's just what we know now about how it all works. I wish you a meaningful month of using these tools to feel and heal in ever-expanding, empowering ways.

KEY 5

Sort the Voices

"Life has always been this scary here, and we have always been as vulnerable as kittens. Plagues and Visigoths, snakes and schizophrenia; Cain is still killing Abel and nature means that everyone dies. I hate this. It's too horrible for words . . . There is no healing in pretending this bizarre violent stuff is not going on, and that there is some cute bumper sticker silver lining. (It is fine if you believe this, but for the love of God, please keep it to yourself. It will just tense us all up.) What is true is that the world has always been this way, people have always been this way, grace always bats last, it just does—and finally, when all is said and done, and the dust settles, which it does, Love is sovereign here."

—ANNE LAMOTT

You've done such amazing work! Have you gotten more automatic about breaking down your reactions to the everyday challenges in your life? Have you done some meaningful feel-to-heal

clearing of your filter, digesting your pain body? If you've been diligent with your practices, I have no doubt you're feeling lighter and
freer already. See how powerful you are?

The skill you'll build this month is an exciting one! You're going
to become aware of two voices that talk to you in your head. The one
you're most familiar with is likely the voice of your Horizontal Self.
That's the loud one for most of us, but everything this voice tells you
is filtered through . . . well, your filter. The thoughts and opinions
expressed by the voice of your Horizontal Self are all born out of your
bucket beliefs, and as you now understand, that means they're not
rooted in anything real or true. Sometimes it's uncanny how much
this voice resembles the voice of one of our parents!

The voice you're going to make space for, by inviting it, is the
voice of your Vertical Self. It's talked to you before, but you may not
remember. Until we build the skill of sorting these voices so that we
can clearly decipher who's talking, most of us go through life following the directional impulses of our Horizontal Self, hearing only its
loud and overpowering voice, while missing the softer, quieter voice
of the Vertical Self, where all our inherent wisdom, peace, joy, and
natural compassion for self and others resides.

One of my favorite ways of helping Joy Schoolers identify the voice
of the Horizontal Self is by making them aware of their ipso facto
switch. "Ipso facto" is a Latin phrase meaning "by the very fact." You
draw ipso facto conclusions all day long, and your personal ipso facto
switch is the product of erroneous, joy-robbing beliefs that are presently mucking up your unique perception filter.

One of my Joy Schoolers recently demonstrated her ipso facto
switch in a situation with her husband. In a nutshell, he was careless
with an object that meant a lot to her. He knew it meant a lot to her,

but he still failed to keep it safe and protected. It was clear and obvious to this Joy Schooler that he didn't care about her feelings. Didn't value her. Maybe to an extent, didn't love her. This is a super common flavor of ipso facto, and the equation basically goes, "They did XYZ thing, therefore—ipso facto—by that fact, they don't care about me."

Another Joy Schooler came to a similar conclusion recently when a friend stood her up for a lunch date. Similar conclusions are drawn all the time about forgotten birthdays and casual jokes or remarks that could be interpreted in demeaning or dismissive ways.

Another flavor of ipso facto is, "No one is buying my product/service, liking my social media posts, giving me the good projects at work, responding to my online dating profile—therefore, ipso facto, by this fact, it follows that my product/service is no good, I'm no good, I'm not likable, I'm failing again, I'll never be loved/respected/included/deemed worthy." You get the picture. Another example might be as simple and commonplace as being cut off by a driver on the road and your ipso facto voice coming to the "irrefutable" conclusion that "People are jerks!" or "People are idiots!" or "The world is scary and unpredictable, and therefore I am in danger and must stay hypervigilant at all times!"

All these events I'm mentioning are just that—events. They're things that happen. We have no idea why any of these things happen. There are countless possible reasons for these things to occur. The ensuing pain is the result of the thoughts/meanings that we've ascribed to the events. The guy who cut you off might have been having a stroke! When your ipso facto switch is flipped on, it's super hard to see any possibilities other than the one you're seeing. It feels like your deduction is clear and obvious—the only logical conclusion. But that is almost *never* the case. It's extremely limiting to your joy to assume that the way you are looking at a particular event or circumstance represents its only truth.

We tend to want to keep the world tidy and neat by fitting everything that happens into our pre-established categorization system. But for most of us—unless we have a carefully curated, deliberately upgraded bucket system, this is to our massive disadvantage. (Don't worry; we're working on getting you that upgraded system.)

Here's a tool we use in Joy School: We take an event. A circumstance. A thought. A conversation. Any triggering thing at all. And we pretend it's a statue. Let's say you're standing in front of the statue. You can see it clearly from where you're standing. You can describe it. You see all these details. It feels super real and concrete, this statue that you're looking at. But if you walked around it a quarter of the way, you'd see parts of the statue you couldn't see before. And if you walked all the way around to the back side of the statue, you might see something entirely different from the thing you thought you were seeing so clearly just moments before when you were standing in front of it.

This is how it is with every single thing that's bothering you. There's always more than what you're seeing. How could that not be true, when there are 400 billion bits of information swirling around you in every moment, and you're only processing 50 of those bits, based on where your tiny keyhole is positioned? Every perception you've ever had in your life is like this. Most of us never walk around the statue! That means all your memories, beliefs, and opinions—and all your present and ongoing thoughts, too—are all just tiny slices of objective reality—flimsy, unsubstantiated, unreliable representations of what's real.

As I've mentioned, according to many sources, we think approximately 70,000 thoughts per day, with 80 percent of them negative. The vast majority of those are repetitive thoughts on a continuous loop.

These thought loops have been wearing physical, detectable grooves in your brain. Imagine a mountain with streams running down its face. When it rains on this mountain, the rainwater naturally flows into the existing streambeds, cutting them deeper into the earth as time progresses. It's just like that with the grooves you've worn in your brain with all that repetitive thinking. If most of your moments are blissful and beautiful and love-filled, you've worn some grade-A grooves there—good on you! But if you're like most humans, conditioned to feed your mind with thoughts of stress and worry, you've probably worn at least a few grooves that aren't serving your joy. The trick is to get out of those thought loops and wear some new grooves. That's what you've begun to do, and we're just getting started!

I know I'm being kind of repetitive here, and I'm guessing that from an intellectual perspective, all of this is obvious to you by now. But I want you to tap into that kerklunked perspective where it's a little mind-blowing. You do this in your life. We all do. And it becomes the water we swim in, so we don't see it.

Discerning Between the Voices

This month is all about discerning the voice of your Horizontal Self from the voice of your Vertical Self. Becoming aware of those grooves you've worn—becoming aware of your ipso facto switch—is one of the best tools for doing that. Once you start observing the ipso facto conclusions you draw, you'll be able to clearly recognize the voice of your Horizontal Self. You'll begin this month's practice by simply tuning into that recognition and paying attention to the attributes of this voice. Just like the voices we hear from the people around us, it has its own patterns, mannerisms, ways of addressing you and getting your attention.

From there, you can get even more nuanced in observing your default patterns of perception. When a thing happens, and it triggers a negative feeling in you, you want to start asking yourself, *What flavor of negative is this? Does it make me feel anxious? Undervalued? Unseen? Does it confirm my suspicion that the world sucks and gets suckier all the time? Does it say something specifically disappointing about humanity? About my loved ones? About me?*

You've already practiced noticing the distinction between the thing that happened and the meaning that you gave it. Now you can apply your understanding of the ipso facto switch to gain extra clarity about those habitual thought patterns that have worn grooves in your brain, and how they're coloring your experience of reality in unnecessarily joy-robbing ways.

Are there incredibly optimistic, positive people out there with an ipso facto switch that's working in their favor? Sure. Probably. These are the people who are always going to, by default, consistently choose the best, most optimistic belief available in any situation. And guess what—they're manifesting amazing lives for themselves.

But most of us, for all those reasons and biases I've already laid out, tend to have an ipso facto voice that's not in keeping with the joyful, blissful lives we came here to live. Between the built-in negativity bias, the confirmation bias that keeps us creating and attracting evidence to shore up unhappy beliefs we formed about ourselves and the world, and the conformity bias that drags us down to the vibrational level of those around us, it can feel like our joy doesn't stand a chance!

All these oh-so-human tendencies contribute to us perpetually drawing negative conclusions about ourselves and others when there are *always* equally valid and true interpretations that would serve our higher good and greater joy. It feels like these negative assumptions keep us safe. They don't. They keep us focused on what we don't want, and the more attention we spend there, the more certain it is that we'll create more and more of what we *don't* want. We have to become the observer of our weird assumption that keeping our eye on the danger will keep us safe from it. That was true, back when the danger was tigers and crocodiles (that's why we have this leftover setting in our primitive brains) but it's rarely true for the lives we live today. Outside of situations where our physical wellbeing is in fact threatened, our fears tend to be overblown ego-protection instincts more than anything else. Becoming the observer of this tendency is how we dissipate it.

We're spending this much time here because awareness is the golden ticket, darling reader! Not just intellectual awareness, but a deeply kerklunked awareness (born of practice) that lets you, right there in the trigger moment, pull back and say, *Ah. Look at that. Look at how I'm interpreting this event. It sure does feel like there's no other rational way to interpret it. I feel my body chemistry kicking up in that way that it does. Let me check to see if my ipso facto switch is involved. Oh, yep! Sure is. Okay, so I know, then, that the voice I'm hearing in my head is the voice of my Horizontal Self. I'm bringing my powers of reasoning in now, which remind me that this voice is extremely unreliable and often simply inaccurate. Let me see if I can deliberately tune in to a different angle here. Let me see if I can make this thing/thought/event a statue and walk around it. Maybe there's another truth—another equally likely perspective—that I could subscribe to, that would raise my vibration instead of pulling it down.*

Internal dialogue like this takes practice, but it is an absolute gamechanger. The part that you really want to practice is the recognition that your bad-feeling assumption is just as likely to be wrong as it is to be right, no matter how strong the feeling it's generating in that moment. In most cases, the strength of the feeling is an indicator of how off-base the assumption is! You're not asking yourself to do "positive thinking;" you're asking yourself to do *more objective* thinking; it just doesn't feel that way in the moment.

You've probably started to get kerklunked on the truth that any time you are convinced that you are unequivocally right, you are most certainly wrong. (Just like everyone else who thinks they're unequivocally right.) Prior to reaching this understanding, you will continue to seek your own wins and gains by pitting yourself against an imaginary "other" you need to make wrong. Isn't escaping this insanity kind of joyful to contemplate? Our default setting is to feel fear when our certainties crumble around us, but just beyond that irrational fear is exhilarating curiosity and wonder. With a little practice, it starts to feel a lot like awe.

You want to watch for patterns. Most of us have a just a few themes our ipso facto voice likes to harp on over and over. They're the natural extensions of our bucket beliefs. Super common ones include, "People can't be trusted." "He/She/They don't love me." "I'm powerless in a scary world." "They're out to get me." "Someone's trying to take what's mine." "I have to hide who I really am in order to be accepted or loved."

If you keep your understanding of this dynamic in the forefront of your mind this week, you'll spot it in other people. It's a lot easier to spot in other people—especially your spouse or partner! Don't bother pointing it out to them; they're probably not ready to hear it. Share this book and tell them to start at the beginning.

But you're ready. You've been inching toward this powerfully evolved moment when you can step fully into that observer role, observing your own joy-robbing dynamics in action, and take the steps to begin habituating a new pattern, a new way of being. Remember, everything Out There in your external landscape that you want to be different—it doesn't stand a chance of happening out there until it happens inside you. It's all about the energy you bring to your life, darling reader. You're an energetic creature operating in an energetic world. And you're ready to start taking control of that now.

Becoming ever more aware of your ipso facto switch means deliberately directing your attention to notice all those places in your life where you've been hearing the voice in your head imply this message: *The only natural conclusion to be drawn here is . . . blah, blah, blah.* You want to notice that kind of messaging in your headspace and answer that voice with something like, *No. Of course that's not the only conclusion to be drawn; that would be absurd. It just feels like it's the only conclusion because it's the only one I'm conditioned to see through my tiny keyhole of perception. Let me check what other perspectives are available here.*

HOMEPLAY FOR KEY 5, WEEK ONE

The first of your homeplay assignments this month will be to watch for where your ipso facto reasoning gets switched on. You've been practicing being the observer of you, so this is just the next step in that ever-evolving skill. When you recognize yourself in any situation where you're making an ipso facto assumption, you'll deliberately integrate what psychologists call a "pattern-interrupt." Basically, a pattern-interrupt is anything you intentionally do to change the direction that your default setting of thought/response/behavior is taking you in. My psychic sister Lisa Campion calls it "catch-and-release" thinking. I love that!

My phenomenal friend Paul Boynton teaches a pattern-interrupt involving an imaginary fairy godmother, so let's borrow this general idea. Whenever you notice your energy pulled down by an ipso facto assumption you're making, push the pause button on your mind. (It's so cool that we have the power to do this with a little practice!) Once you're in the pause, direct your imagination to this question: "If I had a fairy godmother right now who could wave a magic wand and make this event/circumstance/thought that's triggering me mean whatever I would most like it to mean—instead of this ipso facto conclusion I'm drawing—what would I choose?"

Let your imagination come up with the most delightful scenario, even if it feels impossible that it's true. Just letting your mind go there will loosen the drag on your energy and maybe bring some lightness to the moment. Then consider how extremely unlikely it is that your ipso facto voice is a reliable indicator of objective reality. You know better than that by now. Even if your wildest-dream happy scenario is too far-fetched for you to believe, you'll have stretched the keyhole enough to consider the probability that the "truth" likely lies somewhere between these two extremes.

There! Now you have a first week of homeplay designed to make you extra aware of one of the biggest telltale signs that you're tuned into the voice of your Horizontal Self. I challenge you to have fun with it! Remember that you're just pushing pieces around the gameboard. Try to laugh at yourself. It's all funny, really. We human creatures are so bizarre and silly and laughable—all the defaults we have for getting in the way of our natural, own joy. We'll keep pulling these tendencies up into the light of our awareness so that we can set them aside. So that we can be our free, naturally joy-filled selves. I'm sure it's shifting for you already. I want you to see that for most of your life, you've been turning lemonade into lemons. The lemonade is all around you for the taking. And you've begun shifting your vibration to let it in. Hold on to your hat because we're (still!) just getting started.

Invite the Voice of Your Vertical Self

Your longstanding ipso facto switch is just a habit. Are habits easy to break? Nah. Not usually. But can they be broken? Absolutely. You're at the point in your joy journey where you're ready to get solidly acquainted with the one voice that we're inviting to take center stage now—the wise, true voice of your deepest inner knowing, the voice of your soul, your Vertical Self. It's time to get excited because alignment with this voice comes with a tremendous upgrade to your joy.

You started this month off by recognizing what the voice of your Horizontal Self sounds like because that is what makes it easier to find the voice of your Vertical Self by comparison. If you're new to tuning into it, the voice of the Vertical Self might sound unfamiliar. It might suggest things you hadn't been thinking about before, at least not consciously. Perhaps it's been waiting for some time for you to tune in, so it has a lot to share with you once you open that door.

My favorite clue to help you in your discernment practice is to remember, *your soul doesn't think you suck.* Again, that means any thought that crosses your mind that tells you any version of how you suck is simply not a true thought. It's nonsense, born of your bucket beliefs, and reinforced by your confirmation bias, negativity bias, all those unfortunate patterns inherent in us silly humans that we've been talking about. A thought like that is not in alignment with your soul's wisdom; that's why it feels bad to you. Stop subscribing to those thoughts. Cancel your subscription. When a thought like that comes up, call it out for the fake that it is and drop it like it's hot! Remember that even if there's seemingly lots of evidence around you to support this idea of you sucking, all that evidence was created out of bullcrap bucket beliefs that you are now in the process of replacing!

Another thing we do at Joy School when we're learning to distinguish between the voice of the Horizontal Self and the Vertical Self is to see how a thought feels in the body. Thoughts that are coming from your negative bucket beliefs (Horizontal) often feel like contraction. They might feel muddy and dark. You experience the weight of them dragging you down, like you're bracing yourself for some anticipated struggle. Sometimes they take on a frenetic expression in your nervous system, and other times a dulling, clouded-over expression of heaviness.

The voice of your inner knowing (Vertical) feels expansive in your body. That doesn't mean it's the Pollyanna voice, because it's often the one telling you to choose a more challenging experience. But it feels clear. Simple. Uncomplicated. Constant. The true soul voice of your Vertical Self doesn't have a lot of accessories or bells and whistles. If there's a choice between A and B, and A feels right, but with B you'd get this goodie and that goodie, and get to avoid that thing you don't like, and there's a long list of reasons attached to it that your brain keeps cycling through—that's a sign. All those rationalizations belong to the voice of the Horizontal Self. The purity of the Vertical Self doesn't need that kind of embellishment.

If it's a thought with some fear attached, you have to tease out the fear to see what kind of fear it is. Fear is a sneaky emotion that likes to hide itself behind other things—all kinds of protection stories and seemingly logical rationales. Of course, there are situations in which genuine fear is warranted, but far more often what presents as fear is really just unnecessary protection of ego. It's just the loud voice of the Horizontal Self wanting to protect its positioning in the forefront of your experience. Typically, the more complicated, protected, guarded stance is the stance of the Horizontal Self.

There's a purity and simplicity to the inner wisdom of the Vertical Self. A neutrality. It's the voice that's in alignment with a higher vibratory frequency. An excellent question to ask when the voices in your head are competing over some issue is, *which path has the most integrity?* The voice that's suggesting the shortcut, the bypass, is usually not the true voice of your Vertical Self. The one that is ultimately the most loving to you, *is.* And often that means choosing what appears, in the moment, to be a more difficult path.

Your Vertical Self *wants* you to risk it all for love of the journey, for joy, for expansion—because this part of you knows the riskiness is just illusion. When you remain firmly and earnestly committed to the path your soul came here to take, everything you encounter along the way is a reward. Some rewards are easy to spot, and others temporarily wear unpleasant disguises, but when you're aligned with your soul's wisdom you trust that every bit of it is for your ultimate benefit.

For a few months now, you've practiced tapping into the non-physical aspect of your being—through meditation and mindfulness, through focusing on the buzzing vitality within your flesh, and through intentional dialoging. Building these skills has primed you to begin this rich inner dance with your Vertical Self. It might not feel real at first. Sometimes, Joy Schoolers tell me they wonder if it's "just" their imagination. I want you to reframe your association to the word "imagination," to understand that imagination is the language of the soul. It's the vehicle your Vertical Self uses to communicate with you.

Thanks to this valuable communication device, with practice, you'll eventually be able to tune into the vibration of *anything* and know whether or not it's right for you.

You'll know what's right for you, *and,* kind of ironically, one tremendous benefit of building this communication tool is that you become less invested in your human habit of desperately needing to get it right in the first place. It becomes more automatic for you to metaphorically take that walk around the statue, because you see that most decisions you make aren't nearly as black-and-white as you once assumed them to be. Most questions simply do not have a 100 percent right, and a 100 percent wrong answer. You grow in your trust that you can be light about it. You understand that you can be most powerful and effective when you're *able* to authentically stay light about it.

HOMEPLAY FOR KEY 5, WEEK TWO

Ready for the second week of this month's homeplay? You'll begin this week by writing a letter to your Vertical Self, stream-of-consciousness-style, in your Joy Journal. Tell it you're sorry for not paying more attention to it until now and tell it you're ready to open a more robust and meaningful dialogue. Once you've opened your heart to this part of you through your letter, let your Vertical Self write a letter back to you. Just invite it in and start writing. Put the pen to the paper before your head knows what you're going to write, even if you have to scribble loops until some words start kicking in.

As awkward as this exercise might feel, it will introduce you to the voice of this incredible inner wisdom you've been neglecting. Then, every day this week, check in with this part of you. Put your hand on your heart, slow your breathing, and ask, *Vertical Self, what would you most like me to know right now?* Journal whatever impressions come to you, even if they don't seem to make any sense. You're learning one another's language, so some patience is called for. You might see symbols or shapes in your mind's eye. Draw them in your Joy Journal. A memory might come to you of a person or prior event in your life. Jot it down. Maybe you just see, or sense, or feel a color, a flavor, a weather condition. At this point, your only job is to allow whatever surfaces to surface and to record it.

Then, as you go through your week, pay attention to any synchronicities between the messages you've recorded and the things you notice or experience. Connecting these dots might feel random and insignificant when you're new to doing it, but over time you'll become more aware of the deeper value of these communications. You might have heard this process described as watching for "signs from the Universe." Maybe that sounds hokey to you. If so, I invite you to entertain the idea that your Vertical Self is wise in ways you have not had access to in the past. It knows what will move you forward in your journey, and it wants you to have a beautiful life. Once you invite it to the table, it's going to show you directional signals to help you with that.

Occasionally, my Joy Schoolers have scoffed at the idea that these "signs" could be placed in our experience as if by magic. But when you relax into the scientific truth that there are 400 billion bits of information that you could be perceiving in any given second, the vast majority of which you typically miss, it becomes easier to allow for the possibility that inviting your Vertical Self to show you "signs" is just another way of expanding the keyhole. Maybe it's not a matter of the signs suddenly appearing out of thin air, but simply a matter of your perception filter lining up with certain things that were there all along. I hope that helps to normalize the concept for you of receiving signs from the Universe (or from your Vertical Self.) We'll do more with this in coming months!

HOMEPLAY FOR KEY 5, WEEK THREE

Another way to discern the voice of your Horizontal Self from the voice of your Vertical Self is to notice what kinds of messages they're sending you about your feelings. Your Horizontal Self is burdened with the daunting task of preserving your ego at all costs and that makes it easily offended. The Horizontal Self believes identifying and pointing an accusing finger at all your offenders keeps you safe from them, but, again, the opposite is true. The attention you give to anything only strengthens it in your experience. (Your Vertical Self cannot be offended because it knows you are an unlimited being of light and love, as is everyone else.)

Your Horizontal Self is also tasked with protecting your orientation in the world, which means keeping you certain about all those bucket beliefs you've stored away. Anything that questions the validity of your bucket beliefs, or enables their dissolution, will be threatening to the Horizontal Self.

Since the way to drain your buckets of those unbeneficial beliefs is to reveal and feel the emotions that are trapped there (your feel-to-heal practices), the voice of your Horizontal Self will always try, in myriad ways, to shut down any challenging feelings. Since the Horizontal Self is made of your bucket beliefs, it needs you to keep your bucket beliefs alive and thriving to maintain its position in the forefront of your existence. This means, when you hear a voice in your head that suggests you distract yourself away from your authentic feelings that are unpleasant, it's always the voice of the Horizontal Self.

It's nuanced territory we're in now, because much of the work you've been doing has been about recognizing when you're having a bad-feeling thought, that you don't necessarily need to believe that thought. This is where it becomes important to remember that even when a feeling is coming from an untrue thought, the feeling itself is still real and valid and needs to be honored with compassion and your full acceptance. The Horizontal Self would rather you continue to repress your feelings, thereby fortifying your bucket beliefs. Your Vertical Self will instead invite you to compassionately feel them to heal them. To again use Eckhart Tolle terminology, this is how you "digest your pain body" so that these stored energies can be cleared out to make room for joy.

That's the discernment practice you'll be working with next, so here's the recap of the points you'll need to keep in mind for this third week's homeplay: All of us store away energies that limit us, based on misperceptions we formed early in life when we didn't have the emotional maturity to properly feel and process our frightening feelings. Not feeling them caused them to become lodged in our cells, where they still reside. These stored energies are blocking us from experiencing the natural joy we are at our core. Our work is to allow them to surface via different masks, different wrapping paper, presenting through the vehicle of our day-to-day experiences, so that we can say, *Ah! There's one! Let me do the thing I know I need to do to clear a bit of this energy away, so that I can live more closely aligned with my core, my source, my joy.*

And the way you've learned to do that is to *not* rush away from the feeling, *not* distract yourself from it, but instead invite the fullness of the feeling to be expressed while you hold yourself in compassion and full acceptance, right where you are.

To this end, and to crank up your observer skills to ninja level, this week you're going to notice when the voice of your Horizontal Self tells you to deny, suppress, or distract yourself away from feeling something. Here are some of the suggestions this voice typically makes to us susceptible humans: eat, drink, use recreational drugs, shop, have sex, scroll social media, watch television, complain and have meaningless conversations with others who are also wanting to avoid their feelings. For some of us, its strategy is to coax us into retreating into the mind to overanalyze the feelings instead of simply feeling them. We've all established these coping mechanisms in different ways and to different degrees. We've all habituated certain routines for avoiding experiencing the full extent of our difficult feelings.

Avoiding these uncomfortable feelings seems like a great idea to the Horizontal Self. And even some spiritual seekers have mistakenly gotten the message that it's better to force "positive thinking" than it is to feel anything negative. But this is not what your Vertical Self wants for you, and here's why: Every time you suppress, deny, or neglect feeling an emotion that's naturally there for you, the energy you exert to keep the feeling suppressed just *adds* to the already-established bucket. The reason it's come up (triggered by something in your current experience) is to give you an opportunity to feel it and heal it. When you miss that opportunity, you instead contribute *more* to that particular pocket of repressed, stored energy.

One of my most influential teachers, the author and consciousness expert Debbie Ford, had a beach ball analogy I've taught in Joy School for decades. She said that keeping these emotion-bundles repressed is like trying to keep a beach ball under water. You can do it for a while, but keeping a beach ball under water is going to require more and more effort (energy expenditure) over time. Eventually, it's going to wear you out and the ball's going to pop up in your face. Most of us human-y humans have *multiple* beach balls we're trying to keep down at any given moment. It's exhausting and draining all our valuable energy!

Let's invite our inner wisdom to the table on this. Take out your Joy Journal and ask, *Vertical Self, show me the things I habitually do to keep the beach balls down. What are my go-to methods for avoiding feeling the full expression of my challenging feelings?* Shake the Etch A Sketch and invite whatever emerges.

Your Vertical Self probably provided a decent list of your top offenders. You're going to observe yourself this week and add to that list as your default patterns emerge, brought up into the light of day by your intentional focus on spotting them. By using your ever-developing skills of observation, you're bringing valuable, healing consciousness to these damaging patterns! With practice, you'll find you can catch yourself in the moment when you're resisting a feeling. You can decide to say, *No, I'm not going to repress this emotion this time. I'm going to give myself compassion while I feel this in its fullness.*

And sure, there will be times when a challenging emotion surfaces and you're in the middle of a situation where it's not practical to invite up the full expression of that feeling. In these instances, you'll simply make a commitment to revisit the situation and invite the emotion into full expression at a later point when you have the privacy and right setting to give yourself that gift. The sooner after the triggering situation, the better. My beautiful friend, renowned psychic and author Sunny Dawn Johnston, suggests scheduling bath time for this sort of intentional feeling practice. Sitting in a soothing warm bath can feel especially nourishing for the authentic expression of long-stored emotions.

Now that you have some clarity around what your go-to habits for avoiding your emotions are, you can set some healthy boundaries with yourself. You can simply make a rule to no longer engage in these distraction behaviors. It's straightforward, but not always easy.

Okay, it's hardly ever easy.

That's because, as you've probably noticed, several of these behaviors lend themselves to addiction. It's pretty possible that you're addicted to your emotion-avoidance strategies. Many of the common substance addictions in our culture have reached their level of popularity for that very reason—they numb us from things we don't want to face or feel. I point this out not to make your task more daunting, but to encourage you to give yourself all the love and patience and tenderness you can muster as you set this new healthy boundary for your sweet self.

To whatever extent you succeed with this homeplay, I want you to acknowledge it as a tremendous achievement! This is a showdown between your Horizontal Self that's powerfully going to pull you toward distraction (whatever your distraction-addiction may be), and your Vertical Self, the part of you that only desires your healing and sustainable happiness. This is what spiritual gurus mean when they say the magic lies beyond your comfort zone. This part of our work isn't terribly comfortable! It's all about recognizing that the benefits will far outweigh the temporary discomfort.

The goal is to notice when the first glimmer of the challenging feeling comes up, then notice the urge to do the thing you always do to avoid it, and then *pause.* Get grounded, take some centering breaths, and make the choice to not follow the distraction urge, recognizing it as the voice of the Horizontal Self. You'll instead tune into the voice of the Vertical Self, coaxing you to honor whatever is present for you, hold yourself in compassion, and invite the feeling to unfold. No judgment. Just allowing.

The more you practice this level of self-honoring, the more you'll witness how that unpleasant feeling you were tempted to block really *does* just want to be witnessed. When you give it that space, it can flow through you and naturally release. The more you do it, the more confident you get about your capacity for doing it. And each feel-to-heal opportunity not *only* keeps you from storing more problematic energy in your buckets; it also drains away some of what you previously stored there. (I keep going back to Eckhart Tolle's terminology of "digesting the pain body" for good reason. Digesting something means processing it in such a way that it can be released!) Eventually, you'll have cleared enough of these old, stored energies, that those triggering situations will stop showing up in your external experiences. They won't need to anymore. They were always just opportunities for you to do this clearing work.

Of course, there's going to be discomfort with this process. But we can get to the point where we welcome even that! We can recognize that we're basically invincible once we've learned to live at the edge of our comfort zone. This is why people do fire walks and ropes courses as tools for personal growth. It's a mind-over-matter paradigm that shows you that your personal will in committing to moving past your fear is stronger than your egoic, protective impulse. And that feels really good to acknowledge about yourself!

Could you imagine doing this so successfully that you got excited every time a new opportunity came up to digest some of your pain body? That's personal mastery of life, right there! It allows us to escape the prison of what my Hay House colleague David Kessler calls "capture." He says that "capture" is "a common mechanism that underlies many of our emotional struggles. Simply put, a stimulus—a place, a thought, memory, a person—takes hold of our attention and shifts our perception. The theory of capture is composed of three basic elements—narrowing of attention, perceived lack of control, and change of emotional state. Sometimes these elements are accompanied by an urge to act. When something commands our attention in a way that feels uncontrollable and, in turn, influences our behavior, we experience capture. Capture arises from a vast and complex circuitry in the brain. The brain is composed of neurons, organized in discrete layers, networks, and regions. Every time we experience something new, a neural pattern is created in response. When we remember this kind of experience, or something connected to this experience, or even when we do something that calls to mind a thought or feeling we associate with this experience—these neural patterns are reactivated."

He's talking about the way most humans go through life when they're not aware of their filter, their bucket beliefs, and the methods for moving beyond their habituated patterns of thought and behavior. He's describing the common scenario of being triggered by something that occurs in our present life and mistakenly believing our thoughts and urges around this triggering are valid, instead of recognizing they're based in old, stored energies. Taken to extremes, psychologists call this reactivity "maladaptive stress response."

You've already taken powerful steps to distance yourself from this all-too-common state of "capture," but it's good to remember that long-standing habits require diligence and patience and self-compassion along our way to breaking them. If you notice yourself in this state of capture, instead of judging your sweet self for that, please instead celebrate yourself for noticing! The noticing is what puts you in the position for healing! The bottom line is that the better you get at recognizing these tendencies, the more released you become from their power over you.

After decades of working with these tools and witnessing my Joy Schoolers in their application of them, I can tell you that there's no point at which anyone feels they're 100 percent nailing it. Yet, every step in that direction yields incredible rewards. As you become less and less reactive to the things that once triggered you, more and more space is freed up for joy, awe, and love to flood into your experience. You'll start to see it with the very first efforts you make with this practice. It will give you all the incentive you need to continue honing this powerful skill.

What sages have for thousands of years called the pursuit of enlightenment, or elevating consciousness, is just about getting better and better at recognizing these patterns through your advanced skills of observation and healing them by rising above them as the compassionate witness. You're doing the work of masters, so give yourself a good, long, congratulatory hug.

HOMEPLAY FOR KEY 5, WEEK FOUR

Your fourth week of homeplay is borrowed from my workshops for kids. When I'm helping young people find the voice of the Vertical Self, I don't use that terminology. I ask them to imagine a glow stick inside them. I teach them to connect with that glow stick by making YOU-turns. (I spell it Y-O-U turns.) It's a playful tool that I invite you to make use of this week. Whenever you find yourself caught up in some issue in the Out There that's pulling down your vibration—which you've been training yourself to notice and feel—it's always an opportunity to make a YOU-turn, and go into the glow stick, the real you. That's where all the resilience is, the peace, the higher consciousness allowing of whatever is happening out there.

I'm sure you're clear by now that the only way to uplift any situation is to energetically align with a positive outcome more than you're energetically aligning with the problem. That takes some creativity and some vision, and some skillful management of your attention, all of which you've been practicing. It becomes your natural default setting the more you tune into the voice of your Vertical Self, so noticing where your attention is pointed becomes another way to sort the voices.

Your Vertical Self knows that the way to positively affect a negative situation is always to imagine the feeling of the desired end-goal—not obsess about what the next step should be, just jump right to the prize. How do you want this to look/feel/be, ideally? Holding this vision to the point where you feel your own vibration rising up to match it is what allows the staircase to appear. You have to hold the vibration of the end-goal so solidly that the Universe has no choice but to fill your order. That might happen by just one step of the staircase appearing at a time, or you might get the insight of several steps at once. But the staircase can't appear while you're stuck down there in the low vibration of the problem itself, listening exclusively to the voice of the Horizontal Self. It can only show itself to you when you're holding the higher vibration.

This is what Mother Theresa was talking about when she was asked why she doesn't attend anti-war rallies. She said she didn't feel aligned with something so focused on war, but she said she'd happily attend a pro-peace rally. She knew that whatever you spend your attention on is what will grow. She listened to the voice of her Vertical Self.

For your final week of homeplay, you'll notice when your focus is pointed outward, toward the problem, and you'll choose instead to make a YOU-turn, where you can tune into the glow stick, the voice of the Vertical Self showing you how to hold the energetic space for the outcome you desire.

Please make all of this month's homeplay practices regular fixtures in your life. They'll clear your filter and elevate your Joy Setpoint to ever-expanding realms of wonderful!

Spot the Mirrors

"*Every relationship that you're in is something that you carry around with you. If your relationship is lousy, it's because you think of it that way. The person you're in a relationship with isn't with you in this moment, or when you're at work, or when you're in the bathroom, but your thoughts about that person are always with you. The only way you can experience another person is in your thoughts. You can't get behind their eyeballs and be them. You can only process them with your thoughts. If you look for what's wrong about them and store that negative image in your mind, then that's where your relationship exists. If you change your thoughts to what you love rather than to what you label as wrong, you've just changed your entire relationship.*"

—WAYNE DYER

*Y*ou're almost to the halfway point in your Joy Journey! You've done powerful, remarkable work, and I'm sure you're seeing that reflected not only in your inner landscape, but in all those tangible, external circumstances as well. You have undoubtedly begun manifesting a different reality by changing, steadily and incrementally, the shape and contents of your filter. Please celebrate your wonderful self!

This month, we're going to shift our focus to an aspect of that external landscape that is important to most of us: our relationships with all those other people out there. We haven't talked much about them yet because joy upleveling is truly an inside job, so our first order of business has been to build your skills of redesigning that all-important inner landscape to raise your personal vibration. It's likely, however, that the list of external circumstances you most want to create has an item or two on it involving other human beings.

Manifestation gets a bit more complicated when it involves other souls on their own soul journeys. Here's an example of an area in which it's *not* hard to manifest regarding other people: if you are single and want to manifest a like-hearted romantic partner, this is not difficult to do as you continue to raise your vibration. Beings who are vibrating similarly to you will be drawn to you as you move forward with this work. They will seem to appear out of nowhere. This manifestation goal works in perfect alignment with the energetic laws, benefiting both of you and furthering you on your paths. As you elevate your vibration, this manifestation will be effortless. I see it again and again. This is one of the easiest scenarios when it comes to manifestation involving others, and the same goes for new friendships, business partnerships, and relationships of all kinds. As the vibratory signature you send out changes, so do the people around you—for the better!

Here's a more difficult scenario: Maybe a particular person in your life is not behaving/responding/thinking/acting in the way that you would like them to. If your manifestation goal is about changing an existing human in some way that they are not interested in being changed, I'm sure you can see that this becomes a more complicated matter. It is true that the frequency you emit is always affecting everyone around you. However, the strongest influence in reality-creation for each of us will always be where we, *ourselves*, are vibrating, including this person you'd like to change.

Wanting to bring someone to a higher vibratory state is an admirable goal, and I'm not saying it can't be achieved to an extent. You will definitely benefit the vibration of this person simply through your involvement with them. You cannot, however, do the work of their journey for them. Ultimately, this person's own predominant intention (conscious and subconscious) will dictate if, when, to what extent, and how speedily they progress in elevating consciousness.

Let's do something fun. Right now, call to mind someone you're annoyed with, or angry with, or who has disappointed you. It's best if you can think of someone in your day-to-day life you don't feel great about. If you can't find anyone there, the next best thing would be someone you know *of*, even if they're not a personal acquaintance. That could mean even a politician or anyone in the media you don't like. If you still can't find a specific person, you can let it be a representative person—a *kind* of person that is challenging for you. For me, for instance, it might be the transphobes since I have a lot of personal investment in the kind of world I want for my daughter. For you, it might be the polluter, or the bigot, or the dishonest politician, or the greedy corporate magnate.

Come up with someone now. I'll wait.

Next, tune into what it is, specifically, that you dislike about this person. If you had to come up with a word or short phrase to describe their terrible traits or actions, what would it be? It might help to consider these points: Without the specifics, what did this person do? If you took away the detailed story, what's the *category* of what they did or how they behaved? Did they lie? Were they selfish? Lazy? Inconsiderate? Disrespectful? Fake? Ignorant? Annoying? Close-minded? Did they betray you? Hurt you? Ignore you? Misjudge you?

You want to boil your complaint about his person down to its general essence, stripped of the specifics, so that it sounds like "He lied," or "She was selfish," but inserting the trait you came up with. When you have it, write it in your Joy Journal.

I'm going to ask you to do something now and it requires action on your part, so don't just keep reading without doing the action step! Promise?

Now, with as much drama and indignation as you can muster, bringing intense energy to it, I want you to declare *out loud*, "I would *never* do that!" Then say it again, but using the specific quality you identified in this person, so it sounds like, "I would *never* tell a lie!" "I would *never* let someone down!" "I would *never* be inconsiderate!"

Say it again, bringing even more intensity and indignation to your declaration! Pull up your best drama queen or drama king self! "I would *never* . . ."

It's fun for me when we do this in my workshops. As you might have guessed by now, the indignation in the room typically shifts into some laughter.

Did it feel kind of silly to exclaim such a thing?

Nod your head if you've ever lied.

If you've ever behaved selfishly.

If you've ever betrayed anyone, including betraying yourself.

Maybe you've done some of this type of work. It's called "shadow work." I learned it from Debbie Ford who learned it from Deepak Chopra. It originated with the famous analytical psychologist Carl Jung. The above sort of exercise shows up in most shadow work trainings, but I'll credit my heart-sister and phenomenal Passion Test facilitator Beth Lefevre for this one because she makes it extra fun.

Shadow work involves unearthing all the traits we don't like about ourselves that we've been repressing and denying. To put it in the framework we've been using, these are the bucket beliefs you formed about yourself that tell you how bad and wrong you are. The particular traits you associate with being bad and wrong will depend on the specific things you felt judged for when you were young. Since you carry shame around these traits, you deny them within yourself, which results in you projecting judgment of them onto those around you. Carrying this subconscious shame often leads to fear of expressing yourself authentically, difficulty making healthy decisions for yourself, and trouble setting and maintaining firm boundaries.

Our shadow traits are most often not in our conscious awareness, so our best tool for locating them is to see where we're judging others. Any area where we judge another is showing us where we're out of balance within ourselves. It's another handy tool we have for identifying what we're storing in our filters.

My Joy Schoolers get to the point where every judgment they observe themselves making is a cause for celebration because it's always carrying a gift when we're willing to unwrap that gift. Shadow work is a super-deep rabbit hole we go down at Joy School; for our purposes here, we'll just dip our toes in it as another way to stretch our perception filter and see what we've been missing outside the view of our keyhole.

• • •

Revealing Your Shadow

"When you understand that every opinion is a vision loaded with personal history, you will start to understand that all judgment is a confession."
—NICOLA TESLA

Look again at the complaint you recorded about this person you're judging. Take a peek inward and see if this thing you judge in another is something that you're judging in yourself. It doesn't necessarily mean you think you exhibit this trait; it could even mean the opposite. A superficial understanding of shadow work makes it confusing for some people because they think it means "I judge my coworker for being selfish; so shadow work says I must be selfish. That's not true at all! I'm the most giving, altruistic, selfless person in the world. This shadow work is bullcrap."

That's where there's a misperception. Shadow work *can* be as obvious as "I judge that person's laziness because I judge myself so harshly when I am lazy." It *can* show up in an obvious way like that, but that's not the only way it shows up.

It's more about showing you where you judge a trait itself too harshly, often a trait where you could use some balance. So, in the case of the person who judges selfishness but knows herself to be the opposite, the message could be that she needs to move a bit more in the direction of healthy selfishness and putting herself first sometimes. It's almost like an underlying jealousy of someone out there taking good care of themselves when you know you're not taking care of you in that way. You judge the *trait itself* so much that you, yourself, have gotten out of healthy balance with it.

To continue with this example, you'd want to consider this: If you identified someone you judge as being inconsiderate, where might *you* be out of balance on the spectrum of considerateness? It's possible you're bothered by it Out There because you're someone who tends to go overboard on being considerate, to the point where it tips into resentment, and the mirror in this case would likely be showing you a suggestion that you work on setting clear boundaries with those around you and expecting those boundaries to be honored.

You want to look for where you might be projecting *your* judgment of *you* onto this person to discover how it's a mirror for you. Try that now. Open your Joy Journal, take a few slow, deep breaths, put your hand on your heart, and ask your Vertical Self, *If this judgment is a mirror, what can it show me about me?*

Jot down any messages you receive in your journal.

HOMEPLAY FOR KEY 6, WEEK ONE

Here's your first homeplay for this month. No matter what you've already just recorded, come back to this inquiry throughout the week. Once you've earnestly gone to your Vertical Self with a question, it will provide you answers. Sometimes not right away, but perhaps in the next few days you'll have an awareness sparked by a song lyric, an animal, or any other kind of sign your filter pulls in for you to consider. We've just begun to develop your language with your Vertical Self, so please treat this emerging skill with all the reverence, patience, and gratitude it deserves.

Every night for this first week of homeplay, go into dialogue with your wise Vertical Self and explore this one trait through the lens of shadow work. What might have caused you to store the energy of shame around this trait? Where has it shown up in your life previously? Understanding that it's just a bucket belief, born of faulty information you interpreted, what could you do to give yourself more grace and compassion around this issue? Invite your Vertical Self to show you impressions, memories, or signs that can assist you with this healing.

Liberating the Energy Stuck in Your Judgments

Now that you understand how filters work, and how everybody has one, and how everybody has their own wildly unique keyhole they're looking at reality through, you'll find that this growing awareness makes it much harder to judge people. Including yourself.

The people around you are there because you pulled them in with your vibration, and while we're on a healing journey we often bring in the very people we need to alert us to where the next phase of our healing could be directed! It's a beautiful system!

Even bullies and victims are attracted to one another because they vibrate similarly. Their actions may seem opposite, but they couldn't be in a shared experience if they weren't matching frequencies. They're both coming from a low vibration, low self-worth energy. One expresses this lack of self-worth by trying to dominate their environment, possibly in violent, persecuting ways. The other expresses their lack of self-worth by collapsing into victim energy. It's fear that's running both of them. Both are experiencing low-vibration, low self-worth; they're just expressing it differently. And it's nothing to judge ourselves for! The people we pull into our experience are always our teachers. It's up to us to open our perception filter enough to benefit from the lessons.

I hope that gives you even more incentive to keep up all this amazing work you've been doing to elevate your own vibration and raise your consciousness. The more you do it, the more you'll see that effort reflected in the beautiful beings that will start to surround you. I want to pinch myself every day when I look around at the friendships and community I've attracted and created. The level of authenticity, intimacy, and shared joy is like nothing I'd ever experienced in my earlier life. I had no idea there were so many purely loving and high-consciousness beings even walking the planet until I elevated my vibration enough to find them. That's what's possible for everyone who commits to this work.

According to Carl Jung, every time we feel the desire to change another person, it's showing us a displaced need to change ourselves. It *feels* like everything would be fine if *they* would just finally come around to seeing things the proper way and doing what they should do. Remaining in this unconscious way of being does nothing to grow us and does nothing to grow the other. Attempting to change another person in a meaningful way is generally futile and a thief of our joy. For the most part, you can count on every person in your life to stay the way they are until such time as something within *them* catalyzes their own desire to change themselves. (Your nagging insistence probably won't be that thing.)

Plus, as Abraham/Hicks explains here, attempting to control others only attracts more to be controlled. "It is easy to understand how you would come to the conclusion that your path to feeling good is through influencing or controlling the behavior of others. But as you attempt to control them (through influence or coercion), you discover that not only can you not contain them, but your attention to them brings more like them into your experience. You simply cannot get to where you want to be by controlling or eliminating the unwanted."

When we unconsciously project our own need to change onto another person, psychologists call it "transference." Often, the relationship dynamic is similar to the dynamic we had with one of our parents. It's common to project these past relationship patterns (embedded within our bucket beliefs) onto our romantic partners, friends, employers, coworkers, and anyone else we encounter on a day-to-day basis.

A weird-but-well-documented side effect of this tendency is that once you transfer this projection onto someone, that person will typically step into the role you've unwittingly assigned them. This goes on beneath the radar of conscious awareness for both of you. For example, if you transferred onto your boss the relationship dynamic you had with your father when you were growing up, your boss will likely start relating back to you in the ways your father did, in accordance with that relationship dynamic.

Maybe you can spot this in your past or recent situations. It's the reason we so often attract the same kind of partner, in essence, again and again, even when the outer packaging might look very different. The same can happen with friends and people we interact with in our careers. It starts looking like "everyone is selfish!" or "every partner I attract turns out to be emotionally unavailable!" It only seems that way because you're attracting these people based on where you're vibrating. To attract differently, you only need to elevate your personal vibration. (It's exactly what we've been doing together!) Here's my favorite reason for doing shadow work with my Joy Schoolers: when we're able to find and forgive these things in ourselves, we liberate our own energy to unprecedented high-vibration levels! Yes, it also makes forgiveness of those offenders out there much easier, but far more importantly, it's about forgiving ourselves because we also have that in us, and we've been judging it harshly (consciously or unconsciously) which only causes it to *grow* in our experience. It creates a focus lens in our filter, so that we see more and more of it; we attract it into our experience because the energy we're carrying around this thing is dense. It's concentrated.

So, declaring "I would never . . ." is supposed to make us laugh. We want to see the absurdity around such a statement because that's what will loosen up the old, crusty energy. Once we see how silly it is to judge this thing, the concentration around it dissolves, and our filter is released from searching it out and bringing it to us in the form of our external experiences. This is how we stop the radar from going *ding, ding, ding* and just amplifying the presence of this trait we don't like, both in ourselves and in our experience of others.

Shadow Work Lets You Get Youier

It's all about getting to that next level up in your self-love. It's about accepting and loving all the bits of you right where you are, and then realigning your keyhole to *magnify* those best aspects you naturally love most about yourself. In my joy training programs, we call it becoming "youier," or raising your "You IQ."

This requires a bit of unpacking because you could be thinking, *Um, I'm not sure I want to become entirely "me-ier" because there's a handful of things I don't like about who I authentically am, so I don't want to become more of those things.* The realization to solidify here is this: Just the fact that you've decided you don't like this thing about you means that you are not truly *that* at your essence—at your true core being. It's just something that got into your experience via your bucket beliefs; it's not really you.

To put it in an archetypal framework, a supervillain who loves that he's vicious and cruel and greedy and evil is different from a super-villain who recognizes he can be those things but dislikes that about himself. If we're watching *that* movie, we might get a glimpse that at his core, his true inner being, he's not really a supervillain at heart, right? Even if he's created some evidence of being one.

On a less dramatic scale, we can apply this logic to ourselves. If there's anything about you that you don't like, that discomfort around it is your indication that this aspect of you is simply not a reflection of who you truly are. If you continue to pour your judgment and attention on this part of you that you dislike, you're just continually feeding it, re-energizing it, and creating more of the same expression of it. Whatever we give attention to is going to grow.

You also have things you *love* about you. (Think hard!) By focusing on things you already love about you, you'll enhance *those* aspects. You'll grow them. And since those other parts of you (those parts you don't like so much) will be starved of your attention, they'll naturally dwindle away. Nothing can exist without your attention to keep it alive in your experience. The things you don't like about yourself are only vivid in your experience because you've been feeding them your attention.

The best kerklunk that happens with shadow work is when we deeply remember that all human qualities exist on a spectrum, and we all have the full spectrum for each of these qualities within us. That means it's likely that those things you don't like about yourself also exist within you at the *opposite* end of the spectrum.

Remember when we talked about the stick metaphor I learned from Abraham/Hicks? Within you exists the whole stick for this issue, with the two ends representing the extremes. If you think you're greedy, you want to acknowledge that you have the whole stick—representing incorrigible greediness to saint-like generosity—within you, and you can probably look back and find a time or two when you were generous and not at all greedy. All you're doing, by putting your attention on *those* times, is just using the energetic power of your attention to align yourself with the better end of the stick. Your attention determines what you create going forward. The whole stick is always going to be in you; it's in every one of us. Where you align yourself on it is just going to be a matter of where you direct the bulk of your attention.

This is the process by which we grow in our acceptance and love for ourselves, which uplevels simply everything in our entire experience and recalibrates our Joy Setpoint.

HOMEPLAY FOR KEY 6, WEEK TWO

I'm sure you can see by now that your filter has been filled with judgments of yourself and others. You've already spent a week observing yourself around your top-identified judgment. For your second week of homeplay, you'll look for other aspects of your shadow self that you've repressed. You'll keep in mind, as you go through your daily activities, that we only ever judge in others what we're judging in ourselves, even if that's on a subconscious level. Anytime you feel judgment flare up, it's a great opportunity to look at how you're feeling about you with regard to that issue. It's always a valuable message!

Throughout this second week of homeplay, you'll hold your understanding of shadow work in the forefront of your awareness and take intentional note of where you judge—the biggies and the smallies! You'll gather up every example of your judgments of others and record them in your Joy Journal where you can explore what each of these examples says about your judgments of yourself. Then, like you did during the first week of homeplay, you'll work to find grace and compassion and forgiveness for yourself around these issues. I'll point out again that even if you have some evidence in your circumstances to prove that you are shameful with respect to this issue, it's the energy of your stored bucket beliefs that caused you to create that evidence. You're shifting that energy up now, so you'll soon be manifesting a different kind of evidence.

Yes, Even Them

We've done a lot of work in Joy School applying these principles to social issues in the past few years. Between pandemic-related controversies and egregious political divide, it's been an awfully judgy time! It helps to recognize that what many of us *most* desire when it comes to any controversial issue, without being consciously aware of it, is simply to be right—to be on the side of the controversy that ends up "winning." As we've discussed, we are programmed, from a young age, to desperately want to get it right. So, of course, underlying our position-taking on any issue is going to be our Horizontal Self's desire to be right. Recognizing that allows us to instead choose to pull back our perspective far enough to contemplate what we most want as an outcome—from the higher perspective of our Vertical Self, not our ego-focused Horizontal Self.

We talked about how, once we're clear on our highest intention for the matter, our work is to then get our ego out of the way so we can move toward that intention most effectively. That means recognizing that the far more effective way to affect any kind of change is to approach it *without* the energy of judgment. We're going to be so much more effective in our conversations with people once we've moved into this higher-consciousness frequency. The way to do that, and loosen the judgment, is to simply remember that this person who disagrees with us has a filter that is different from our own. None of us has a clear filter, and we're all just as likely to be "right" on any given issue because "right" is a unicorn! We're all just looking at our own unique world through our own unique keyhole!

I'm not asking you to give up the causes you believe in; I'm just suggesting you become a bit more loose and compassionate in the way you view those who are not on your bandwagon with you. This is like forgiveness work in that it really isn't *for* the other person. It's a way for you to release the dense frequency of judgment so that your energy field can be lighter and more high-vibe. This is how we drain the heavy energy out of all our disagreements with others.

We have an expression in our culture; we say, "In *my* world . . ." And there's such truth in that expression. The more deeply we can understand that we're all, each of us, living in a wholly unique world, the more joy we're going to have access to.

And, yeah, there's also this communal reality playground that we're all trying to share, and this is where all the division and polarity comes up. If we truly have a pure, abiding desire to make that communal reality a better one for us all, we'll be led, through alignment with our Vertical Self, in the best ways for doing that. But judgment of those who don't agree with us won't play a part in that process. It's just not of the right vibrational frequency to make any kind of positive impact.

It comes back to remembering that however harshly you're judging anyone Out There, you can be sure that's the exact extent to which you're judging yourself in some way. These judgments of others, and of ourselves, are among the commonest ways we unnecessarily drag down our own vibration and deplete our potential for joy.

It's always fun to apply the "I would never . . ." game. The bottom line on all of these issues that have polarized our nation practically to the brink of civil war is that we're all simply convinced that the information we subscribe to is accurate, and the information *they* subscribe to is inaccurate. No matter which flavor of controversy you apply it to, when we're so sure that the information that we subscribe to is correct, and *their* information is incorrect, it's helpful to stay aware that our Horizontal Self's desire to be right is what's most often driving our emotions, no matter what subject matter we're debating. Each side is judging the other for believing false information. When we take a moment to pause and say in our head, "I would *never* believe false information!" it becomes apparent how silly it is to judge anyone for that. Surely, all of us, at some point in our lives, have believed false information. It's hardly a thing to judge a person for. If there were such a thing as objective reality, it would certainly reveal some truths and some untruths on *both* sides of this crazy fence we've collectively erected between the "us" and the "them" for each of these issues.

Even when other details are brought in (the Horizontal Self loves its bells and whistles!) just keep bringing the issue back to its bottom line. When you judge someone who opposes your political/cultural/ social opinion, you are saying, "You are believing something that I do not believe." And when you think about all the experiences that have shaped *any* particular person, all of their influences, all of what caused them to have the filter that allows in a teeny-tiny percentage of the bits of available information, you see that you know nothing about what has shaped this person's filter. And they know nothing about all the influences that have shaped your belief system and your filter. When you really get clear that all that's happening over there is the same thing that's happening over here where you stand, just with different input—then it's easy to loosen your energy around those judgments.

It doesn't mean you have to agree with this person in front of you. You can even keep trying to show them what you believe, but if changing their mind is truly your end-goal, you'll be far more effective at doing that once you've dissolved the energy of judgment around it. This lovely, inherently worthy human just came to a different conclusion based on the sum of their life experiences thus far and what's gotten lodged in the thick, tangly perception filter that's dictating their reality. Same with you.

HOMEPLAY FOR KEY 6, WEEK THREE

To recap the homeplay we've discussed so far for this month, you'll spend a week with that first judgment you identified with your shadow work exercise, holding up the mirror to see what you can discover about yourself and where you might be out of balance with this trait. For the second week of homeplay, you'll identify as many other judgments as you can and investigate them similarly, writing your observations in your journal to supercharge the practice!

For week three of this month's homeplay, you'll observe yourself in your interactions with others through the lens of these words by Eckhart Tolle: "Observe the attachment to your views and opinions. When you become involved in an argument or conflict, watch how defensive you become, and feel the force of your own aggression as you attack another person's position. Feel the mental-emotional energy behind your need to be right and make the other person wrong. Then let go of the force inside you that is fighting for power."

That "letting go" is truly a choice you can make! We are so habituated to our reactivity that we forget it's a choice until we do the conscious work of this week's homeplay. Letting go, as Eckhart describes here, right in the red-hot moment, is your task this week. It's ninja level, superstar! All this week, see if you can catch yourself as these situations arise (even when the arguments you have with others remain unspoken), and practice the "let go." If it's too difficult to do it as the situations are occurring, commit to reviewing your day before you go to sleep each night, and visualizing what the let-go would have looked and felt like in each moment that you had an opportunity to do it. That will train you for bringing the skill into your life going forward. Record your observations in your journal.

HOMEPLAY FOR KEY 6, WEEK FOUR

In addition to noticing your need to be right, you've probably noticed another default tendency now that you're observing yourself in your relationships with others. Have you noticed how much you contort yourself in an effort to be seen in certain ways? In your interactions with your loved ones, your workmates, your casual acquaintances, observe your behavior and conversations with them, and take note of how often you shapeshift.

We're all chameleons. Usually, our motivation is to be seen in a light we prefer to be seen in. We think we'll fit better into the tribe by projecting what we believe the tribe wants to see in us. But this tendency is limiting our true connection potential because what fosters true and deep connection is realness. When others sense that you are presenting your most deeply authentic self to the world, it gives them permission to do the same, and what we all secretly want, deep down, is that permission. That's why people who have done the work of presenting themselves authentically are so magnetic to others.

As president of my local PFLAG chapter (the country's oldest and largest LGBTQ+ support organization), I often witness the crippling trauma transgender folks suffer due to the belief they have to hide their truth in order to be loved. We're so egregiously hardwired to meet society's expectations that we sacrifice ourselves in heartbreaking ways. Once these beautiful souls feel seen and accepted in their truth, a whole new world of possibility opens up for them.

• • •

"Become more authentic and you will have a flowering. And the more authentic you become, by and by you will feel many things are falling away—of their own accord. You never made any effort to do it; they just fall of their own accord."

—OSHO

In the words of one of my most influential teachers, Michael Bernard Beckwith, "Imagine the relief of removing your carefully crafted masks fashioned by societal forms of conditioning and instead responding to what comes into your experience directly from your Authentic Self. One of the first principles to honor in your relationship with yourself is to respect and trust your own inner voice. This form of trust is the way of the heart, the epitome of well-being."

Mucking up most of our filters is the pervasive belief that we need to make other people like us. Are you starting to see what a losing proposition that is? In reality, there are countless versions of you in existence right now. Every person you've ever met, whether they are a regular fixture in your life or it's someone you've barely brushed past, has created a version of you within their minds while layering the distorting filter of their perception all over you. None of these "yous" are identical, and none of them are even close to being some sort of objectively "true" representation of who you are.

This should blow your mind to consider. You exist, in hundreds if not thousands of versions on the planet right now. I hope this helps to loosen your concern about what anyone thinks of you. Each person who perceives you is creating a you that is based primarily on their own unique filter. There's nothing you can do to change that. Clearly, a better objective than trying to get anyone to like you, would be for you to simply focus on continually upleveling the degree to which you like yourself. This elevates your vibration more than anything and will make you a beacon for wonderful others who will easily, authentically adore you.

That brings us to this final week's homeplay. Take out your journal and think about the last time your feelings were hurt by something someone said about you or to you, or by some action they took. What was the underlying message that you perceived from these words or actions? (You might recognize how it ties into one of your bucket beliefs.)

Now go into dialogue with your Vertical Self to ask, *Do I believe that about me?* Ask your wise inner knowing to show you what your honest answer is. There is much wisdom for you in this answer and opportunity for clearing these old hurts from your filter's storage system.

If your wisdom shows you that you do not believe that about you, realizing this deeply will allow you to not feel so hurt by them. You'll see that there's no objective truth to their judgment of you, and you can begin to understand that their erroneous thought is simply an extension of what's in their own buckets.

If you discover that you do believe this thing about you, it's an opportunity to question the validity of that self-assessment with the tools you've been practicing. Make it a statue and walk around it.

Apply the wisdom of the Abraham/Hicks stick metaphor. It could also be an opportunity to see where you can move in the direction of becoming more of who you are at your core essence. Anything you judge yourself for has the potential to be an area where you've gotten out of alignment with your true core being.

Whether you discover that you believe this thing about you or not, it's a gift! Explore some other times you can recall where you've been hurt by the words or actions of those in your life and record all of your observations in your journal. After you've done this insight-inspiring journal work, you're ready to test out this skill in your day-to-day life. When you bump up against anything in your world that gives you an uncomfortable feeling about yourself, go through this now-practiced inquiry for challenging the thought. It's amazing how we become immune to slights and insults with some repetition of this process, so commit to practicing it full-out this week. (And beyond!)

Your inconvenient Horizontal Self is programmed to be concerned about how you are coming across to others, and that includes being right about things. But whenever you worry about what others think about you, you're saying that what they think is more important than what you think of yourself. If you want approval, the key is to stop needing it. Think about who you know who gets the most approval. They're so busy being themselves, they don't worry about how anyone else perceives them. Self-actualization researcher Abraham Maslow called it being "independent of the good opinion of others" and considered it a trait of higher consciousness.

It's not about walling yourself off from the world with a petulant attitude of "I don't care what you think!" You want to find that sweet spot where you're unconcerned about others' opinions of you while still keeping your heart open to them and wanting good for them.

That never means allowing them to abuse to you. In my beautiful friend Paul Boynton's new book, *Remember: A Little Book of Courage, Comfort, and Joy,* he writes, "We need to learn the difference between having a willingness to be kind, open and forgiving, and being a doormat . . . Trust your intuition. It's almost always right."

OPTIONAL ADDITIONAL HOMEPLAY FOR KEY 6

I'll give you one additional, optional homeplay assignment this month. If a relationship you're in is "making" you unhappy, a good question to ask is, *What do I feel is missing in this relationship?* Then, using your ninja-level shadow work skills, you next ask, *In what ways is this something that I am failing to bring to the relationship?* And please note that while it could be something you're not offering the other person, it is often something you are failing to give *yourself.* You aren't showing yourself the kindness, or respect, or unconditional acceptance, or generosity, or patience that your soul desires, so you are projecting this complaint onto the other. It is only when we are failing to give ourselves what we need that we accuse others of not giving it to us. (That doesn't mean you excuse bad behavior in the other; when you're clear about showing yourself respect, it could very well mean ending the relationship.)

Ultimately, if you haven't been able to show your own sweet self the abundant love you crave, it's only because you've got some bucket beliefs saying you don't deserve that love. Let's keep draining these pesky buckets, shall we?

Create Tomorrow Today

"What shape waits in the seed of you to grow and spread its branches against a future sky?"

—DAVID WHYTE

The title of this month's key is inspired by one of Louise Hay's memorable quotes that helped me to spiral in my kerklunk on this critical concept. Louise said, "Today is the future I created yesterday." This month is going to be all about manifestation! In truth, you've always been "creating tomorrow today." The difference is now you've begun doing it with intention and control, and this month you'll crank that mastery up to a whole new level!

As my beautiful friend Christian de la Huerta reminds us: "Too often, we don't even

"What you are aware of, you're in control of. What you are not aware of, is in control of you."

—ANTHONY DE MELLO

know why we do the things we do! And we can't do anything about what we can't see. Becoming self-aware is the first step toward personal freedom and empowerment." Most people on the planet today will remain utterly unaware of the mechanics of manifestation throughout their entire lives, endlessly creating scenarios and tomorrows that they could have manifested more to their liking if they had reached this awareness. You are not most people. You've undoubtedly been coming to ever greater levels of kerklunk on the understanding that you are an energetic being in an energetic Universe that is ceaselessly responding to the vibration you're emitting by delivering to you that which is similarly vibrating.

As we've seen, due to outdated biases that still encumber the human race, we're programmed to vibrate in accordance with fear, even when fear is not at all warranted by our circumstances. The habit of feeding endless energy and attention into our fearful imaginings is all too prevalent at this point in our collective evolution. Yet, as Abraham/Hicks tells us, "You cannot look at that which you do not want and not join and perpetuate that vibration. Take your attention from that which is not in harmony with who you are, and your 'now vibration' will adjust to who you really are, and then you can uplift others." *Who you really are* is your Vertical Self, the part of you that is not comprised of your illusory filter smeared with erroneous bucket beliefs that stir up fear.

Your Vertical Self is clear, effective, and calm—always. Accessing it is accessing your joy. The obvious truth that most of us overlook is that joy is a right-now thing, or it's nothing at all. We are all so conditioned to look for joy Out There, in some next moment. But the only time we can ever have joy is right now, in this moment. It takes practice and commitment to build the habit of present-moment joy, and, let's face it, most of us have never given much thought to cultivating that habit.

One of my teachers used to say that your life is a beaded necklace, and every day is a bead on the string. We have a tendency to always be looking out at some distant goal as the time when our days will be good. We think once we've gotten that degree, or that promotion, or that partner, or that home, then we can finally experience the joy we long for. We treat the day we're in like some insignificant stepping-stone, never stopping to savor what's right here, right now, putting our interest and attention into beautifying and enriching this moment we're presently in.

But this right-here moment—that's our life. It's the individual days, strung together, one after the next, bead after bead, that make up the necklace. If we give time and energy to making each bead, each day, as beautiful and meaningful as we can make it, those beads, all strung together become our existence. You can only make a truly beautiful necklace by paying attention to each bead.

We elevate our Joy Setpoint tremendously when we begin valuing our individual days, hours, moments as the precious opportunities that each one is, instead of rushing through them unconsciously, thinking we're paving the way for some future happy payoff. We didn't come here with that unconscious habit. Babies and toddlers live exclusively in the present moment. That kind of thinking has been programmed into us. The society we were raised in has a collective bucket belief that says, *Suffer now so you can play/relax/rejoice/retire/whatever in the future.* It makes sense to our Horizontal Selves because it's what we've been taught, but energetically, it simply doesn't work that way.

• • •

"If every morning, you can find a reason to say, 'Yes, it's going to be a beautiful day.' And every day you find a reason to say, 'Yes, it is a beautiful day.' And every night, you find a reason to say, 'Yes, it was a beautiful day,' then one day, you'll look back and easily say, 'Yes, it was a beautiful life.'"

—DOE ZANTAMATA

When Louise Hay said, "Today is the future I created yesterday," she knew the energy that you're embodying and sending out right now, in this very moment, is an order you're placing with the Universe, telling the Universe what kind of next moments you'd like to have. The Universe will comply; it's here to fill your order. And maybe your external world isn't set up right now to give you what you believe to be the reasons for you to have a high vibratory state. We all know what that's like, here in this puny human experience.

That's why we learn the skills of becoming less affected by the Out There. We learn to turn inward, where we all are joy and peace and love at our core. It's what my friend Marci Shimoff calls being "happy for no reason" in her books. My heart-brother and teaching partner Rob Mack calls it "happiness from the inside out" in his books. Christians call it "the peace which surpasses all understanding," and Eckhart Tolle simply calls it "presence."

Are You Wanting Correctly?

As I've touched on previously, having desires from an energetic state of joy and presence (Vertical Self) places an order with the Universe that is vibrationally very different from the order we place by having desires from a state of scarcity and fear (Horizontal Self.) Wanting has got to feel good when you're doing it; that's where so many well-intentioned manifesters go wrong. When you're wanting that thing *so bad,* and you're visualizing it *so hard,* you're just keeping it perpetually at arm's length. One of the juiciest things I teach at Joy School is how to want. Because most of us are just wanting wrong, and wanting correctly is the secret to having.

Alan Watts called it the "backwards law" in his teachings, and here's what Rumi had to say about it:

> **When I run after what I think I want,**
>
> **my days are a furnace of stress and anxiety;**
>
> **if I sit in my own place of patience,**
>
> **what I need flows to me, and without pain.**
>
> **From this I understand that**
>
> **what I want also wants me,**
>
> **is looking for me and attracting me.**

Feel that? That's the state you want to achieve. You want to be the still magnet, not the engine out there chasing it all down. This magical sweet spot is nothing more than the result of clearing away the gunk in your filter, which is why we've been focusing on that filter so much. And it's always an ongoing process. No human has a completely clear filter, but it's always possible to nudge our filters gently in the direction of clarity. The clearer your filter, the faster and more extravagantly you manifest, and the faster you get on track with your impassioned, vibrant, joyful experience of life.

Let's do a bit of journaling now. If you'll indulge me this request, please stand up, jump up and down, wave your arms around, swirl your hips, do a little dance to get your heart pumping. I want you to elevate your oxygen level before we dig in because this writing prompt won't work well if you're sitting there in dense, static energy.

Ready? You're going to playfully write down something that you want, as if it could fall out of the sky into your metaphorical lap right now at this second. You're going to do it by starting with this prompt: "Wouldn't it be cool if . . ." and just see what pours out of you from there. Anything you desire! It could have to do with an ideal job, ideal health situation, ideal relationship situation, big money, success. The only rule is to keep this desiring *playful*.

Let yourself be surprised by what pops into your head when you invite your imagination to run wild with that prompt. Pause your reading and do that now. Come back when you're ready.

Okay, why did I ask you to keep it playful? Because playful equals detached, at least to some degree. You need a sense of detachment in order to want correctly. If you're sending out an energy of desperation around this order your placing, it's clear to the Universe that you're afraid it won't happen. Your subconscious knows when that's the case, and the bulk of your manifestation energy is coming from your subconscious beliefs. That's why we do the work of bringing those long-stored subconscious beliefs up into our conscious awareness.

Whenever wanting feels bad, that's your indication that you're not in the right dance with the energetic laws of manifestation. That's not a sweet spot for bringing your desires to fruition. Being the magnet can only happen when the wanting feels yummy to you, when your desire elicits delicious, tantalizing anticipation. Wanting *effectively* means getting yourself to the place where the wanting feels purely positive, because that means you actually believe you can have this thing you desire. Remember how I've told you that manifestation can never outrun your deep-down beliefs about your deservingness? If, on a deep-down (even unconscious) level, you don't believe you deserve to have this thing, you've handcuffed the Universe. There's no way, energetically, that it can deliver.

One of my teachers, Joe Vitale (who inspired the above exercise), says, "You can have anything you want as soon as you don't need to have it." The need adds an energy to your intention that, ironically, pushes the thing you want away. It seems so unfairly set up; I'm sorry for that. But it's not for us to judge the energetic laws; it's just for us to understand them and work with them.

Whenever you have a strong desire that remains unrequited, and you notice the desire doesn't feel good, it means there's another energy you're emitting that's eclipsing the energy of what you want. It's the energy of *not* having it. Maybe you have a strong desire that does feel happy to you sometimes, and at other times you notice feeling dissatisfaction about not yet having this thing (because we sometimes vacillate between these feelings.) The problem, even in this scenario, is that, at best, the energies you're emitting are just canceling one another out. You have to get the positive one bigger and stronger than the negative, so the signal that you're sending is clear and unmistakable and carries the energetic signature of already having this condition or situation or thing that you desire.

Okay, let's look back at what you wrote playfully in your Joy Journal. Maybe you focused on one wish, or maybe you created a little list. If more than one desire bubbled up from your writing, feel into the list and circle the desire that calls to you most in this moment. Let your intuition show you which one to work with now.

Does feeling into this desire bring your energy up or down? Does it feel like contraction in your body, or expansion? Does it bring a smile to your face, or create a pit in your stomach? This is how you assess whether or not you've been wanting correctly.

Since I insisted you approach this prompt playfully, there's a better-than-usual chance that you chose a desire you can feel good about. Hold this desire in your imagination now and ask yourself, *What will the fulfillment of this desire feel like?* You picked some specific thing to wish for based on what you've been able to identify through the limitation of your keyhole, but the bottom line is that it's the feeling you're after. Always, the things we identify as our desires are just best-guess placeholders for what we believe will bring us a certain feeling we want to feel.

Now it's time to get clarity around this feeling you assume the fulfillment of this desire will bring you. Probably joy, happiness; sure. But see if you can get more specific than that. What's the nuance you're craving? Is it a feeling of adventure? Of accomplishment? Of fun and novelty? Of deep connection with someone? Of serenity and relaxation?

Pause your reading again so you can spend some time feeling into that and writing down what you discover.

Ready? Now that you've identified the feeling you're hoping this thing you playfully decided you want will bring you, look around at your existing reality, the life you've got right now, and find something that brings you this feeling. It doesn't have to look like, or in any way resemble the thing you're desiring; it just has to give you the feeling that you believe the thing you want is going to give you. Identify those things that are already in your life now, even if they give you this feeling to a smaller degree than you'd like.

For example, if you desire a romantic partner, look for where in your life you feel loved and/or desirable, or joyfully, authentically connected with someone. Maybe you have a fur baby who makes you feel deeply loved. Maybe you have an admirer at work. Even if it's someone you have no interest in, this would go on your list because it gives you some degree of the feeling of being desirable. Past partners who have loved and/or desired you could go on the list. You'd include everything in your life that gives you any degree of feeling lovable and desirable.

Or, if your wish was about abundance, you'd list everything in your life that makes you feel abundant to any extent, in any way.

Pause your reading to make this list. I'll be right here.

Done? Then you're ready for the magic ingredient! Now, you're going to tap solidly into immense *gratitude* for the things on your list that are already giving you this feeling in your life. The magic ingredient is gratitude. "Gratitude is the ultimate state of receivership!" In Joy School, I reference Joe Dispenza's work a lot and that's his #1 mantra for manifestation.

Are you underwhelmed to learn of this magic ingredient? Gratitude is one of those rather tired concepts. If I had started out saying, "your task for this month is to practice gratitude," you might have indulged me and gone along. But I've noticed that many of us experience the suggestion to be grateful as a minor burden. We struggle when we feel like we *should* be grateful for things that just aren't naturally exciting us that much. It's okay. It's human. But I want you to start looking at gratitude from a different angle and recognizing it as a powerful tool, not only for your present-moment joy, but for your powers of manifestation as well.

It's commonly recognized as energetic law that gratitude in general will always pave the way for more and more good to come into your life. That's at the heart of every spiritual and metaphysical school of thought I've ever studied. But with this exercise, we're fine-tuning that energetic principle a little by honing in on a specific *flavor* of gratitude, so that you can pull in more of what will bring you that flavor of joy, since that's what you've decided you're wanting right now! The Universe might deliver the exact, precise wish as you identified it, but it's been my experience that it's to your benefit to give the Universe some wiggle room. From the view through our tiny keyhole, we often select what looks like it will bring us the feelings we want, when the

Universe (privy to a far more expansive perspective) knows there's a much better option for us having that feeling. That's why many teachers of manifestation suggest we add the following tagline to all the orders we place with the Universe: "this or something better, please!"

I remember when author Joe Vitale used to tell his rags-to-riches story, including the pivotal moment when everything turned around for him. He was living in poverty at the time, but he went to the library and listened to free self-help talks and read books on manifestation. He noticed all these teachers kept talking about gratitude. He thought, *yeah right. There is absolutely no way for me to be grateful about a single thing I have going on right now. I'm living in squalor, my wife and I are fighting and about to call it quits, I have no self-worth whatsoever, I've acquired nothing, accomplished nothing, there is nothing for me to be grateful for.* At the time, he'd been in and out of homelessness for years, and he was committed to this idea that he needed to get something to be grateful for before he could possibly feel gratitude.

One of these gurus he'd been following explained to him at one of the free talks that he had the sequence wrong—that in order to get something to be grateful for, he'd have to feel the gratitude first. So, he's not too happy with this advice. He goes back to his rat-infested, one-room rental with a toilet in the corner, and he looks around and feels there's nothing there to be grateful for. Then he picks up a pencil. His heart's not in it, but he says, *okay, I've got to do this. This pencil is the only thing in the room that's not making me want to kill myself right now.* And then his heart brightens a little at the thought *well, if I did decide to kill myself, I could write a suicide note with this pencil. So, there's something to be grateful for about it. I use this thing to make lists, and I do like to make lists, so I'm grateful for that. I've been using it to write affirmations, and that's been helping me, so I guess I can be grateful that I own this pencil. I've thought about writing a screenplay, and maybe even a book, so it's a good thing I have a pencil to do that stuff with.*

Then, he noticed the eraser! What a cool thing that was! He went on to muse, *with an eraser, I can change my mind about things; I can improve the things I write down as I gain more knowledge and grow. Somebody invented this thing called a pencil with lead on one end and an eraser on the other end, and people throughout time have written things that have changed the world! Thank God for the pencil!*

Joe said he could feel his energy changing inside of him, like he'd been plugged into an electrical outlet! And that thing that I've been calling the kerklunk, where a concept you've heard a million times suddenly goes kerklunk from your head down into your whole being—that's what happened to Joe Vitale in that moment around the concept of gratitude. He looked around his hovel and realized, *this time last year I was on the street! I was homeless and hungry, and now I have shelter and running water and . . . a pencil!*

He shares that story from stages, describing it as the most pivotal moment in his life, because that was the moment he *knew*, at the deepest level, that he had to crank up that gratitude and appreciation every single day. He soon saw that the more he did it, the faster and more dramatically his situation improved. The more he intentionally cranked it up, the more he opened that valve of receivership, and he says he still thinks about that pencil while kicking back in his hot tub in the mansion he's since manifested. Out of all the accomplishments and material accumulations he now has to be thankful for, he says the thing he's *most* thankful for is that pencil, because that's what provided the understanding that turned his life around. Once he elevated his vibration to the point of feeling abundant, he attracted more and more abundance into his life. So elegant in its simplicity!

It works. It truly does. In the morning, you say thank you for this coffee, thank you for whatever parts of my body are working great today, even if some aren't. You only have to find a sliver of gratitude for one little thing, and then intentionally go into that feeling. Then let it build from there. It's the way to expand your valve of receivership, and there's no limit to how wide you can expand it! In the words of Neville Goddard, as soon as you're able to "assume the feeling of the wish fulfilled," you've done your part to place an order the Universe will have no choice but to fill. And the quickest way to assume that feeling is by tapping into gratitude for where that feeling is already in your life.

That's the nuts and bolts of manifestation, dear reader. It's a practice, just like all the other new skills we're building. To make sure you're emitting the most effective, high-vibe signals possible, find your pencil. Discover what you're truly grateful for and use it as the entry point into an even more cranked up, sincere flow of gratitude that you make a point to spend time with every day.

Gratitude is the opposite of resistance and that is a big part of its magic. I'm sure you've heard the wisdom "What you resist, persists." It's been a bit of a theme for us in your joy training thus far. Anything you shower with negative attention will increase the negative situations in your life. Anything you shower with positive attention will increase the positive situations in your life. "Gratitude" is just another word for positive attention, so any situation you shower with gratitude will bring you more goodness.

HOMEPLAY FOR KEY 7, WEEK ONE

For your first week of this month's homeplay, you'll get creative in cranking up your gratitude for the things you already identified as bringing you the feelings you like. Every day this week, challenge yourself to add to the list you made. Every morning, before you get up, list ten things in your head that already bring you this feeling and shower them with your appreciation. Every night, before you go to sleep, do the same.

Pro tip: If you notice that it's difficult for you to assume a sincere attitude of appreciation, that's a surefire sign that you're overly identified with your Horizontal Self. The Horizontal Self is rooted in fear and scarcity; it doesn't want you to get complacent about what you've accumulated or achieved because it's afraid you'll stop achieving and accumulating if that happens. The author Robert Wright offers a fascinating perspective on this tendency. He says that our human brains are programmed, above all else, for propagation of the species. Again, this programming goes back to our primitive days (which span a considerably longer period of time than our "civilized" days.) To ensure that our genes got passed on to future generations, humans were wired to hoard resources, compete over desirable mates, and stay hyper-focused on self-preservation and protection. None of that lends itself to basking in a blissful state of appreciation for what you have and who you are. So, when you're struggling to feel appreciative, it's helpful to remember that you're just taking cues from some long-outdated brain programming. You've been working to cancel subscriptions to those erroneous influences, but it's likely that's still a work in progress.

Why Do You Want It?

I've mentioned that the bulk of your manifesting energy comes from your subconscious. We've all seen that diagram of an iceberg representing conscious awareness, right? There's the little tip of the iceberg sticking up out of the water that represents the thoughts and beliefs you're consciously aware of, and then there's that enormous mountain of ice under the waterline that represents the unconscious beliefs and programs that run you. Our work together has been to lower the waterline, and we'll continue doing that, bringing to light more and more of the thought patterns you've been unaware of so that we can divest them of their control over you.

Let's do a slightly repetitive bit of journaling now. Off the top of your head, make a quick list of things you desire. Notice this time I'm not asking you to be playful about it. You don't need to try to be in any particular frame of mind. Without overthinking, simply make a brief list of what comes to mind for you when you're invited to have some desires. Write that list in your Joy Journal.

Since aligning more fully with our Vertical Selves is our primary goal, it's important to understand where it is we're typically aligned so that we can feel the difference between operating from our limited Horizontal Self perspective and operating from the much higher, broader perspective of our Vertical Self. Getting clear on how often our actions and choices come from our unreliable, faulty bucket beliefs and skewed definitions is imperative to the journey, so we're going to get some clarity around that now.

Many years ago, I interviewed the world-famous shaman William Whitecloud on my radio show, and one of the most profound things I learned from him was a dynamic he calls our "compensating tendencies." Often the things we identify as our desires are merely attempts to compensate for our underlying, long held feelings of unworthiness, powerlessness in a scary world, or any of those other erroneous beliefs we form in childhood. We make decisions about what we want in attempts to compensate for the pain these beliefs cause us, often unconsciously.

Unfortunately, when a desire springs from a compensating tendency, it means the signal we send out is coming from a low-vibration belief that corresponds more with what we *don't* want than what we do want. This sends out a convoluted signal that sounds something like, *I want this thing in order to make up for not really feeling worthy of it,* or, more simply, *My bottom-line belief is I'm not good enough to have this, so I desperately want it so I can show myself that belief is wrong.* You can see how this would impede successful manifestation of our desires.

With this understanding, look at the list of desires you just came up with. For each item on the list, ask yourself, *Why do I want this?* See if you can identify whether it's a "run to" feeling, or a "run from" feeling. A "run-to" desire feels good! A "run-from" desire would be one that's about compensating for a feeling based on an uncomfortable belief. One insight that can emerge from this exercise is the identification of your primary unmet needs. We all have them, and they shape our path in seen and unseen ways.

For a little extra clarity, try this writing prompt: What do you wish had been given to you or done for you in your childhood? Again, no overthinking! Top-of-mind answers are always more likely to be coming from your truest inner knowing.

Our compensating tendencies take on different flavors depending on the flavors of our bucket beliefs. Maybe some connecting threads are starting to emerge for you. No worries if not. We're not done poking around here. We're just looking to gather some insights around why you want the things you believe you want.

As we've discussed, we create the framework of beliefs that dictate our reality early in life, before we've individuated, while still at the developmental stage when it feels like everything is about us and our fault. We think, *If I'm not getting the love and validation I need, it means there's something wrong with me.* For almost all humans, compensating for that becomes a way of life. All our decisions become about compensating for these early beliefs. We don't put our energy into developing our true potential because we're so caught up in this compensation tendency.

Let's break that pattern, shall we? We'll do it by observing our desires and developing the habit of asking, *Why do I want this?* Here's an example. Maybe you identify that you'd like to own a boat. The next thing to do would be to go into your imagination to access your fantasies about boat ownership and observe, without judgment, what those fantasies feel like. If you see yourself telling your friends and associates about your boat, posting pictures of your boat, inviting people to your boat so you can impress them and feel the pride of ownership, you might want to consider whether your main reason for wanting the boat is to make yourself feel more important and successful. That's nothing to judge yourself for! It's a common compensating tendency for the widespread bucket belief called "not worthy/not successful/not important." It's the same reason many people desire designer clothes, flashy cars, degrees from prestigious schools; the list is endless. What's important to understand, is that whenever we want something in order to relieve the tension of any of those unworthiness bucket beliefs, it's a compensating tendency, and when that's the case, it means the strongest manifestation energy we're sending out carries the vibration of "I want this because I don't believe I'm worthy of it."

See how that makes manifestation a sticky wicket? The vibration you're emitting is not likely to easily, smoothly manifest you a boat because the bottom-line belief is the energy of "I'm not worthy of owning a boat." What's most likely to be created from that energy is remaining boatless. The Universe is simply fulfilling the order you placed, even though you thought you were placing a different order. This is what I mean when I say the bulk of your manifesting energy comes from your unconscious (the big chunk of ice under the water) and not your conscious mind (the tiny bit of iceberg that's visible over the waterline.)

Your desire for boat ownership was a strategy to resolve the tension you felt about being unimportant or unworthy. That's how our tension-resolution strategies perpetuate our cycles of experience. When your motive for wanting something is coming from your untrue and unhelpful bucket beliefs (consciously or unconsciously), the underlying energy of the desire is about fighting the beliefs in your filter, trying to defeat them. You know by now that fighting anything keeps it alive in your experience. What we fight, we ignite. That's why it's so important to bring this dynamic into your conscious awareness!

It's possible you'd still, through lots of struggle and effort, manage to manifest the boat. But if the desire for boat ownership was driven from the compensation-tendency dynamic described above, the fruition of this desire wouldn't bring the happiness you expected. We simply cannot find sustainable joy by manifesting from a "run-from" positioning, because creating anything from the energy of what we don't want will always eventually lead us to create more of what we don't want. Getting the boat from that energy wouldn't relieve the core wound in the long term. You'd have fleeting moments of pride of ownership and impressing people, but it wouldn't do anything to actually quell the unmet need. Soon, you'd just be looking for the next way to do that.

Now let's look at this boat desire from another angle! Go back to the step where you tap into your imagination to see what the fruition of this desire feels like to you. This time, let's say you're shown something like this: You feel the wind in your hair and the freedom and exhilaration of being out in the open sea. You imagine loving the feeling of using your muscles to hoist the sail. You feel the sun and sea spray on your face, the salty air on your skin, the excitement of the speed, maybe glancing over at your friend or significant other laughing and enjoying the moment with you. Feel the difference? If that's the kind of energy you find underlying your desire, you'll know it's a "run-to," and not a "run-from." Same desire, different manifestation energy!

In this second example, you're tapping into a scenario for generating the kind of happy, joyful feelings you're here to experience. It's not compensating for any weighty belief, so there's no lower, conflicting vibration attached to it. This is the manifesting position that yields miraculous results. My Joy Schoolers will attest! The reason so many people got excited about the Law of Attraction and then found it didn't work for them is because the things they wanted were so weighed down by their compensating tendencies they were unable to send out clear signals.

In another common example, if you're urgently desiring a romantic partner, but the underlying reason is you need someone to validate your worth by picking you, by admiring you, I'm sure you can understand now that the predominant vibration you're sending out is *I don't feel worthy of romantic love, so I really want it in hope of proving my unworthiness belief wrong.* It's a muddy signal to send out. That's why all the consciousness gurus suggest we clean up our own stuff before looking for partners. It's not impossible to attract a partner from this low-vibe frequency, but the result in that case will be more about matching puzzle pieces as a way to continue growth for both of you. Same story for all kinds of partnerships like friendships or job offers. It's fine for it to go this way, and often does as we go about the business of evolving. It's just not the most joyous, high-vibe route, and you've been doing such good filter-clearing work that I want something more for you.

HOMEPLAY FOR KEY 7, WEEK TWO

Your homework this second week is to start paying attention to all your desires, small or large. Write them in your Joy Journal! Any time you notice yourself wanting something, look at it from this new understanding of your compensating tendencies. Ask yourself, *Why do I want this? Am I joyfully running TO it, or am I running FROM something by having this desire?*

Journal your responses. Becoming aware of your compensating tendencies can reveal even more bucket beliefs you might not have yet uncovered. You may notice your desires shifting. Often, things we thought we wanted fall away as we do this work, replaced by desires more aligned with what would truly light up our soul.

It's been said that money is one of the most difficult things to manifest, and I believe that's simply because money, in itself, is meaningless. When you identify your deep-down reason for wanting money, it's usually easy to see whether it's a run-from reason or a run-to reason. If you determine that it's a run-from reason, you now understand why you've been unable to manifest money! If you can switch it to a run-to, you will see a difference in your manifestation results. Whatever it is you believe money will bring you, you have to deliberately get excited about that (not the money itself.)

It gets tricky because sometimes the reason a person wants to manifest money is tied to an inherently low-vibe situation, like being uncomfortably in debt. If you want to get out of debt, you need to come up with a purely wonderful scenario for what that would look like. What would a day in the life of a debt-free person be? Let your imagination paint you a picture that feels good, that raises your vibration when you imagine it, and then go to that daydream as often as you can. Don't let the word "debt" be any part of the daydream. Take control of your immense powers of attention to turn a run-from into a run-to.

Remember when we talked about giving the Universe some wiggle room? It's good to keep in mind that money is often a step that can be skipped. When we focus on the run-to thing we truly want, and we take out what we think the middleman has to be, we give the Universe the room to deliver our desires in novel ways that we might not have imagined. If you really want a vacation in Bali, for instance, and you're trying to manifest money so you can do that, you might be missing some other opportunity for the Universe to get you directly to Bali without needing that middle step. As long as the desire is a run-to, and not based in compensating tendencies attempting to relieve false beliefs you've been harboring, the magic around this kind of manifestation can astound you! Instead of working on manifesting money to get there, simply focus on all the pleasures and delights you anticipate feeling in Bali. Let the feelings you generate with this imagining be the magnetic signal you send out.

So again, your homeplay for this second week will start with you noticing all of your big and small desires and writing them in your Joy Journal, then determining which ones are a run-from and which are a run-to. You might notice that some desires have a bit of an element of both. Your next job is to curate this list to be more in alignment with your soul-level desires, then finesse each of these desires into a pure run-to scenario. You'll know you've hit on the right visualization when the thought of this desire feels good and not bad. You probably are able to notice by this point, when your vibration is pulled down by a thought or elevated by a thought. Wanting correctly means wanting that's accompanied by an elevation of vibration.

HOMEPLAY FOR KEY 7, WEEK THREE

For your third week of homeplay I want to bring you back to the most basic, critical understanding for successful manifesting, and that is that you are in control of where you put your attention. It's how you place your orders with the Universe. I love this classic Abraham/Hicks analogy: Imagine a train with an engine at each end, the engines pointing in opposite directions. One engine represents the problem; the other engine represents the solution. Whichever engine you're giving your attention to is the one you're fueling. You're making *that* engine the strongest by feeding it your attention, so that's the direction the train is going to move in. If you want the train to move in the direction of the solution, you have to pay more attention to *that* engine than you're paying to the engine that represents the problem. (You don't need to see the specifics of the solution; just sense what it will feel like when there is one.)

Your homeplay this third week sounds simple, but it is profound. Just like you did early in your journey when you checked in with yourself throughout the day to see how you were feeling, you're going to schedule those check-ins again this week. This time, the question you'll ask yourself, right in these random moments of your day, is: *Which engine am I fueling right now? Am I holding the vision of what I want, so that the steps can appear to take me there, or am I focused on what I don't want?*

Don't beat yourself up if you discover you habitually feed the wrong engine. It's how we've all been programmed! The discovery itself is the cause for celebration. Once this tendency is brought to your awareness, you can commit to fueling the engine that's headed in the direction you want to go.

My beautiful romance-expert friend, Arielle Ford, has this to say about manifestation:

> The core basis of my belief and understanding about manifestation (whether you are manifesting love, a car, a new career, or a new little black dress) is this: There is no "time." The past, present, and future all happen simultaneously. When we have a desire for something, it's because some part of us already knows that this is possible for us on an unseen level. Your dream is not some random thing out there somewhere; it is already in existence, calling upon you to dream it into *your* existence. To do this, we must be willing to own and embrace the dream or desire and then take the necessary, appropriate action steps to bring it into 3-D reality.

We're always creating tomorrow today. How we're vibrating in this present moment determines what we'll create for our upcoming moments. Failure to understand this is what causes most humans to stay "stuck" in situations they'd rather be released from. They're taking thoughts and feelings from the past and layering that energy all over their future, so the future has no chance to deliver anything fresh or new!

The people you witness breaking out of their ruts and creating better lives for themselves are the ones who have changed their internal state *before* the desired external conditions showed up. Some have learned this skill by studying spiritual principles, like you're doing now, but I've known many who arrived at that vibrational juncture via a crisis or dark night of the soul. Desperation can sometimes jolt one into new perspectives and shifts of thought. My remarkable author and poet friend S.C Lourie describes these life-altering crisis points like this: "You implode from the inside. And you are left with millions of pieces of your identity, belief system, and memory bank splattered on the soil of your life that you at first can't help but stamp on in disbelief, in fury, in sorrow. But the shock soon enough disarms you. Time is a blur. You are surrounded by a fog. The screams are silenced in the shock. You become nobody in that very moment. And, eventually, as the loss becomes you, you realize out of all this piercing pain, you are given a bulb of opportunity to rebuild all these demolished areas inside you any way you want, without any of the falsehoods and conditioning of before, if indeed you want to."

In such a scenario, your long-conditioned thought patterns and bucket beliefs are wiped clean, which allows your natural state—your Vertical Self—to organically fill the void. It's a painful way to achieve this transformation, but for many people it's the only way the Universe can find to provide them the gift of a fresh vibrational start.

By paying attention this week to which engine you're feeding, you're consciously reprogramming your default patterns of thinking. This is a far more smooth and pleasurable method of shifting your vibration.

HOMEPLAY FOR KEY 7, WEEK FOUR

One last pro tip regarding manifestation: The whole process becomes so much more streamlined and miraculous when you reach the point in the elevation of your consciousness that your manifestation desires are at least as much about others' happiness as they are about your own. It is not impossible to manifest desires that are purely for your own gratification, but it is also extremely unlikely that those manifestations will bring you the deep inner joy and peace you were hoping they would.

One of my most impressive manifestation successes (of the outwardly measurable ones, that is) is my book-sales total. Combined, my books have sold over nine million copies as a direct result of my manifestation abilities. I'm fully aware that it's my authentic desire to uplift and improve the lives of my readers that has allowed me to manifest this glorious number. I've long harbored the crazy notion that I'm here to elevate humanity by bringing more joy and love to the table, and that's the energetic position I've always taken when manifesting book sales. It works like a charm, but it must be authentic for the magic to kick in.

For your fourth week of homeplay, make a new list of your desires (because they may have changed since your last list), and rate each one on how its fruition would affect others. The Universe adores you, but it also adores everyone else. Any desire you have that conflicts with the wellbeing of others will have some energetic resistance attached to it. It doesn't mean you won't be able to manifest this thing; it just may not bring you the high-vibe feeling you're looking for. Throughout this final week of this month, consider ways you may be able to tweak your desires in the direction of them benefiting more than just yourself. It's a miraculous manifestation accelerator!

As you divest yourself of the heavy trauma energies you've been storing, you'll naturally become more self-loving *and* loving of others, which leads us beautifully into Key 8.

Be Love

> *"What you will see is love coming out of the trees, love coming out of the sky, love coming out of the light. You will perceive love from everything around you. This is the state of bliss."*
>
> —DON MIGUEL RUIZ, JR.

Joy and love are sister emotions. It's difficult to feel one without the other. I've been telling you that you are joy at your core, your truest essence, your Vertical Self, and now I'm asking you to consider that joy and love are basically fungible terms in our discussion of what comprises this eternal essence of you.

I do understand that it's not easy to tap into the full experience of joy every minute of every day here on this roller coaster of human existence we've all opted to ride. What you might find a bit more doable, and what we'll be exploring this month, is to build a stronger default setting for tapping into the *love* that you are at your core. Just as I've been claiming your Vertical Self is joy, it is also love. When joy feels out of reach, perhaps love will feel more accessible. And once you've aligned with the love you naturally are, through that alignment, you'll undoubtedly feel joy. See what I did there?

We've had fun in prior months with my friend Lee's terminology for reminding you that "your soul doesn't think you suck." To extend this cheeky wisdom a bit further, it's time to open your heart to the understanding that your soul doesn't think *anyone* sucks. It doesn't even think any *situation* sucks. Your soul (Vertical Self) knows that everyone is being precisely who they're here to be and whatever is happening is just what's meant to be happening in this moment.

We all have a continual mix of thoughts parade across our minds. Any thoughts and feelings rooted in love and joy—we don't need to mess with those. Those are already in perfect alignment with our truest selves. That's who we naturally are. The thoughts and feelings that drag our energy in the other direction are the ones we need to gently challenge. Not to go to war with them; resisting them only perpetuates them. Our goal is simply to recognize their false nature and funnel our attention in a better direction.

As we become more habitual with our enthusiastic questioning of everything we think and believe, we increase our chances of tapping into the blissful recognition of oneness that runs through most spiritual traditions. As the author Robert Greene puts it, "In the face of the Sublime, we feel a shiver . . . something too large for our minds to encompass. And for a moment, it shakes us out of our smugness and releases us from the death-like grip of habit and banality."

• • •

"Everything is connected. The greatest tragedy of human existence is the illusion of separateness."

—ALBERT EINSTEIN

Most of us only get tiny glimpses of it in the beginning. But if you celebrate them when you catch them, give thanks, and earnestly invite more; the glimpses will present themselves with ever greater frequency until they've expanded your perception filter in sustainably joy-enhancing ways. Once you get a taste, you want more, and that makes full commitment to a spiritual practice so much easier.

My energy-healer friend Avilone Bailey says, "You can choose your mood, choose the energy you emit, by monitoring and choosing your thoughts. Thoughts need maintenance. It's like dusting. You dust, and then you notice it's gotten dusty again. Where did the dust come from? Doesn't matter. You like it dust-free, so you dust again."

It reminds me of the time a student of motivational guru Zig Ziglar complained that all this positive thinking stuff was great, but it doesn't last. Zig replied, "Neither does showering. That's why I do it daily." Stick with your homeplay practices, my precious reader, and I promise you they will afford you benefits beyond your imagining.

The author Ian MacLaren famously wrote, "Let us be kind to one another, for most of us are fighting a hard battle." If it's true that most of us are fighting a hard battle, then I have to believe there's a reason for it. What if the all-knowing source set it up this way on purpose? Maybe the reason most of us are fighting a hard battle is so that we can better learn the part about being kind to one another. That's the love piece, and the piece each of us is here to ever more fully awaken within ourselves.

Heaven and Hell

You may have heard the story about the long spoons. It goes like this: A passed-over soul arrives at a banquet hall laden with fabulous soups and stews. Everywhere he looks, he sees people holding spoons that are longer than their arms. The people all look emaciated and miserable. When they try to eat the soups and stews, the length of the spoons makes it impossible for them to get anything into their mouths. He asks, "What is this place?" and he's told it's Hell.

Next, he's taken to another banquet hall, laden identically to the first. The people are all holding the same long spoons, but they look plump and happy; they're smiling and conversing with one another, having a grand party. He's confused, until he notices the difference. In this banquet hall, all the people are using their long spoons to feed one another. Clearly, this is the place called Heaven. This parable leads well into our discussion of a body of work by Emmanuel Swedenborg, an eighteenth-century philosopher theologian I recently learned about through my delightful friend Curtis Childs.

I met Curtis when he was a speaker at a conference that featured acclaimed scientific visionary scholars Gregg Braden and Bruce Lipton as headliners. I mention that to make the point that science and spirituality, for so long relegated to opposite corners of the ring, have begun playing together with greater and greater overlap and synchronicity! It's incredibly cool to watch the extent to which modern scientific research has begun validating ancient spiritual principles! Curtis explained the following concepts on my *Do Joy!* podcast, and you can learn more about his fascinating Swedenborg Foundation through the Joy Kit at my website.

Curtis teaches, in eloquent modern fashion, the principles set forth by the genius inventor and highly accomplished renaissance man Emmanuel Swedenborg, who, in his mid-fifties had a spiritual awakening wherein he started having lucid, complex, spiritual experiences. He recorded all that was shown to him, devising a system of living that he claimed would result in Heaven on Earth. According to Swedenborg, Heaven and Hell are both right here, and we all get to choose which one we experience.

Living in Heaven, he said, could be accomplished at any moment by subscribing to the following basic tenet: Heaven is wishing better for others than for ourselves with all our heart, and serving others for the sake of their own happiness, not for any selfish goal, but for love.

He explained that when you walk the planet looking at everyone you pass as an opportunity for you to experience Heaven, it changes the entire trajectory of your experience. You do that by continually concerning yourself with the happiness of others.

He says our more common tendency is to see other people as either obstacles, rivals, decorations, or frustration release. In describing our tendency to see people as obstacles to our own happiness, Curtis pointed out how we complain about being stuck in traffic without ever pausing to consider that we *are* traffic. For someone else, we're the car that's in the way of them getting where they want to be.

We see others not only as obstacles, but also as rivals, believing we can only be happy if we're getting more attention, more stuff, more accolades, more respect than others are getting. We also tend to view others as "decorations" to our own experience. Instead of recognizing a whole being in our presence, we consider them only in the context of how their existence in our life is affecting us. The final way Swedenborg claimed we tend to see our fellow humans is as a form of frustration release, someone to take out our own unhappiness on.

All of these tendencies, he says, create Hell on Earth. But we have the opportunity to change all of that by shifting into seeing each person we encounter as an opportunity for our own Heaven. We do it by intending for each person, *I want this person to be happier than I am (in a good way.)*

This helps us to remember that this person is having a conscious experience, just like we are, and that automatically adds complexity to the picture, making it less likely we'll see them as an obstacle, rival, decoration, or frustration release. Instead, we'll see them as fully conscious beings who have moods, things that make them happy, and— they have a trajectory beyond this moment in time when they happen to be showing up in our life.

Building the skill of immediately seeing each person this way gives us the opportunity to decide how we're going to interact with them, knowing that the interaction has the potential to shape *their* experience. We want to become super aware that every moment we interact with someone, the potential is there for us to have tremendous impact. They might think about or talk about our kindness for years to come for all we know.

Let me get back to that disclaimer, "in a good way." What that means is we don't just give people what they want if it's not what will lead to their highest good and ultimate happiness. It's not about being a doormat and dishonoring ourselves, because allowing another to mistreat us keeps them in "Hell," and therefore would not serve that person, so it wouldn't fall under the category of helping them be happier "in a good way."

Remember when we talked about David Kessler's term "capture" for the state we find ourselves in when we're triggered by our bucket beliefs without the tools to beneficially process our triggering? Curtis uses this terminology to explain the condition of what Swedenborg considers Hell on Earth.

It's up to those people wanting to create Heaven to spread that light to those still creating Hell by remaining in the state of capture. He says when Heaven-creators notice this Hell tendency in a person, they're careful not to associate it too closely with the person. They talk about it in abstract language instead. They'll say the person in "capture" is "inhabited by Hell." It's not who they are. To tie this concept into the work we've been doing, it's simply a person who is still overly identified with their Horizontal Self and unconsciously reactive to their circumstances.

Right now, bring to mind a person for whom it feels challenging for you to wish good things. This will be someone you judge, someone who does something you don't like, or has done something you don't like. What would you call the thing they did? We did a similar exercise when we were exploring shadow work a few months ago. Just like you did then, sort this undesirable behavior you've identified into a category. Was/is this person rude? Mean? Unfair? Hateful?

Now, consider the concept of "capture." Whatever this person does or did, they did this thing as a result of being triggered. They were compelled by their bucket beliefs, which have representation as neural pathways they've worn in their brain. With this in mind, you want to create a phrase that acknowledges the person is not their objectionable trait. It will sound like this: "_____ is not their _____." For instance, (Name) is not their rudeness. They are not their hatred. They are not their *fill in blank*. This is an extension of work we've done before, but I like this additional tool of creating a phrase to hold in our minds as an easy way to separate the behavior from the person.

HOMEPLAY FOR KEY 8, WEEK ONE

Your homeplay this first week will be to make a list in your Joy Journal of people who are challenging for you and create this phrase for each of them. It's important to practice this reframe skill when we're not face-to-face with these people, so that it becomes more automatic and natural when we're out there doing life and running into them. Whatever we don't like about someone, we want to get automatic about recognizing this trait we're disliking is not *who* they are. It's just an aspect of their Horizontal Self that they innocently picked up somewhere along the way. Once you've practiced creating these sentences in your journal, challenge yourself to remember this trick out in your life.

There's an important side benefit to this practice. Remember how our shadow work explorations revealed that the less we judge others the less judgmental we are of ourselves? The same dynamic applies here. As we become more habitual in recognizing that the negative traits of others do not define who they are, the better we get at realizing the same thing about our own sweet selves!

The idea is to always count the trait or behavior itself as a separate player in the equation, separate from the people involved. Curtis gave an example of a boss yelling at an employee. We think of that as a victim-and-perpetrator situation, but he suggests we count anger itself as a third participant. There's the anger itself, and there are two victims of the anger: the boss (who is in "capture" mode and therefore in Hell) and the employee. After the drama is over, the boss might realize her mistake, might feel terrible, embarrassed to have lost her cool. She might end up suffering more in the long run than the employee she yelled at. Or even if she doesn't feel bad, she's still prone to capture and that means she can't experience Heaven. Therefore, she's a victim of the anger, too.

Anger and negativity produce addictive chemicals in the brain. They've done MRIs that show where dopamine regions light up when anger is activated. And one thing known about the addictive brain is that it does not have normal memory function. The reward center of the brain is so powerful it actually blocks out relevant memory data. That means that when an alcoholic is tempted to drink, there's no memory of the havoc that resulted from the last drinking binge, and all the commitments to not do it again are basically, in that moment, erased from the memory center.

It's the same with anger chemicals. Raging at someone releases a flood of dopamine that is so addictive it makes you not remember your remorse from the prior time you raged at someone. This is why, by Swedenborg logic, we need to have compassion for those who harm us. And he said we're always self-sorting. Those who choose Heaven will attract a life around them where others are choosing the same, and the experience of Heaven will be created for these groups and communities. And those who are trapped in capture (who keep reinforcing their bucket beliefs) will be drawn together with others vibrating similarly, and together they'll create Hell on Earth.

It's just like how, if you click on a certain type of social media link or post, the site will provide you with more and more of that type of content. What you're choosing in one moment shapes the next online experience you'll have. It's a perfect corollary to how the Law of Attraction brings to us everything that vibrates where we're vibrating.

Even for those who create Hell on Earth, we're cautioned to remember that no matter how negative their behavior, there's no evil in them; they're just trapped by their "capture," and are going to live accordingly in Hell until they do the work to free themselves.

As an extension to this week's homeplay, try this exercise: Bring to mind your top challenging person again, and create the phrase that says, "_____ is not their _____." Now, in your imagination, subtract that attribute that made them challenging. Just delete it from the person. Then, vividly imagine this person for one full minute *without* the offending trait. Once you do that, you're seeing the truth of who they are.

We touched on this earlier, but another thing to remember to keep in mind is that this person has a future. Everybody here is on a journey with a timeline. Any one snapshot of a moment is not going to be representative of their full journey. We don't know where they've come from, and we don't know what leaps in consciousness they might be on the brink of making. When you hold that realization, you see that judging them based on this moment in time when they're displaying this particular trait is failing to take the full picture into account.

Swedenborg says each of us is destined for Heaven, and we all play different roles for one another along the way. All of our interactions with others are part of a divine plan. It's not about letting anyone walk all over you or abuse you, because that wouldn't be in their interest either. It's about seeing every person as an opportunity for *you* to be in Heaven simply by wanting to influence their happiness. You don't give them what they want in a way that reinforces their own capture that's been keeping them in Hell. When you truly want happiness for another, you understand that their happiness depends upon *them* wanting happiness for others too, so you don't perpetuate any cycles that would impede that!

To recap, this week's homeplay is to apply the teachings of Emmanuel Swedenborg to your life in these ways: Journal a list of people you find challenging, determine the trait you dislike, and apply the phrase: "_____ is not their _____," plugging in the name of the person and the trait for each person on your list. When you've practiced the technique with your journal, see if you can apply it in your life when you come across people who offend or annoy you. Journal about those experiences! And finally, to perfect the skill further, spend some time with the exercise of holding an offending person in your imagination after deleting the offending trait from the person. Such a beautiful practice for cultivating a felt sense of oneness!

HOMEPLAY FOR KEY 8, WEEK TWO

Once you've practiced draining some more of your judgments and resentments toward the people in your life, you can bring this fresh new energy into your communications with them. For your second week of homeplay this month, I'm going to share this communication wisdom my world-changing heart-sister Kayse Gehret teaches and let her describe your practice this week: "from the moment you wake up till the moment you fall asleep:

- Be impeccable with your word . . . Say what you mean. Mean what you say.

- Is it kind? Is it true? Is it necessary? When you speak, place all your words through the filter of kindness, truth, and necessity.

- Don't take anything personally. This is such a powerful practice! Continuously remind yourself that what other people say or do has nothing to do with you. Be open to feedback, criticism and uncomfortable truths shared, and practice not being defensive.

- Refrain from gossip.

- High vibe, positivity only. Use your speech exclusively to encourage, uplift, solve problems and promote positivity. Eliminate judgment, criticism, shaming and—especially— complaining. While complaining feels freeing and relieving in the moment, the temporary fix fades quickly and lowers the vibe of everyone around you. Complaining is contagious, and not in a good way!"

Kayse explains that when we bring a new level of consciousness to our communications with others,

> Relationships that are not healthy, or stuck in immature patterns, will fall away. As you grow, evolve, and find your voice, people in your life will either need to uplevel along with you or remain in their old, stuck reactions. Consequently, some of your relationships will grow stronger, while others fade away and—while sad—this is natural; it is not your responsibility to stay stuck and small just to enable or comfort others unwilling to grow or mature . . . The more we know ourselves, the more we can stand in our own authentic voice. Trust that the people and situations who resonate with your up-leveled frequency will gain in closeness, while those who require pretense or camouflage will vibrate out. All of life—your intuition, decisions and actions—will become more clear, uncomplicated and effortless as you find your voice and ability to communicate with kind clarity and loving truth.

Your second week of homeplay is outlined for you in the above communication instructions from Kayse. When you are operating in the world *as* the love that you are, this is what communication looks like. Speaking personally, the more I commit to communicating this way, the more my life rearranges itself accordingly. Yes, I've lost people from my life who couldn't meet me here, but I've gained many more who can! It's just as Curtis described; life becomes Heaven on Earth when we align with others similarly wanting to create that Heaven.

HOMEPLAY FOR KEY 8, WEEK THREE

Much of what I teach at Joy School is rooted in Buddhism, and Buddhists are all about cultivating what they call "the qualities of the heart," which are loving kindness, compassion, sympathetic joy, and equanimity. (These are natural qualities of your Vertical Self!) The most widely discussed is "Metta" or the quality of loving kindness, and I'm sure you can recognize its influence in many of your practices so far. For your final two weeks of homeplay this month, you'll be practicing the quality of the heart known as "Mudita," which translates to "shared joy," or "relational joy," or "sympathetic joy."

Mudita is described as an inner wellspring of joy that is always available, in all circumstances. The idea that underlies Mudita is that happiness can be found when we direct our attention to finding it, and we don't need to limit ourselves to experiencing our own happiness. We can feel into the happiness of others as a way to elevate our own joy. This is a kind of a shortcut, or hack, because often it's easier to spot other people's good fortune than it is to acknowledge our own.

According to the idea of Mudita, there's always positivity all around us; there's always love all around us. Most of us just block it to different degrees with our beliefs, filters, habituated thinking, and all those biases we've talked about. So, the way that this is a bit of a hack, is that to have positive feelings on behalf of another, or to send positivity to another, it has to flow through us on the way. We're being the conduit for it, so it has to come through us. It puts us in the flow. And it kind of tricks your energy system into thinking you've got surplus. It's similar to how, when you donate money, that triggers a feeling of abundance, which of course leads to more abundance. Same with positive energy. Giving it away sends your consciousness the message that you have a surplus within you; you have it to spare.

Vietnamese Buddhist monk Thich Nhat Hanh said that developing the skill of feeling joy for others' joy is a way to plant a garden inside you, and that garden becomes a resource for you—a refuge during challenging times.

Mudita meditation is done by calling someone to mind and then mentally sending them a phrase. In traditional language, some of the phrases sound like this: "May your happiness and good fortune continue. May they increase. May they never wane." To keep it simple, I'll invite you to choose between the following two phrases: "I'm so happy that you're happy." Or "I'm so grateful for your blessings." You can decide which of those feels most natural for you.

While Mudita is typically done with people, sometimes a pet is easier to start with because our relationships with our beloved animals are often simply less complicated and it's easier to feel pure joy on their behalf. We can all appreciate how watching a happy animal play can lift our own spirits; there are YouTube channels dedicated to such things! Grab the audio from your Joy Kit, or read through this description of Mudita meditation and give it a try.

You can close your eyes, or you can keep them open and just soften your gaze out in front of you if you prefer that. Get comfortable, grounded in your seat. A quick, easy way to get grounded is always to just bring your attention to your feet. You can do that any time you want to feel more settled in your body, in any kind of anxious situation or stressful moment. Just feel your feet, solid and heavy on the floor. Maybe imagine them melting into the floor a bit.

Register the contact your "sits" bones are making with whatever is holding you up. Feel the support. As your sits bones are rooting down, think of the center of your chest lifting slightly, so the collar bones can spread. Feel the back of your head anchor with your spine, your chin level with the ground, and then imagine the crown of your head lifting toward the ceiling. Whatever's underneath you, imagine it's a nest for your hips and pelvis. Sit tall with the crown of your head rising up.

Now find your breath and direct your attention to evening out the lengths of the inhales and exhales. This is a gentle breath technique Buddhists call "the breath of equal measure," to connect the mind and body with your awareness. You can listen to the sound of your breath, or observe the ambient noise in your room to center you in the present moment. After a few moments, let your breath return to normal.

Next, invite into your awareness someone for whom it is easy for you to feel joy. It's usually easiest to think of someone who you already perceive as joyful, or someone very dear to you. If you're a parent, you probably get happiness from seeing your child or children happy. (Don't forget that pets work too!)

Next, picture this joyful being in your mind's eye. Or simply bring their energy into your awareness if you prefer that to a visual conceptualization. Once you have them there, drop down to the center of your chest, into your heart space. With your lips closed, silently to yourself, repeat one of the following phrases, directing the energy toward this person (or being.) The phrase is either "I'm so happy that you're happy." Or "I'm so grateful for your blessings." Use whichever feels best to you.

Gently repeat the phrase for another minute or so while you keep this person in your awareness.

Then just let that person's image or energy dissolve.

The next person you'd bring in, according to the traditional sequence, would be a benefactor—someone who has supported you in some way, been there for you, or given to you. Spend a few minutes working with the benefactor using the same steps as above. Observe any sensations that come up.

When you feel ready, let this person's image or energy dissolve. Drop all doingness and just sit in your awareness, feeling and allowing. Then, when you're ready, if your eyes were closed you can open them and give yourself a nice stretch.

This week will be about incorporating a daily practice of Mudita meditation. Additionally, you might naturally think of your Mudita practice this week when you see someone demonstrating joy. Maybe you'll remember to mentally send them the message, "I'm so happy you're happy." Notice how it truly does elevate your own vibration to put your attention there!

HOMEPLAY FOR KEY 8, WEEK FOUR

After one full week of this introduction to Mudita, you'll crank it up for the following week. You've started with people you find relatively easy to wish well upon. In the full traditional sequence, you'd create a progression in terms of your immediate gut feelings toward the person you call to mind. You'd go from loved ones to someone neutral, to wishing well for strangers, and eventually you'd build up to someone who is truly challenging for you to be happy for. With mastery of the practice, you'd develop impartiality, so that sympathetic joy is extended on behalf of all beings, yourself included.

Work your way through this traditional sequence this week to the best of your ability, both in your meditation moments and out in the world. Set an intention when you wake up each morning to find people to wish well upon throughout your day. Standing in line at the grocery store next to the drooling kid in the cart with the cookie, you'd project "I'm so happy that you're happy with that cookie." Just silently, in your head. You'd pull up to a red light where you can't miss the big energy of the heavily inked and pierced teen blaring loud music in the car next to you, and you'd beam "I'm so happy you're happy and enjoying your music."

The people you encounter in your own household might be easy for you to be happy for. You might even want to say it out loud to those people. You are probably already doing this to some extent, so the idea is that whatever your baseline default is for enjoying the joy of others, you consciously, deliberately crank it up this week.

When you're deliberately looking for it, there's always someone to be happy for. If you can't find anyone, turn on the TV to a random, dumb sitcom and spend a moment thinking about how hard it is to break into TV for a new actor. Imagine the moment when that actor got the call saying they'd been cast in that show, and how over-the-moon excited they must have been. When you've got that feeling solid in your heart, send the phrase, "I'm so grateful for your blessings."

There are times when "I'm grateful for your blessings" is a better fit than "I'm happy you're happy." An example would be when a friend calls you on the phone with a problem, and you hear them out. They're not happy, so "I'm happy you're happy" doesn't really work in this case. You might wrap up the call by holding the highest vision for your friend and saying something like, "I know you've got this. You're resourceful, and resilient, and you have XYZ going for you." Then, when you hang up, you could focus on that highest vision you're holding for them (which is always the best thing you can do for anyone, energetically) and silently send the message, "I'm grateful for your blessings." You acknowledge what their blessings are, even if they're not seeing them, and you feel genuine gratitude for their blessings.

Like all the homeplay practices I've given you, I hope you find this so rewarding that you make it a part of your ongoing routine, either by doing the meditation regularly or simply bringing the intention of Mudita into your daily interactions. Or both! As always, a way to supercharge the vibration elevation is to incorporate this week's activity into your journaling practice. If you like journaling at night, you could look back on your day and record the times you did Mudita that day. Who was it toward? How did it feel? Was it harder in some cases than others and what factors might have been at play to make it harder or easier? Or if you prefer journaling in the morning, you could just look back at the prior day and record your observations.

• • •

"If you could look inside the heart of any and every human being, you would fall in love with them completely."

—MOOJI

Practicing Mudita is a powerful way to open to your felt sense of oneness. Oneness is one of those concepts we've all paid lip service to. We know what it means; we might fundamentally agree with the idea in an intellectual way. But this practice lets us *do* oneness. And it's the doing that creates vibration elevation, not the learning; not the intellectual agreement. It's the doing—again and again—that creates a lasting, delicious uplevel to your Joy Setpoint!

A scientifically controlled study conducted by German researchers at the University of Kassel found that while the chest area of an average person emits only twenty photons of light per second, someone who meditates on their heart center and sends love and light to others emits 100,000 photons per second—5,000 times more than the average human being! Many studies have also shown that when these photons are infused with a loving and healing intent, their frequency and vibration strengthens to the point where they can literally change matter and heal disease for themselves and other people. My long-time teacher Dr. Joe Dispenza has been conducting well-documented research on this kind of energy healing for decades.

In *The Book of Joy: Lasting Happiness in a Changing World,* His Holiness the Dalai Lama tells us it only takes ten minutes to change your vibration for the entire day: "Ten minutes of meditating on compassion, on kindness for others, and you will see its effects all day. That's the way to maintain a calm and joyous mind." This timeless wisdom is so simple and yet so little utilized in today's distracted, overscheduled, chronically anxious society.

This month has been all about *being* love, which is nothing more than being the truth of who you are. I hope you're feeling and experiencing that truth in ever-expanding ways.

Flow Intuitively

> *"Your heart knows the way. Run in that direction."*
> —RUMI

My darling heart-brother Scott Stabile, author and love guru extraordinaire, reminded me the other day that "each of us can be the sky, and not the weather." He means, of course, that our journey to greater consciousness and joy entails becoming less reactive to those external circumstances we bump into, recognizing ourselves as the vast, constant container of it all so that we don't get bogged down with the transient details.

Here's another beautiful thing Scott wrote: "Sometimes it's not the pain that changes, but your ability to be with the pain that shifts over time. You grow larger than what debilitates, until the mighty boulder crushing your heart becomes a single stone that rests upon your chest. The pain remains, real and even heavy at times, but no longer suffocating, no longer the only story. You have expanded too far, (a Universe all your own) to stay oppressed by its weight."

So many of my highly tapped in, authentic, and sensitive friends are dealing with various flavors of upheaval in these heavily charged times. Me, too. In the Preface, I mentioned the painful resurfacing of an old, deep, family-of-origin wound I would have sworn I'd already addressed to completion. This is how it is for those of us on a sincere and persistent journey of spiritual growth. It's the spiral, and it continues for as long as we're breathing! We heal from our early traumas to the extent we're able, plateau for a while, and then, when the Universe sees that we've grown into the required emotional bandwidth for the next level of evolving, it provides the just-right challenge to allow us to further digest those long-stored-away energies. To do so requires a personal commitment to use pain as an instrument for growth (along with the tools you've been practicing!)

Before that recent heartbreak, I'd gone over a decade without much drama to speak of, so the Universe that loves me decided I was ready for an uplevel. I learned so much as I healed that pain, and a tremendous part of the gift was a huge spike in the closeness and love I share with the many friends I've mentioned in these pages. I'm so deeply grateful for my loving, same-vibing, chosen family that so eagerly stepped in to help heal me upward along the spiral. Another aspect of my healing centered around deepening my connection to my own inner knowing because that's where the healing reframes reside. That's our imperturbable resilience to all that we bump up against.

This month's key is about the expansion Scott describes above. Look, I know it's tricky out there for the kind of sensitive souls who are likely reading this book. But maintaining a high vibrational frequency in your own personal "universe" doesn't have to mean sticking your head in the sand. You can do so much to contribute to the elevation of all humanity when you become skilled with your own nonreactivity and emotional flexibility.

Here's how my delightful heart-sister, transformational healer Kayse Gehret, expresses our predicament:

> Those of us alive today are witnessing human evolution in real time, with one foot in the past—a mechanistic, unnatural existence built upon toxic individualism, tribalism and separation—and one foot in the future—a cooperative, interdependent existence based on respect, reciprocity and natural balance. Today, we straddle two realities, almost as if different species walking the earth. This is our moment! We need all lightworkers and heart-centered citizens on deck for this critical moment as we step across the arc of history and welcome a new age. We are the regular people doing the extraordinary work of evolution. It is our personal work to first heal ourselves so we may give people the tools, inspiration, embodied example, awareness, and support to step forward. This is how we heal our world.

It's a big ask, darling reader; I know. You're being invited to help direct the trajectory of humanity. And as we've discussed, the way to do it is simply to keep up your diligent commitment to upleveling your own vibration. By now, you've no doubt begun reaping more benefits than you ever anticipated, so let's keep this engine moving forward by getting you even cozier with your own precious Vertical Self.

Decide.

Take one of the most unsettling things you feel exist in your life and decide.

Decide to meet it with love and understanding.

Decide to meet it with a proactive spirit that believes that a solution, an ease, a peaceful resolve rests in the meeting.

Prepare your heart for what it feels like to be joyous over the result. Give life to this solution with your breath.

Let any fear be a helpmate, let it actually support and lift you to an awareness that your next opportunity for growth is revisiting you through this present unsettling because you are now more than capable and authentically ready to meet it.

Learn and value the lesson and transcend its repetitive nature.

—DAVID AULT

That "solution, ease, peaceful resolve" that my wonderful friend David Ault is talking about here is the reward of tuning in to your soul's wisdom, like you've been practicing doing. As we've discussed, the communication from this voice is always found in the stillness, and there's always a gentle simplicity to its directives. My remarkable heart-sister and energy healer LaRue Eppler makes the additional distinction that your Vertical Self won't necessarily tell you why. The voice saying "do this because yada-yada-yada" is more often the voice of the overthinking Horizontal Self. It's common to not understand the reason for the suggestion the Vertical Self is making until you look back on it later in hindsight. I hope you're getting more comfortable distinguishing between these voices, but please don't worry if it's still unclear. We're not close to being done!

One benefit of your practices up until now is that they've reduced your reactivity to external stimuli. This month, we'll enhance that joy-skyrocketing skill by paying close attention to it and honing it from a new perspective. Now that your Vertical Self is more accessible in your daily experience, it's time to deepen that communication system we dabbled with a few months ago when we learned to sort the voice of the Vertical Self from the voice of the Horizontal Self.

As you've undoubtedly noticed by now, your Vertical Self is sublimely peaceful and accepting of whatever silly nonsense is unfolding in the Out There. All your anxiety, stress, busy-ness, and mental chaos springs from your Horizontal Self. You've probably recently found yourself in situations that triggered you in the past, but that have triggered you to a far lesser degree now that you've begun loosening your identification with the Horizontal Self and all its inflexible insistence on ridiculous joy-robbing beliefs and frameworks that imprisoned you for most of your life.

You know how we've been working to let go of our need to know and be right about all those stiff, unyielding thoughts we previously subscribed to? We've been freeing up some space for a new way to "know" or perceive things. This fresh new method for knowing things has been called intuition, psychic ability, trusting "hunches," or trusting your "gut." You've accessed it all your life, but likely nowhere near to the extent available, because it's always been so eclipsed by your loud, insistent Horizontal Self. Intuition is simply not a skill our society values or encourages, but it's the key to you flowing beautifully and effortlessly through all the lifey life-bumps that happen. This month you'll come to understand what a tragedy it is that you've never been taught or encouraged to develop this life-enhancing, natural gift.

Most of what I know about intuition, I learned from my personal brilliant guide to awakening my own abilities, (another dear heart-sister), Victoria Shaw. I'd taken many courses and trainings on the subject matter previously, but it wasn't until I started working privately with Victoria that I was able to push beyond my own doubts enough to see my abilities skyrocket. She is the most authentic, empowering teacher of intuition I've ever experienced, and you can find some additional materials from her in the Joy Kit at my website.

According to Victoria, the primary purpose of our intuition is to keep us aligned and on track with what we're here to do. All the other ways we use our intuition are just bonuses. She says that developing your intuition is more a process of re-discovery than one of learning, since every one of us is naturally equipped with intuitive gifts! The more you trust, the more comes through; it mostly comes down to a decision to invite and welcome your intuition to the table. We're all being guided, whether we're acknowledging that guidance or not, and we can all choose to get in alignment with those nudges and start cooperating with their suggestions. According to Victoria, "the single best tool for awakening your intuition is to use your intuition."

You want to start by recognizing how and when you're already doing it. You've probably noticed your intuition has increased in recent months, simply from your attention to your Vertical Self. The Vertical Self is where all your intuitive wisdom resides, and you've no doubt been hearing it with more frequency as you've brought this part of you more to the forefront of your existence. But instead of saying "hearing" it, I should point out that you might be more inclined to "see" it, or "feel it," or simply "know it." Each of us experiences our intuition differently, or as Victoria likes to say, "We're all snowflakes in the best possible way."

Maybe you have a sense about where your intuition has already been enhancing your life. It probably happens in those moments when your brain is taking a mini break from the myriad things that occupy it throughout the day. Many of my Joy Schoolers report moments of insight while driving, showering, or walking in nature. If you know what I mean by "moments of insight," ask yourself now, *Where do these moments most often occur for me, and how do I experience these "aha" flashes? Do I see an image in my mind's eye? Do I hear a word or phrase? Do I feel a sensation somewhere in my body? Do I just somehow know?* All of these methods for receiving intuitive information can be developed, but it's helpful to determine which one(s) already come most naturally to you.

Any skills or hobbies you consider yourself naturally good at, it's likely that's an area where your intuition is coming through. Intuition has often been linked to creativity. If you've ever been lost in the flow of a creative project, you can feel into the memory of that flow-state now as a way to recognize what intuition feels like. Victoria says it comes to you when your mind is soft and slowed down a bit. It's gently feeling into the space between the thoughts, the way music relies on the space between the notes. Take a moment with your Joy Journal now. Ask your Vertical Self, *Where is my intuition already strongest in my life?* See what flows from that inquiry.

Like any other muscle you're wanting to build, your intuitive muscle grows stronger with use. You'll be setting the intention this month to use your intuition more than you've ever previously done. That includes paying attention to random signs from the Universe as well as specifically asking for those signs and acknowledging their appearance when they show up. It also includes more consistent, less formal dialoguing with your Vertical Self. Up until now, I've had you practicing this dialog by posing questions to your Vertical Self and answering them through your journaling. This month, you'll take that skill into your daily life by pausing and inviting those internal dialogues whenever your day presents a question or choice to make.

Early in your journey, I had you place your hand(s) over your heart and ask, *Is this thought/feeling/impression coming from my highest wisdom?* That's a beautifully simple and reliable tool that you can use any time for clarity. You'll get a sense of an answer right away. It's common to not trust or believe that we have this ability when we first start utilizing this tool. The way to expand your trust and belief is simply to use it more frequently, trust the answer you get, and then watch for verification that the answer was correct. Time and time again, my Joy Schoolers have been blown away by how simple and reliable this technique is once you've practiced it for a while.

When you have a more open-ended question to pose to your wise Vertical Self, you may be able to intuit an answer right away, or get an answer through doing automatic writing in your journal. ("Automatic writing" is what you've been doing every time you've listened to your inner wisdom and captured its messaging without overthinking, self-editing, or judging what comes through.) Sometimes there's a delay. The important thing to know is that your question will always be answered. As I've mentioned, the answer could surface as a sign that shows up in the regular activities of your day. Your subconscious might zero in on an animal, or an image in a storefront you pass by, or a word on a license plate, or a phrase uttered by a radio DJ or sung in a song you hear playing. (Repetition is confirmation!) The fact that your subconscious selected that bit of information to allow through the thick, tangly web of your perception filter means something! The more you can ease into that belief and understanding, the more magical your life will become.

I'm not sure why, but I can attest that becoming more confident in your intuitive abilities leads to a tremendous boost in your personal confidence overall. It's like those movies where the kid suddenly becomes aware of a superpower they've always possessed but never acknowledged before. It's tremendously exhilarating to awaken this superpower within yourself! It not only helps you to know what's best for you, but it helps you to know how to best love and support all of those you encounter. One of the most important things Victoria taught me is that when you live in accordance with your soul's wisdom, you do what's in your highest good, and when you do things for your highest good, it's also for everyone else's highest good. Being a lifelong people-pleasing addict, this was a tough one for me, but again and again, by trusting my intuition, I saw that if an action I'm taking is not honoring to me, it won't serve the highest good of anyone I'm trying to please.

According to Victoria, "Over-givers think because they have more love, compassion, and kindness, they need to make up for where others are lacking that capacity. They think because it comes more naturally to them, it's their duty to compensate for where it doesn't come naturally to others. But doing that ultimately does those others a disservice because it blocks their path to raising their own consciousness."

One of Victoria's favorite ways to keep her intuitive dialog flowing is by scheduling regular "walk-and-talk" sessions with herself. She loves being in nature and she's found the most reliable way to open the flow of her own intuitive communication system is to take walks in her best-loved nature settings while using the record feature on her phone to pose questions and capture the guidance that comes through. She's comfortable with the term "guides" so she conducts these conversations with what she perceives to be spiritual guides that are always working with her.

If you're uncomfortable with the idea of guides, you can substitute any word that feels most right to you. I have intuitive friends who talk to angels, animal spirits, and specific deities and crossed-over figures from history. Victoria and I agree that none of those labels are important. Since our imagination is the communication vehicle, it stands to reason that our human minds will enjoy coming up with whatever concept lets us feel most comfortable with these communications. For our purposes here, I'll continue referencing these dialogs as conversations with your Vertical Self. Just know that you're free to conceptualize this dynamic in whatever way feels best to you. The only rule of thumb is to make sure the messages you receive are high-vibration and feel nourishing and wholesome to you. If you feel you're hearing "messages" that aren't of this quality, it's more likely you're confusing your intuition with some old, untrue programs running in your Horizontal Self.

Your overarching homeplay assignment, which you'll do through-out the entire month, is to let your intuition show you how to build your intuition! Using the suggestions above, try out different approaches to enhancing the intuition that's always been available to you, waiting for you to acknowledge, appreciate, and grow it. As my longtime friend, the renowned shaman and author Dr. Steven Farmer, PhD, says, "The more you listen, the more you will hear."

HOMEPLAY FOR KEY 9, WEEK ONE

Your first week of more specific homeplay will combine some of the work we've been doing with this new focus on receiving intuitive guidance. First, carve out a bit of time when you won't be disturbed. You're going to be doing some automatic writing, as we've done before, but I invite you to use your intuition to feel into any routine you might want to put into place to enhance this connection. Some of my Joy Schoolers like to light a candle or burn incense, play some soft music, chant, or meditate before they begin. You might want to experiment to see if any of these mood-setters enhance the dialogs you have with your Vertical Self.

In your Joy Journal, you're going to create a numbered list. Let it be quick, off the top of your head. You'll write 1, 2, 3, etc., as you rattle off the items on this list. The numbering is not meant to be hierarchical; there's no greater importance to the first things on the list than the latter things. The automatic writing prompt for making this list is "I love _____."

So, start by writing 1 followed by something you love, whatever first comes to mind. It could be a significant person, thing, or circumstance; or it could be some trivial aspect of your life. The biggies and the smallies—you're just going to capture them all here in list form. People, things, abstract ideas, hobbies, pets. Record whatever pops into your mind while making this off-the-cuff list. The only rule is to continue numbering these things as you add each one. Go as long as you'd like. You'll know when you feel complete with it.

Ready? Go!

No matter how long or short your list, it's perfect. It's a treasured collection of things in your life that are already bringing you joy. What a beautiful list to have!

Your practice this week will be to build up your appreciation reflex even more than you already have, while also inviting your intuition to participate. Each day, you'll take a cue from your ever-burgeoning relationship with your Vertical Self to select one item on this list to pour extra love and attention onto.

Here's how you'll achieve this particular communication with your Vertical Self: First, determine the best makeshift random-number generator that works with all the numbers on your list. For instance, if you have pairs of dice in your home—enough to match the highest number on your list, you could use a dice collection as your random-number generator. Or, you could write each number on a small slip of paper and keep them in a bowl to draw from. There are free random-number generators online, but when I investigated them for my Joy Schoolers, I found them a bit dodgy (one tried to give my laptop a virus when I opened it), so I'm going to recommend you steer clear of those.

My personal favorite method is old-school and easy. Grab any book off your shelf and open it to a random page near the beginning of the book. (If you open to a page where the page number is higher than the last number on your list, just open it again closer to the start of the book.) You now have a divination tool as a communication device for working with your intuition. Shamans and spiritual leaders throughout recorded history have used tea leaves, runes, pendulums, coins, crystal balls, dowsing rods, and countless other objects for divination. The most common divination tool used today is card decks. All of those are fun to play with, but since for our purposes here we only need a system for selecting a number, I'll use the example of opening a book to a random page to explain the rest of this homeplay.

Every morning this week you'll open the book randomly and see which page number you've opened to. (Decide in advance if you'll look at the page on the left or right.) Next, find the item on your list that corresponds to that number. That's how your intuition is going to provide the "sign" that tells you what to pour extra love and attention onto that day!

When you see which item your intuition has selected, spend a few moments really feeling your love for this thing you listed. Then, dedicate your day to expressing your love for this thing, person, or idea in some manner that exceeds your ordinary expression of love for it. For example, if it's a tree in your backyard, you might go sit under it at some point in the day, bathing it in your appreciation. You might photograph it, hug it, write a poem about it, or spend a few moments gazing out your window in mindfulness watching how the wind tosses its leaves around, offering it your love.

If it's a person, send them an extra text or email, and spend time holding them in your thoughts and bathing them in love energy. Brag about them to someone else. Think about your favorite recent moment with them, and your favorite long-ago moment with them. What's your favorite thing about this person? Tell them. If they're in your physical space, give them an extra-long hug. Tell them verbally or show them you love them in some way that's beyond what you'd normally say or do. If they're deceased, talk to them in your heart and imagination, and listen to what they have to say back. Trust that real communication is happening, because in truth, from an energetic standpoint, it is.

Do this every day for the first week of this month, and journal about your experiences with it! The point of this week's practice is to invite your intuition's participation while you train yourself even more to amplify your appreciation for what's good in your life. Whatever you love, you want to build the habit of loving it *hard!* It's such a simple, timeless way to elevate your vibration. And the Universe, via your divination tool, will always select for you the precisely best way for you to expand this love capacity!

Love is all around us all the time—I know that sounds like a sappy song lyric, but it's just a time-honored spiritual truth. The consciousness that binds every bit of us and everything here together *is* love. Nearly every spiritual tradition from every corner of the world has said so. We cut ourselves off from it because we're habituated to pay more attention to the things that *threaten* our happiness than we pay to the things that *contribute* to our happiness. Becoming skillful observers of this tendency is what allows us to flip it and begin creating new habits to skyrocket our joy! As we know, whatever we pay attention to, grows.

The cool thing about love is that even though it's all around us for the experiencing at any given moment, in order to love something, we have to pull love *through* us. It's not like we just grab some love from outside of us and throw it at the object of our affection. To love something means to pull love through our own being and direct it toward this thing or person or idea. And pulling love through our own energy field raises our vibration better than just about anything we could do!

We increase the presence of love in our lives through this practice of intentional loving. That means, whatever loving we do right now, as our default, we need to deliberately, through a structured practice, go to the next level up in our experiencing and expressing of love. The structured practice I've given you not only trains you to a more love-centric default setting, but it supercharges the process by inviting your intuition to show you what will be most beneficial for you to shower love upon on that particular day.

Another benefit is that if you're intentionally directing your focus throughout the day to loving this one thing, it's just that much more time that you won't be focused on those other distractions that pull at your attention—those low-vibration thoughts and circumstances that we've all got going on. It's making use of that replacement-habit tool we've talked about!

Some days, it might be funny. Maybe you love pepperoni calzones, and that made your list, and that's the number that the Universe shows you when you open the book that morning. If it's silly and makes you roll your eyes to have to show your love for pepperoni calzones all day, all the better. Embrace the silly! If that happens, on the most obvious level, you could plan your day around, at some point, enjoying a pepperoni calzone. And if your chock-full calendar just absolutely prohibits it, then at the very least, you could make a plan that day by scheduling lunch with a friend, or some other path to get that next pepperoni calzone. And maybe that day, you'd extend your love-intention to just loving and appreciating your sense of taste. Maybe you'd stretch it to really savoring the taste of your coffee that morning. Or whatever you choose to put in your mouth that day, you'd take extra care to make it something you really enjoy, and you'd focus your love on every bite. There are always ways to get more creative with it. Tap into your ever-expanding intuition to show you how!

Here's one more piece to think about with this homeplay. You want to acknowledge that whatever your intuition chose for you that day, there was a reason for it. Often the reason will be startlingly apparent; other times you might need to give it a bit of time to emerge.

If you don't get any clear ideas about the reason, you could always wrap up the day's homeplay by journaling with this question: *Vertical Self, why did you choose that item for me to shower with love today?* The answers that come forth from your automatic-writing response can be so insightful!

HOMEPLAY FOR KEY 9, WEEK TWO

After spending a week with that homeplay, you'll switch it up for the second week, but only slightly. You'll set the stage for some journaling and dialoging with your Vertical Self, just like you did the previous week. But this time, off the top of your head, you'll make a numbered list of things you love *about you.*

Again, you'll capture the biggies and the trivial, in no particular order. The number of each item on the list doesn't connote any kind of weight or priority of some things over other things. Your free-flowing list might include an assortment of characteristics and traits you love about yourself that bounces back and forth between meaningful and totally playful ones. You might love your integrity, and then love your cute butt. You might love that you're a great parent or great employee, and then the fact that you're a consistent flosser. Nothing is too big or too small for this list. Maybe you love your regard for nature, and that you escort spiders outdoors instead of squishing them. Maybe you love your commitment to your joy—hey, you've already been knocking that one out of the park, so make sure that goes on your list! Just let your Vertical Self show you all the things you love about *you.*

Then, just as you did the previous week, use your dice or your book, or whatever you choose for allowing your intuition to select one numbered item from the list—one thing each day—for you to focus on that day. Once you've been shown what your intuition chose for you, sit quietly and direct your attention to this thing you appreciate about yourself. Think about all the ways you exhibit this trait and all the people who benefit from you *being* this thing. Then think about the upcoming day and feel into all the ways you'll highlight this part of you on this day. Think about how you could crank it up even bigger.

If you love your honesty and that's the trait your intuition chose for you to focus on, think about some place in your life where you could bring just a notch more honesty to the table, and commit to doing that. If it's your sense of humor, find an extra way to amuse yourself or those around you. If it chose your appreciation for your eyes, take a few moments throughout the day, whenever you come across a mirror, to stop and find your precious, divine soul in those beautiful eyes. We all have the capacity to do that and most of us don't take the time for it.

If it chose your ability to be a good friend, think of one extra thing you could do to honor a friendship. You might be shown an idea for bringing a new piece of connection to an existing friendship, or a way to revive an old one. If it chose your love of your organizational skills, create a new flow chart for something you want to accomplish. The point is to make the whole week a celebration of these things you love about you and to work with your intuition as part of the project. Don't forget to stay on the lookout for the reason your intuition chose each item for you each day. The resulting events that unfold from these little actions you take will amaze you!

If you find it difficult even to make the initial list for this week, don't beat yourself up about that. It's sadly common to have trouble loving ourselves. If you're struggling to make the list, try priming the pump by doing some automatic writing with these prompts:

"If I really loved myself, I would . . ."

"One way I could love myself more would be to recognize . . ."

I hope you throw yourself into this week's homeplay and have fun with it. Nothing will elevate your vibration more quickly and easily than practicing loving yourself in ever bigger and better ways! You'll soon start noticing there's a ripple effect of seeming "coincidences" and serendipitous events that flows from these practices of intentional loving. Record all these "miracles" in your journal! The more you acknowledge them and celebrate them, the more you'll get!

HOMEPLAY FOR KEY 9, WEEK THREE

Your third week of homeplay is going to follow the same pattern as the previous two weeks, but we're going to up the game a bit. Remember when we talked about thankfulness, and I mentioned that we sometimes feel burdened by pressure to feel gratitude for things that we know we're more inclined to take for granted?

It's human and it's okay. That tendency comes from the antiquated program in our brains that still operates from a position of scarcity. Back when propagation of the species needed to be a biological imperative, our ancestors were programmed to hoard resources to ensure passing along their genes. That's where we get our leftover default setting to ignore what we already have and instead focus on getting more of it. We don't need this setting anymore; it's part of the erroneous programming of the Horizontal Self. Understanding where it's coming from helps us to unsubscribe to thoughts based in scarcity so that we can, instead, expand the keyhole of our perception filter to let in the awe and appreciation for the myriad conveniences, blessings, and abundances that surround us!

This week, you'll once again set the stage for that dialog with your Vertical Self. You'll make a new numbered list in your journal similar to those you've made the prior two weeks, but this week it will be a list of things you're grateful for. And you'll push yourself to include not just the top-of-mind things you love (you've already made that list!) but the things you might forget to be consciously grateful for, like water, electricity, the view from your kitchen window, the fact that you're healthy in whatever ways you are, the fact that your loved ones are healthy, the car that gets you around from place to place, even if it's not the car of your dreams. You get the point. (Think of Joe Vitale's pencil!) This list could get ridiculously long, so let your intuition tell you when to cut it off. You might be surprised by what bubbles up for you.

From there, you know the drill. You'll use your chosen random number generator system to invite your intuition to select one of these things you've listed each day this week, and then you'll spend the day showering gratitude and love on this item. You'll feel the stretch with this one, but the prior two weeks have built your gratitude muscle to a new level, and you'll see that reflected in how easy it is for you to recognize and tap into the awe of so many wonderful things in your life that you'd been taking for granted. Pay close attention this week to that final step of tuning into why your intuition chose each of these things for you. There's amazing self-knowledge to be unearthed there. And watch for the related miracles to surface!

This is powerful keyhole expansion, superstar! Congratulate and celebrate yourself!

I'll let my heart-brother Jacob Nordby inspire you even further with his gorgeous interpretation of gratitude:

Gratitude isn't an obligation, like the universe is some neurotic parent and requires us to say 'thank you' just right or you won't get another cookie for the rest of your life. It's the warmth given off by the flame of life. It's a feeling that grows by being noticed. If I pay attention to the millions of tiny miracles that are always there, I mysteriously enter a space in which more of them are possible. In this way gratitude is magic. In this way I enjoy what's good. In this way I clear the junk of fear, anxiety, and meanness so that life's generous nature has more room to show itself. Gratitude is the opposite of denying any of the awful facts. It is a different honesty by which we notice and relish what is already working so that more of it can come in. Like the eyes that are reading these words. Like the small glow of sunlight on your skin right now that tells the story of a good earth and how life goes on and on and on; how you are part of that.

HOMEPLAY FOR KEY 9, WEEK FOUR

For your final week of homeplay this month, you'll try out some more intuition-enhancing practices. Here's one I love: Every time I shower, I imagine light pouring down along with the water, cleansing my energy body of any frequencies that aren't for my highest good and evolving. I imagine any of these lower-vibe frequencies flushing out through the soles of my feet and swirling down the drain to be transmuted by Mother Earth. It always leaves me feeling lighter and clearer—an open channel for intuition to speak with me! Once you've practiced it in a real shower, you can do this visualization any time you sense you're carrying some funky vibe you'd rather release. Call on the imagery of your light-shower in your office, car, or home. Just let the light pour through you and gently nudge any unhelpful frequencies out through your feet to be transmuted by Mother Earth.

Another technique I love comes from Joy Schooler Sonya, a gifted intuitive. She listens to a video of a high-consciousness teacher she admires and then immediately gets still and quiet to allow this teacher's energy to continue communicating with her, often personalizing the material to her own situation. If you'd like to give it a try, check out your Joy Kit for some vid suggestions!

Experiment this week. Maybe the idea of Victoria's walk-and-talk method appeals to you. Maybe you're becoming a pro at dialoging with your Vertical Self in your journal. You can pose any question at all and get answers this way.

Trusting your naturally intuitive nature to guide you, rather than the internal voice of your Horizontal Self, is one of the best ways to avoid reactivity and instead flow flexibly with life. I hope you've broken through to a stunning new level of connection with your Vertical Self this month. We'll be continuing to deepen all these practices, so wherever you consider yourself to be with them right now, please give you a hug. You're doing amazing things!

• • •

"For us to truly understand the power of beginnings is for us to wake up every day in a new world. We must embrace beginner's mind, question all our questions, give away all our answers, stand naked in the sunrise, and truly believe in starting over. To begin is to believe down deep in your indestructible soil that transformative change is possible. Right now.

"More than this, to begin is to live in the most immediate right now you can imagine. That all your yesterdays only matter in that they were the vehicle to bring you to this right now, fully enveloping, beautifully poignant, present moment of beginning."

—THOMAS LLOYD QUALLS

Master Your Observing

> *"Nothing imprisons you except your thoughts. Nothing limits you except your fears. Nothing controls you except your beliefs."*
>
> —MARIANNE WILLIAMSON

You've made tremendous strides in your joy journey, beautiful reader, and are undoubtedly aligned more than ever with your eternal, divine Vertical Self and all the magic it offers you. Are you kerklunking on how powerful and beneficial it is to build the skill of being the observer? You have begun experiencing yourself as the entity that observes your thoughts and feelings and all the performances your Horizontal Self is busy playing out. Even if you've only had glimpses of it thus far, please know those glimpses will increase and expand from here on out. You are giving yourself an incredible gift that will benefit every area of your life and every other being it touches!

We've worked with some manifestation techniques to demonstrate that just by turning your attention, your awareness, in particular directions, you are able to powerfully affect the Out There. I want to now remind you that even though you can, absolutely, use your attention to create the things you want, the larger truth is that getting the things you want Out There is not what will make you sustainably happy. The only thing that makes anyone sustainably happy is coming more deeply into the understanding of the true nature of the Vertical Self. Eckhart Tolle says, "The ultimate source of satisfaction in life is to recognize yourself as consciousness. If you miss that, then no matter what you achieve in life, it is not going to make you happy for very long. By going within, we can discover the place where life is born continuously—the source of creation: consciousness itself."

I know you'll want to continue building your skills at manifestation of your Horizontal-Self desires (no one could blame you for that!) and I also want you to hold in your heart the truth that it doesn't really matter what we manifest Out There. The only manifestations that can contribute to lasting happiness are the ones that are in complete alignment with the Vertical Self, whereas most of our human-y desires tend to come from the Horizontal Self. It's okay. We're here to live a human life and there's nothing wrong with wanting to deck that earthly existence out with some cool situations. It's just that we want to do that from the understanding that all these things we're trying to manifest really are not nearly as consequential or important as they seem.

When I teach the work of thought leader Rupert Spira at Joy School, I always start with one of my favorite metaphors of his. Imagine your TV is off, and you're sitting there on your couch looking at the screen. Your friend comes in and asks, "What's going on?"

You answer, "I'm sitting here looking at this screen."

The next day, you're sitting in the same spot with the TV on this time. Your friend comes in and asks, "What's going on?"

You're all flushed and excited and you say, "Marjory's sister killed her husband, but she doesn't know yet and there's a clown with a knife under her bed!"

Friend says, "Looks to me like you're sitting there looking at a screen like yesterday." The only difference is this time you've gotten sucked into what's being projected on the screen.

The metaphor illuminates Rupert Spira's assertion that enlightenment is about becoming aware of the screen, realizing that, in essence, we're always just watching a movie. Nothing we're seeing is as solid and weighty as we think it is when we're sucked into the story (sucked into the egoic mind of the Horizontal Self.) By pulling back and recognizing the screen, we become detached enough to see that we don't have to suffer. We don't have to attach to storylines that cause us suffering.

Spira also wants us to understand that the whole movie we're watching came from within us, from the state of our consciousness. That's never meant to cause anyone to blame themselves or feel like their misfortunes are their fault. Taking control of the state of one's consciousness is still a very little-understood thing. Eckhart recently estimated only 10 percent of people worldwide have begun to awaken to this truth. So, it's not like this is to condemn anyone for unwittingly creating suffering for themselves or others. There's no fault or blame there. This is what we do. But we don't have to. And understanding that is the cusp of enlightenment.

I've always thought one of the most enlightened phrases to have caught on in pop culture is "shit happens." It's meant to be cheeky, but there's a definite spark of highly spiritual understanding underlying that phrase and I think that's why it went viral. There's something comforting in the recognition that universally, for all humans, shit happens. And that's okay. The casualness of the phrase hints at the profound truth that "what we resist persists; what we fight, we ignite."

Being able to feel, on a deep level, the realization that what we're experiencing is just a movie on a screen—being able to see the screen, is what lets us feel safe. Have you ever been with a child who's enjoying a Disney movie, right up until the moment the music changes and the landscape darkens, and the villain's creepy voice starts filling the soundtrack? That's usually when the kid understandably gets fidgety and anxious. You tell him, "It's just a movie, baby. It's not real. It's just a movie." You can do that for yourself when you train yourself to see the screen.

When I teach this next part, I make clear that it's not Rupert or Eckhart, but only Lisa McCourt attempting to manage life and joy here. I confide that there's a part of me that doesn't always love the idea of the screen. I adore immersing myself in the yummy stuff of life, the people-y, earthy stuff that makes my heart explode in joy and wonder. And in those situations, I don't like recognizing the detachment of the screen. So I just decide when I'm going to intentionally lose myself in the movie and when I'm going to pull back and make sure my focus is more on the screen than the movie itself. Because for me, at least, the full, juicy enjoyment of life does mean forgetting the screen to an extent and being full-on immersed when the situation is right for that.

Then, when something feels upsetting, triggering to me in some way, I remind myself immediately that I'm getting caught up in the movie. I know my true nature is love and peace so anything that's not of that vibration is clearly not aligned with my truest self. I pull back my attention so it's more on the screen itself than whatever drama's unfolding there, and I start to look at it with full awareness that I'm the observer on the couch looking at a metaphorical TV.

I turn down the volume, because that helps with the detachment. I have this imaginary button that's not on real TVs but it's on this one, where I can blur out the images a bit. I can still watch, but it's not as crisp and engaging. And I direct my attention to the question "What did my soul want to show me when it made and directed this movie?" and "What am I meant to learn from this so I can grow?" This is a fancy TV, so I can even pause and rewind and re-examine the movie from different angles, which is another way to detach from the emotional entanglement of it. Doing this makes the feeling of the show on the screen go from being a high-intensity drama, to being more of a documentary.

And when I do this, the most notable thing that arises from this practice is I get super clear that I'm the observing presence. The unhappiness is the bundle of thoughts and feelings playing out on the screen. The unhappiness isn't me; it's not who I am. I know that because I know that thoughts and feelings come and go, on a day-to-day, hour-to-hour basis, so they can't be the real me. I'm the one who notices thoughts and feelings moving in and out of my awareness. I'm the eternal, observing presence who observes the thoughts and feelings.

Sure, there was something in me that created the movie, but always for my benefit somehow. It's just up to me to look for clues as to what the benefit might be. And sometimes that includes realizing I haven't gotten to the end of the movie yet. And from there, all I need to do is find that trust that by the end of the movie it will all make sense. Movies almost always have a satisfying ending, and if it doesn't feel satisfying yet, it just means it's not the ending.

I stay aware of the spiritual truth that all our dissatisfaction with any aspect of our lives is simply an indication of dissatisfaction with ourselves in some way. I give thanks for any Out There reminders of this truth because it's always a helpful finger pointing me in the direction of the inner work I need to focus on next. In this way, I stay welcoming of whatever arises in my experience. (At least to the best of my ability at this point in my spiraling!) Mastering our observing always entails learning to observe less judgmentally.

Our Source Is One of Love, Not Condemnation

There's a story about the guru Krishnamurti, whose followers hung on his every word for thirty years, writing everything down, living their lives in accordance with his wisdom. One day he told them he was going to sum up his entire teaching for them in a single sentence, and he said, "I don't mind what happens."

Mic drop. I think what gets in our way of accepting this ancient wisdom is, again, this idea that it means surrendering to things that are unacceptable to us, not working to make the world better, or our lives better. The deeper significance, which I'm sure you're kerklunked on now, is to *first* not mind whatever's happening—meaning basically, don't be reactive to what's happening. Instead, our work is to be *with* the present moment, whatever it's bringing, long enough to invite our Vertical Self to take the lead so that we can come from the most effective, clear place in our efforts to move things in a positive direction.

Abraham/Hicks reminds us, "Our Source is one of love, not condemnation . . . The majority of negative emotions that you feel are not because the subject of your thought is wrong, but instead, because you are condemning something that your *Source* does not condemn."

It's a tough nut for most of us in many scenarios. We see things that we want to condemn, and it's hard to comprehend that our Source does not condemn them. This is the essence of teachings on nondualism, a concept of unconditional acceptance found in many Eastern traditions. To me, what makes the understanding bearable is reminding ourselves that we are not powerless to effect change. As Wayne Dyer has famously expressed, "When you change the way you look at things, the things you look at change." Our job, therefore, is simply to continue faithfully holding the vision of the improved situation we desire and feeding it our powerful attention, while taking any action steps that arise from this position of higher understanding.

It means never forgetting that peace and love and joy are always there, right there in the 400 billion bits of information that are available to us at any given moment. If we leave it to our unexamined, long-ago-created filter to pick the 50 bits we become aware of, we're just leaving cards on the table. Life mastery, taking charge of our joy, means learning to do our selecting from a higher level of consciousness through our deliberately expanded keyhole.

I'll remind you now that when I talk about expanding the keyhole, I'm not implying we'll ever totally annihilate the unconscious beliefs that gave form and substance to our original conception of reality here, our foundational bucket beliefs. What we're changing is the attention and weight we give to them. We're becoming aware of how utterly meaningless they are. They'll always be there. They'll always be setting off our radar and trying to accomplish their original job. The difference is we now know how to turn down the volume, thank them for their service, and lovingly dismiss them.

We now understand that the biggest mistake we've habitually made throughout our lives is believing our thoughts and feelings and acting as though they show us an accurate representation of reality.

We understand now the magic inherent in the present moment, and we're glimpsing the deeper kerklunk that we're never truly in the present moment as long as we're exclusively interpreting the world through a filter that was created in our past. We've begun to peek around that filter to see what the present moment could truly potentially hold for us.

We've seen that we create based on our beliefs, and that our beliefs very often are simply inaccurate. We cling to our convictions because they make us feel safe, but we understand now why all those things we crave certainty around may well be false. For most humans, this idea still sets off anxiety because of that primitive brain we've talked about. We think we need to neatly categorize the world because that's how we protect ourselves from danger, and if the things we think we know start moving around and becoming unknowable, that sets off an alarm for most of us.

You, however, have been doing powerful work to disable that alarm. You know it's not keeping you safe the way we've all been led to think. Much more often than not, it's *bringing about* more of those circumstances we'd rather avoid because when an alarm goes off, what's that meant to do? What are alarms for? They're meant to get our *attention*. And we know that our attention is what we create with, whether we're doing that creating consciously or not.

So, congratulate yourself for getting more comfortable with the idea that we really don't know all these things we think we know! In a Universe as vast and incomprehensible as ours, where there is an angle from which practically anything is true, we can, in most cases, decide which truths we want to subscribe to and which truths we want to cancel our subscriptions to. That's how we create from a new set of *chosen* beliefs, instead of creating from all those beliefs that haphazardly landed in our filter.

A frequent guest teacher at Joy School's live and online events is my brilliant friend don Miguel Ruiz, Jr. His contagious vibration of peace and elevated consciousness is exemplified in this affirmation he shares: "Today I will become aware of my beliefs, realizing that I can discard those that no longer serve me." What a powerful ticket to our joy to know we can simply drop our convictions that aren't serving us—deliberately *un*-believe those things that cause our energy to plummet instead of elevate.

James Allen—one of the pioneers of the self-growth movement back in the 1800s, best known for his book *As a Man Thinketh*, has famously said, "The soul attracts that which it secretly harbors—that which it loves, and also that which it fears."

Marianne Williamson and lots of other New Thought superstars and *Course in Miracles* teachers have echoed this idea that all of life is a dance between love and fear, and we can all probably recognize that those are our two most powerful human emotions, and therefore they're our most powerful attractor-magnets. We're all constantly manifesting a mix of things with the energetic signature of whatever we've previously loved and feared, because our emotions are what pull our attention in different directions, and we create whatever we feed our attention into. We have an emotion, it grabs and directs our attention, and then our attention generates a vibratory frequency that goes into the Out There—and creates our next set of external circumstances. Understanding this cycle is critical to our joy upgrade because it shows us that all we need to do is focus on creating an inner landscape that vibrates more with love than it does with fear.

As we've discussed, the majority of what we fear today is illusory. In our primitive days, threats to our survival were everywhere, and in order for our species to exist and perpetuate, our brains got programmed to stay on high alert for all these potential threats. In our evolutionary journey as humans since then, our circumstances have evolved far beyond that kind of existence. But our brains haven't caught up. That's why our nervous systems are constantly activated by perceived threats that aren't even real dangers to us. They're not man-eating predators and erupting volcanoes anymore; they're just flimsy little thought structures. When your nervous system is jacked up, you create from fear. And when you create from fear, you create more things you don't like. When your nervous system is relaxed and balanced, you're more likely to create from love because love is your natural state. Then you're creating more of what brings you joy—effortlessly.

The only difference between creating things you want versus things you don't want comes down to whether the energy you're creating with is rooted in fear or in love. That's why mastering your observing means calming your nervous system in order to lower the volume on fear energy, so that love can flow in to fill that space. Then you create what you love, not what you fear. It's just the natural, energetic law.

HOMEPLAY FOR KEY 10, WEEK ONE

I'm going to take you through a little imaginative journey. If you'd like my voice to guide you through it, you can access that at the Joy Kit at my website. Otherwise, just read it and then close your eyes and imagine it as vividly as you can.

Imagine a big, heavy, leatherbound, gorgeous hardcover book that's been so well worn that the spine is broken in and you can lay it on a table on its back and it stays open that way. Got it?

Now imagine it's the book of your life and it's open to the page that correlates with where you are in your life's chronology right at this moment. Don't try to get super clear about what's on this open spread. It might be a montage of images, or of words, or both. Don't get caught up in the details of what's there on the page; just acknowledge that these two open pages are full of words and/or images that are representative of your life in this precise moment.

I want you to consider now that if you were to randomly open this book to a page over on the left of where it's spread out open, you'd see some prior snapshot moment of your life. It might be a page of joy and contentment; it might be a page of hurt, frustration, maybe anger. All those pages are back there. You know if you were to randomly flip to a page over there on the left, there's a chance you'd get any of that.

Now consider, what if you were to flip to a page to the right of where this book is open?

The pages to the left are all filled up because the energy that you've sent out in the past has created the contents of the pages that make up the beginning of this book. You're a vibratory creature in a vibratory Universe, so the vibration that you've previously held at different times in your life has resulted in all the things on all those pages. They're all filled up because that part of your life has already been created.

I want you to use your imagination now, to, one by one, turn those pages to the *right* of where the book is open. Again, don't get bogged down with what the specific images and words are (it's better if they're a bit of a blur) but just notice that the first few pages in this future direction are only partially covered (with words, or images, however you've been imagining it.) Notice that there's quite a bit of blank space on these pages.

As you continue to turn the pages to the right, the next thing you notice is that the ratio of empty space to filled space changes. There's more and more that's empty on the page, the farther you go away from that open spread that represents your present moment. As you turn the pages, one by one, you see more and more blank, open space on each page.

The vibration you've most recently been holding has sent out a signal that's been bringing in circumstances, people, and situations to match it. Always, that will continue onward for a bit into the future. I can't tell you exactly how far it will go, or the exact ratio of blankness to filled-in area on each of these future pages, because it depends on how strong the signal you've been sending out has been, and how long and consistently you've held it. But what I can tell you is that the blank portions of those pages are up for grabs. You get to decide what fills them.

What fills those blank spaces is the result of the order you're currently placing with the Universe. That means they'll be filled with whatever best matches the vibration you're holding today, right now. If you continue to basically send out the same vibratory signals you've always sent out, (which is what most of us do, until we take deliberate control of it) you can pretty much count on all those upcoming pages looking a lot like the pages to the left, with some good stuff, no doubt, but also with other stuff you might prefer to be different, better. The details and exterior wrapping will change, of course, but the vibratory essence of the experiences will remain constant.

On the other hand, if you take steps now to raise your vibratory frequency, and you stick with the steps, and you make it a conscious choice because you now understand vibration and how it's creating life for every one of us on this planet, then a new energy will wash into those coming pages. The new energy of your higher vibration will fill the blank spaces with positive situations, pleasing interactions, deepened connections, and abundance in all the areas you'd like to enjoy abundance.

And here's the thing: It's not too far out to the right before the pages in this book are completely blank right now—completely up for grabs! And if you continue to hold this higher vibratory frequency (which is nothing more than your absolute purest, most natural state when you've got your filter cleared up) then eventually that purely positive energy will be what completely fills the pages! Let yourself bask for a moment in the understanding of the book of your life being filled this way. (This is the work you've been doing!)

Next, I want you to consider that the pages to the left (the start of the book that represents your past) hold a pretty consistent vibration. Let that vibration become visible to you in some way that symbolically makes sense for you. For instance, maybe it's a fog that lifts up from that side of the book now, however you imagine it to be in color, consistency, density. Let the energy of these pages take some form in your imagination.

Now look over at the right side of the book in your imagination, the side that represents your future. This time, imagine a different, higher vibration energy, represented again by some sort of symbolism. Maybe it's still that fog or mist, but on this future side it has a different color or texture or feeling. Note the difference between the left side and the right. Make a commitment in your heart that you're going to do whatever it takes to claim that higher vibration on a more consistent basis.

You can reorient yourself back to your present surroundings now.

I hope you felt the truth that imaginative journey symbolized. I hope you're deepening your understanding of yourself as an energetic creature in an energetic world. Cementing that understanding is what will grant you access to the magic. It's the fish *seeing* the water.

Your first week of homeplay this month is based on that imaginative exercise. Every morning when you wake up, imagine that book of your life and imagine that you're turning a new page on a new day. Some things that you'll encounter on this brand-new day are pretty much pre-arranged by the energy you've been sending out, so some areas of the page are already filled in, but not all of them! There's some blank space on the page! You get to *decide* how that blank space gets filled. What kind of energy will you flood onto the page, knowing it's the energy you feed into it right in this moment that will create the experiences that fill in the blanks for that day and begin filling in the subsequent days?

Go back to the images your imagination gave you to represent the different frequencies of vibration. As you go through each of your days this week, stop periodically to check in with your energy. Does your current energetic state feel like the symbolic representation you got for the left side of the book? If so, you'll know that's the order you're still sending out to fill those future pages. Or does your energetic state feel more like the symbolic representation you came up with for the right side of the book when you purposefully imagined a higher vibration frequency? It's always the frequency we're holding *now* that's placing that order with the Universe that's still to be filled. If your check-in shows you that you're in a lower energetic state than you'd like, ask your Vertical Self, *What would be a healthy, self-honoring way for me to elevate my vibration right now?*

Work with this practice for this first week of homeplay and record your observations in your journal.

HOMEPLAY FOR KEY 10, WEEK TWO

For the second week of homeplay, start by journaling a dialogue with your Vertical Self around this prompt: *Taking into account my average vibrational frequency in the last month, what would it look like if I were to wake up tomorrow morning with a noticeably higher Joy Setpoint?*

Whatever "normal" has been for you lately, you want to now consider what it would be like for your Joy Setpoint to elevate even more. If you woke up tomorrow more naturally joyful than you've been on average, how would you walk? Talk? Eat? Dress? Who would you hang out with? How would you fill your time? Let these questions paint a vivid imaginary scenario for you.

Next ask, *Now that I know what it would look like, what would it take for that to be the case?* I know it's tempting to say, *It would take XYZ shifts in my external world.* But by now I know you understand that your external world is nothing more than a creation born of your internal landscape and the energy you've sent out. So, let's look at something more immediately within your control. Let's look at what it would take in terms of your perception filter and where you place your energy and focus.

Returning to your journal, next ask your wise Vertical Self, *What would need to change in my filter—what new belief(s) would I most need to cultivate—in order for me to live this higher baseline experience of happiness?*

Let your Vertical Self answer in whatever thoughts, sensations, memories, or signs come up to be captured. It's showing you personalized guidance on where you can adjust the alignment of your filter's keyhole in favor of your happiness. All the myriad flavors of reality are out there, all the time. It's just a matter of selecting which batch of evidence you want to collect, nurture, and grow with your valuable, magical attention.

This is high-level work. You've earned this ability with all the groundwork you've laid, so trust what emerges for you. Whatever answers you get, trust that your Vertical Self is steering the ship now and pointing you toward a new, upgraded experience of your joyful life. Your homeplay for this second week is to commit to this realignment of your keyhole. You are in control of the thoughts, impressions, and opinions you subscribe to and the ones you do not. Listen to what your Vertical Self has shown you and commit to making those adjustments this week! Whenever you observe yourself believing the old, vibration-tanking thoughts, replace them with the new thoughts your intuition has shown you, understanding that they're just as likely to be true.

HOMEPLAY FOR KEY 10, WEEK THREE

As you've discovered by now, vibration elevation is the single most valuable skill you'll ever learn. It's the key to a peaceful inner world, as well as the key to creating all the things you want in your external life. The most critical piece to keep in mind (because it can feel contradictory at times) is that all your emotions are valid and only want to be acknowledged with your love and compassion in order to be released. Allowing the full experience of a negative emotion can seem like it would lower your vibration, when in fact, it's the *repression* of the emotion that does that. Full acceptance and release will result in a higher vibration than stifling what's true for you. That said, there is a difference between a raw emotion that's come up for healing and a tired, habituated pattern of negative thought. You're at the point in your journey where your intuition will help you with that discernment.

Your third week of homeplay this month is a remedy for dealing with those tired, habituated patterns of negative thought, and it has the ability to change everything in both your inner *and* outer worlds.

We've done some exploring already around the concepts of mindfulness and present-moment awareness. Please open your heart now to the possibility that there is a deeper kerklunk-level of understanding here that could change your life if you were to commit to discovering it. When we're aligned with the Vertical Self, we naturally focus our attention on the moment at hand. We've talked about how almost all of our problems exist in the past or future (and are therefore illusory) so focusing on the present moment is a wonderful trick for aligning with the Vertical Self. Eckhart Tolle advises,

> Ask yourself: Is there joy, ease, and lightness in what I am doing right now in this moment? If not, it's likely that psychological time is covering up the present moment. That's when life is misperceived as a burden or a struggle. See if you can give more attention to an action you're taking, rather than to the result that you want to achieve through it. When you give your fullest attention to the moment, you can't be giving attention to past and future aspects of it that would cause resistance.

This week, you're going to notice when you're having a negative emotion like fear, anxiety, regret, or any feeling you don't enjoy. Ask your intuition if this is a genuine, surfacing emotion that requires you revisit the steps in the Feel to Heal Key, or if it's a habituated thought pattern. The first will feel urgent and alive within your energetic self. The second will feel weary and draining. If it's the first, you know what to do. If it's the second, proceed with this practice.

Begin by noticing how this negative feeling resides somewhere outside the present moment. Regret, shame, resentment, and sadness occur when we move our consciousness back to the past, to some negative memory or old feeling that we've memorized and continue to feed energy into.

An emotion like anger might feel like it's in the present moment, but usually when we're angry it's more to do with being triggered into anger because of a bucket belief from our past. When you get angry about something today, it's almost always because something happened in the past that matches the energetic frequency of what is occurring in the present. In this past scenario you stored the energy of the anger instead of acknowledging it appropriately. So, in that sense, anger is an emotion that's associated with the past.

Fear, worry, and anxiety are examples of negative emotions that reside in the future. They happen when we've moved our consciousness into a future scenario that we feel uncertain about, and we've projected an old, memorized emotional pattern onto it. Even though these emotions also arise because of old, stored energies, in these cases we're overlaying our past onto the future.

Most of these negative emotions show up as a voice in your head, and whenever a voice in your head is pulling you into the past or the future, you can know it's the voice of the Horizontal Self. The Vertical Self lives only in the present.

Here's the thing: In almost all instances of our lives, the present moment contains peace. The bad thoughts about things we regret or bemoan (past) or worry about (future) almost always do not apply to the current situation we're in. It's critical to keep this in mind because the present moment is where we are establishing our energetic frequency, the signal that creates our next reality. Establishing a peaceful energetic frequency happens automatically when we manage to focus all our attention on the present moment. Since our habitual negative emotions are about the past or future, staying in the present allows our emotional cork to float. Floating is what corks do, naturally, when nothing is pulling them down. Your emotional cork is no different.

How do you center yourself in the present moment? You do it by noticing the things around you. Tune into your senses and take note of the sounds you hear, the colors you see, the smells, the tactile sensation of your clothing against your skin. One technique I love to do is to run my fingers lightly over my arm or face and notice how nice it feels to do that. Another effective technique is to smile and notice how just moving those muscles in your face into a natural smile shifts your emotional state, even if ever so slightly. It's fun to notice that, and it brings you right into the present moment.

Another way is to revisit the Eckhart Tolle trick of feeling your energetic presence. Focus your attention on the light buzzing sensation in your hands, and then allow that awareness to lead you to feel the energy in other parts of your body as well. Sometimes I like to feel into where I might need a good stretch, or launch into a moment of intuitive yoga. Anything that gets your awareness into your body is a good pattern-interrupt for those negative thought loops trying to pull you into past or future perseverating. The contemplation inspired by Holly Copeland that I shared in Key 2 is another wonderful resource for centering in the present moment, even if you only do a modified version of it.

For those times when the pull of a negative thought is strong and you find it too difficult to ground your energy in the present, try this trick of making a lateral shift: When you notice you've moved your consciousness into past regrets or anxious future projections, you can deliberately *use* your past or future to create a high frequency state instead of a lower one. As the observer of your thoughts, you have the power to deliberately turn your focus to sweet memories (past) or excitement and anticipation about something wonderful that is to come (future). If you notice that you tend toward negative *past* thoughts, deliberately come up with some go-to happy memories you could choose to focus on instead. If you tend more toward *future* anxious projections, establish some exciting, happy thoughts about the future that you can shift into. It will feel unnatural at first, but that's how it feels to break any long-established habit and replace it with a new one.

Here's a recap of your practice for this third week:

1. You'll start by being deliberately conscious of your emotions throughout the day. Be the observer of your thoughts and feelings. (You should be a pro at this by now.)

2. When you're feeling bad, observe whether you've moved your consciousness into the past (regret, sadness, shame) or into the future (anxiety, fear, helplessness, worry, lack of control). Most of us lean more often in one direction than the other, so see which is more prevalent for you.

3. Notice how seductive the pull of that negative emotion is. That's your clue that you're addicted to an emotion attached to a habitual thought pattern. Becoming aware that it's just an addiction will help you see that it's not anything real or true. It's just a habituated thought/feeling cycle. You can break any habit with some commitment and perseverance.

4. Become the observer of this negative feeling. Get clear that the feeling isn't you; it's just a biological reaction to a thought you're allowing yourself to dwell upon. Accept that. Be okay with this understanding, and then tell yourself, *That's not here right now,* and just bring your awareness to the present moment. Use any of the techniques described above to

inhabit the present moment, or make a lateral shift with your attention.

5. Write in your journal about your experiences with this exercise. Include specific examples so that later in your joy journey you can look back and see how far you've progressed with this practice.

HOMEPLAY FOR KEY 10, WEEK FOUR

Your fourth week of homeplay for this month is inspired by a Jack Kornfield meditation I love. Start by setting aside some time for meditative contemplation and journaling. Get into your meditative zone, however that's been working for you. Shake the Etch A Sketch. Then think about your life and take note of all the things around you or within you that you don't completely understand. We tend to dismiss them, but there are so many mysteries surrounding us at all times! Sure, there are some folks who fully understand how electricity works, but most of us don't. We just like the convenience of utilizing it at the flip of a switch. How does your cell phone do all the miraculous things it does? How does your body digest your food? Journal about these observations, then from there, let your mind wander to even bigger mysteries that no person can claim full comprehension of—mysteries about death, about space and the cosmos, about time and the potential for other dimensions of reality.

Do not work to figure out these mysteries; simply consider them and appreciate them with wonder and delight. Find the glimmer of excitement in the not-knowing. Remember how intoxicating it was to see a magician when you were a child? Be that child again and find the enjoyment in the seeming magic that goes on all around you. Once you've practiced being at peace with the not-knowing and journaling about it, you're ready to take this attitude into your daily life. Make a point each day this week to seek out mysteries and pause to enjoy them. Record your daily observations in your journal.

Take note, also, of the more mundane unknowable things with which you typically negatively concern yourself. Will you get the promotion? Will your toddler cooperate at nap time? Will that online cutie respond to your invitation to connect? Now that you've practiced making peace with the unknowable, see if you can transfer that skill onto these unavoidable issues that surface in your daily life. Can you enjoy the mystery inherent in these unknowable potentialities? Can you trust that whichever way things go, it's always a gift for you on some level?

I'll leave you with this poetic musing by a.h. walker:

Immersed

In

Imaginative

Inquisitiveness

I

Elongate

Inside

Embrace What Is

> *"Nothing ever goes away until it teaches us what we need to know."*
>
> —PEMA CHÖDRÖN

One of my most influential teachers has been Byron Katie. Her bestselling book *Loving What Is* captures the essence of this month's key. I like the word "embrace" for our purposes this month more than "love" because when we're in the thick of a challenging situation it can feel like too big a stretch to say we love it, but by keeping a higher consciousness perspective we can remind ourselves that even this is a circumstance we'll be better off embracing than fighting against. We've already explored the ironic truth that embracing an uncomfortable *emotion* allows it to flow through us and be released. This month, we'll extend that understanding to encompass all the challenging aspects of our life.

Eckhart Tolle tells a story about a wise man who wins an expensive car in a lottery and his friends say, "Oh my gosh, that's great! That's awesome! You're so lucky!"

And he says, "Maybe."

Then he's out for a joyride in the new car and a drunk hits him and he ends up in the hospital. His friends say, "Oh no! How terrible!"

And he says, "Maybe."

Then, crazy enough, there's a landslide that night and the guy's whole house slides into the ocean. His friends say, "Wow! How lucky that you were in the hospital and not in your bed in your house last night!"

And he says, "Maybe."

The understanding, of course, is that there's really no point in judging anything as good or bad, because life's going to keep unfolding and nothing is as knowable and predictable as we'd like it to be! Everything's a statue with multiple sides and multiple coexisting realities that are all valid and true. There are 400 billion bits of *true* reality in any moment that can apply to literally everything we encounter! Nothing is ever *only* the way it first appears to us from the keyhole of our tiny human perspective.

Your joy training has been moving you in the direction of letting go of your urgency around that question "how is it here?" because the more committed we are to fitting everything out there into our neat categorization buckets of "wanted" and "unwanted," the more rigidly we're keeping our blinders in place. The blinders aren't serving our joy. Taking them off can feel disarming, but it doesn't take long to adjust to the broader perspective and all the joy it ushers our way. Purposefully suspending our need to know or understand things is uncharted territory for most of us, but it's the natural progression from realizing, on a deep level, that our habitual negative thinking simply isn't based in anything objectively real.

When it kerklunks that there's so much legitimate *real* to choose from, you begin to see past the filter, opening your perception to so much beauty and pleasure and richness that's always been there, just not accessible to you because of where your keyhole's been lined up.

It's the ultimate position of joyful empowerment.

One of Byron Katie's famous quotes is: "When you argue with reality, you lose. But only 100 percent of the time." Whatever "reality" you're currently looking at, embracing it is the only sane option. Arguing with it feeds it the energy that is keeping it solid and immutable in your experience. It's only by embracing it that you can release its grip so that you can move the keyhole around to find a better reality to line up with.

When your "reality" is showing you something that's unpleasant to you, you can honor and address the feeling it brings up in you while still putting your attention on asking, *Okay, what if this thing I'm resisting is totally supposed to be happening right now?* (Truth bomb: it *is* supposed to be happening because it's happening.) Can we have that faith that anything that's happening is simply supposed to be, including whatever feeling it brings up in us? It's reality doing what reality does. We can resist it, or we can flow with it. The choice is always ours.

Flowing with it doesn't preclude taking steps to change or improve it. It simply means embracing it first so that the ensuing steps will be that much more effective. It's about aligning with your Vertical Self, where you become the observer of whatever is happening in your thoughts and body. Maybe you feel your head getting all activated and busy looking for answers, or you can feel your heart wanting to close in defense, or you feel your gut tightening or the cortisol shooting through your veins. If you've practiced alignment with your Vertical Self, then all of that is simply stuff you notice. You can stay aligned as the witness to it. You can bring compassion to all of that activity you witness happening in your physical self, knowing that who you truly are is so much bigger and more divine than any of that.

We're always going to be interfacing with this Out There construct—people, situations, responsibilities—the minutia of our daily routines. Every bit of it has the potential to trigger feelings within us. Some we like. We're typically more receptive to feeling those. (Though, in many cases, we push away and deny even feelings we like because of a fear they won't last, or a sense we don't deserve them.) For the feelings we don't like, many of us have habituated ways to block or avoid facing those feelings. (You've been working on overcoming that oh-so-human tendency. Good on you!)

One of my Joy Schoolers recently compared a chart I had made for them to the Serenity Prayer. Take out your journal now and create this chart while I describe it to you. At the top of the page, use a few words to describe a situation you don't like. Under that, write the question "Is there anything I can do to improve this situation?" Under this question, draw an arrow to the left side of the paper and make a box with the word "Yes!" in it. Under that box, write "Great! There is something I can do. That means I can relax, take a deep breath, and take the first step toward whatever can be done."

Going back up to the top of the page with the problem and the question, "Is there anything I can do to improve this situation?" next draw an arrow from that question toward the right side of the page and make a box with the word "No!" in it. Underneath that box, write "Great! There is nothing I can do about this, so I can relax, take a deep breath, and realize all I can bring in this moment is acceptance."

Refer to this simple little chart whenever a situation bothers you. Whichever arrow you follow—toward yes or no—the answer is

"Great! I can relax!"

Embracing what is means appreciating the gift of contrast. Many wisdom traditions talk about how each of us is born with a unique identifier to our soul that's the source of all our magic. Part of that package includes our wounding or our shadow. No matter how deep we feel our shadow runs, it's part of the perfect package and it's there to shape us in valuable, essential ways.

Often, our wounds are our greatest gifts. There was a study done at Google a while back when it was considered a model of the company of the future. The researchers took comprehensive statistics on all of Google's employees and found that its best, brightest, most innovative people—the shining stars of Google—were not the ones with the fanciest degrees, or the most relevant prior work experience. But they were all people who had gone through some form of significant pain or challenging obstacle and had come through it.

In our human-y Horizontal-Self moments, we tend to think, *If only I could change that one thing Out There—that one thorn in my side—then I could be happy.* We fail to take into account that if the vibration we're emitting stays the same, whatever we've attracted Out There that we don't like—even if we vanquish it somehow—that consistent vibration is just going to pull in some other circumstance that feels just like the thing we finally got rid of. The *thing* Out There wasn't ever the real problem; it was just the latest symptom of the problem. The frequency within us that attracted it is the problem. If we don't change the frequency, we'll just attract it again, or something similar.

The secret to shifting the frequency is to drop the resistance. You've suffered. You've faced challenges and maybe you're facing some now. Can you embrace all of this now, with authenticity and compassion for your sweet self, so that we can continue elevating your personal vibration and establishing your new, much-improved Joy Setpoint?

• • •

"The most beautiful people we have known are those who have known defeat, known suffering, known struggle, known loss, and have found their way out of the depths. These persons have an appreciation, a sensitivity, and an understanding of life that fills them with compassion, gentleness, and a deep loving concern. Beautiful people do not just happen."

—ELISABETH KÜBLER-ROSS

You—beautiful person—did not just happen. You were artfully designed to be right where you are right now in this gorgeous moment. Our oh-so-human tendency is to view our challenges and upsets as the things we most want to avoid. What if we turned that equation around and learned to welcome each of them as a valuable opportunity for true and lasting healing, and blissful growth and expansion?

Every Challenge Is a Portal

I want you to start recognizing that every uncomfortable situation you face is a portal through which you can enter a newly healed and transformed point in your life. Instead of slamming the door on this portal, as you've been conditioned to do, you'll instead approach this valuable opening with curiosity and readiness to do what needs to be done. The portal is always a window to an old trauma; it's showing you what's stored in your filter as stuck, stagnant energy. Once you've located it, thanks to it vibrationally matching some current-day situation that's pointed it out for you, you can give it the attention and compassionate awareness that you were unable to give it at that prior point in your life when it got lodged there. It's such an exquisite system!

According to physician and trauma expert Dr. Gabor Maté, "You have to understand, trauma is not that bad things happen to people. Because like the Buddha said 20,000 years ago, life brings suffering. So that's just the norm. You know, people die, your pet dies. People might reject you. Somebody you love may not respond positively. You might suffer illness. This is painful. So life brings pain, but pain is not the same as trauma. Pain becomes traumatic when that pain isn't resolved, when it doesn't get the support it needs, when it isn't metabolized, when we don't learn and grow from it. Trauma is not what happens to us. Trauma is what happens inside us."

You, darling reader, are beyond the point now where the circumstances of your Out There, no matter how challenging, can traumatize you. You have been building your skills to the point where your resilience and baseline vibratory state are simply too high for that to happen. If you've stored the energy of trauma in the past, you're now taking regular steps for releasing that stored trauma and your energy is growing lighter every day. Thanks to the spiral, you can forever continue this valuable work, becoming ever more conscious and joyful!

My beautiful friend, the famous spiritual musician Karen Drucker, calls it "moving the boulders." On my Do Joy! podcast recently she talked about how the stream of ease and flow is always running through us, but we put up boulders in the stream. (In my lingo, the boulders are those obstructions we've talked about that keep us from aligning with our Vertical Selves.) We need to spot the boulders we've put in our stream so that we can commit to moving them out of the way. During this conversation I made a small, casual remark about how I feel so lucky to get to sing in the Agape Spiritual Center's Global Choir, as I feel I'm far less talented than most of my choir mates. Karen took the opportunity to school me, pointing out that every tiny judgment we put on ourselves is blocking the stream. Even our innocuous-seeming judgments are pebbles that can pile up to block the stream as egregiously as the larger boulders do.

Your boulders (and your pebbles) are the spots of resistance where you're not embracing reality right now, where you're wishing things were different. We all have them; they're nothing to be ashamed of. Bringing them into our awareness gives us the opportunity to make them a statue we can walk around. What fresh perspective might be waiting on the other side of the statue that would allow you to soften in your resistance to this thing? Take out your journal and ask your Vertical Self, *Where do I still have some boulders in my stream, and if not boulders, what are the pebbles? What in my life am I resisting?*

Whatever emerges for you, love that. Love it right where you are, just as it is. As you've seen by now, that's the magic step that allows these boulders to roll gently out of our stream of flow and ease. Buddhists believe whatever is troubling you is here to serve you. Think of the most serene, peaceful Buddha representation you can call to mind, probably some type of artwork you've seen. Imagine yourself embodying that Buddhist serenity and see if that helps to lighten the resistance you're experiencing to your boulders or pebbles.

Taoist and Buddhist traditions have a practice of sensing a smile up in a wide-open sky, and then inviting that smile energy to come into them. They imagine they can smile with their whole face, smile with their throat, their heart, and all of their internal organs. Elizabeth Gilbert made this practice famous in *Eat, Pray, Love* with the suggestion to "smile in your liver." Try it. Hold the thought of the situation you're resisting while smiling in your liver. Any little trick that lets you feel lighter in your resistance is a powerful manifestation tool for creating a more joyful life!

HOMEPLAY FOR KEY 11, WEEK ONE

Select one of the boulders or pebbles you identified. It could be anything, big or little, that's here right now as part of your existence, that you feel is blocking the stream of your wellbeing.

Take out your journal and ask your Vertical Self, *If this thing were a generous gift from a loving Universe that adores me, what would I need to recognize in order to see it that way?*

You're asking, "What's good about this thing?" Instead of looking at what you don't like about it, which is probably what you've been doing, you want to make a list—even if it's a short list, or even if you can only come up with one thing but it feels genuine—for why this is actually a gift in strange wrapping paper. Walk around the statue.

It's not like you have to get to the point of "I'm so glad this is happening." You don't have to be thankful for the situation on the whole for this exercise to work; that's too big a leap for most of us to make. You just have to find the tiny sliver where there is some genuine gratitude, so that you can consciously start bringing your attention to that piece of it every time you feel the energy flowing in a negative direction around this thing.

You might be thinking, *Wait a minute, Lisa said what I give gratitude for is what I get more of. I don't want more of this, so why am I giving gratitude for it?* That would be a valid point (that you may or may not have been making in your mind just now.) The idea is to thank the Universe in such a way that invites closure by finding the gift and giving gratitude for that aspect alone. You're telling the Universe, "Yep, I see what you did there. I receive that. Thank you." And then make sure you truly do receive it. Often, the gift is an insight about yourself and that is always valuable information! If this situation is allowing you to recognize an energetic order you've been placing with the Universe, so that you can now start placing a different order, that is truly a gift to be grateful for!

You'll know your gratitude is authentic when you feel your nervous system calm down a bit around this issue. A relaxed nervous system loosens the energetic grip that you've had on this thing that you don't want. Gradually then, the energy of love (the energy of your true nature) can flow in to fill the void where you released that fear-based energy. I'm using the term "fear-based" now to represent any of those emotions that jack up your nervous system—any kind of anxiety or displeasure.

In Joy School, I teach the still-pertinent insights of nineteenth century philosophical writer James Allen, who wrote "The more tranquil a man becomes, the greater his success, his influence, his power for good." (We'll forgive James Allen's sexist language since he said this stuff way before sexist language was a thing.) He also said, "They who have conquered doubt and fear have conquered failure." That's solid wisdom right there, and it's been around for so long for those higher-consciousness souls who were ready to hear it, even back then.

Once you've done this dialogue with your Vertical Self and loosened up the resistance that's been keeping this unwanted thing in your experience, your job is to maintain that frequency! Every time you feel the tug of the low-vibe thoughts and fears around this issue, redirect your attention onto the sliver of gratitude you dug up. This isn't about pasting a smiley-face-sticker over a cesspool; positive thinking never works when it contradicts your true feelings and beliefs. Your subconscious isn't an idiot, remember? The point is to deliberately funnel your attention in such a way that you see the true, fuller picture of this situation; not just the part you've been hating. That's how you flatten out the intense negative response you've been having to this thing and get your attraction-point on it nullified a bit.

Remember, whatever gets your big energy is going to grow. Whatever you pour a lot of your love, gratitude, and passion into—probably that would be the good stuff in your life—is likely to stay in your life and even multiply. Yay! You've got a strong point of attraction there from all that positive energy you're giving it through your valuable attention. Celebrate that stuff till the cows come home!

Likewise, however, whatever you hate, whatever bugs the heck out of you, whatever you complain incessantly about is also likely to stay in your life and multiply because you've got a strong point of attraction on it. It's simply energetic law that your attention creates the magnet that determines what stays prominent in your experience. So, this week's homeplay is to help you get closer to neutral about that thing you don't like. If you can find a sliver of where it's actually good, maybe even to your benefit, it drains the bigness of the energy out, reducing the magnetic pull. Ideally, you want to move toward a state of neutrality on it. The things you don't give energy to are always going to diminish and eventually fade out of your experience. They have to. You can literally starve them into nonexistence by refusing to feed them your attention.

If the cute trick of smiling in your liver helps you, use it! But I also invite you to let your intuition show you what kind of pattern-interrupt might best fit the situation you're dealing with. I'll share the example of a little thing that came to me when I was still working to heal the heartbreak I referenced earlier with some members of my family of origin. Whenever my mind would pull me toward the pain I still could not comprehend these family members wanting to inflict upon me, I'd put my hand over my heart, where the pain was strongest, and use my fingers to make the motion of physically pulling the pain out of my heart center, into my hand. I'd hold my cupped hand in the air and imagine a flame of transmutation. I'd say, out loud, "I release this pain for transmutation." I'd watch, in my imagination, while the fire transmuted the pain into love and understanding, and then I'd place my hand back on my heart to allow that transmuted energy to settle back in.

The sliver of gratitude I'd discovered was the realization that the pain was simply an indicator of love. It was grief over losing these people I loved from my life. I'm grateful for having loved them and appreciate the psychiatrist Colin Murray Parkes's assertion that "Grief is the price we pay for loving." While the situation brought me immense pain, it also brought into clear focus all the ways I'd habitually failed to honor myself by never having boundaries with them and always putting my need for their approval above everything else. I was able to make a tremendous leap in my own evolution as a result, so that was another area where I found a way to be grateful. The third area is my favorite: my deep vulnerability in that situation allowed the many people I do have in my life who love me to care for me in incredibly impactful ways I'll never forget. The gift in the contrast of being unloved by those few was that I was able to receive the depth of the love I'm so blessed to experience from so many wonderful other people.

Because I'd been able to find these slivers of appreciation, the fire-transmutation pattern-interrupt I described above worked. Not the very first time I did it; I had to do it many times. But each time, I felt a bit more of the transmutation take effect. I'd been learning some energy-healing skills, so I had confidence in the power of my imagination to affect energy and vibration. Please trust that power when you're coming up with a pattern-interrupt to match your unwanted situation this week! Your imagination is the most under-rated, misunderstood tool in your tool belt. You only gain aware-ness of its potential by using it and taking note of its effectiveness! With those family-of-origin offenders, I also began a daily practice of remote healing and sending love to them, which helped tremen-dously. (To use Swedenborg tools, "They are not their hatred." They are in capture.) All I can bring to any relationship is my half of it; staying clear in my own heart toward them helped neutralize the intensity of the pain.

Again, I need to point out that these techniques are not to be used to avoid pain that your Horizontal Self would rather you repress. I know it can get confusing! To continue with my own example, I did a lot of authentic, unrestrained grieving with the support of loving friends and family before I got to the point where I was ready to incor-porate a pattern-interrupt. Your intuition will let you know the differ-ence. And even when you're incorporating the pattern-interrupt, it's still important to acknowledge the truth of the feeling with compas-sion while taking this step to transmute or release it.

To recap your homeplay for this first week of this month: You'll work with your journal and your Vertical Self to identify a thing you don't like in your life, and then identify at least one small sliver of it that you can authentically be grateful for. Every time you feel your energy pulled in the low-vibe direction of resisting this thing, you'll intentionally focus your attention on the one aspect of it that's good. To deepen the practice, you'll invite your intuition to show you a pattern-interrupt you can use, like my little fire of transmutation.

• • •

"Be confused; it's where you begin to learn new things. Be broken; it's where you begin to heal. Be frustrated; it's where you start to make more authentic decisions. Be sad, because if we are brave enough, we can hear our heart's wisdom through it. Be whatever you are right now. No more hiding. You are worthy, always."

—S.C LOURIE

HOMEPLAY FOR KEY 11, WEEK TWO

For your second week of homeplay this month, we're going to add in the advanced step of committing to *embracing what is,* not only in our hearts and minds, but with our actions. Let's look at how actions tie into all the work we've done now.

We know that all we ever experience is perception; from when we woke up until this moment, we've been swimming through a sea of perception. Our mind always wants to know *How is it here?* So we dredge up our subconscious bucket beliefs, layer them all over the objective scene we're in, and that's how we see what we see. That's how we decide "how it is here" in every situation we encounter. (Even though you've now done much work to counteract this process, it will stay alive to some extent for all of us as long as we're here in our human-suits.)

You also now understand that we then, from whatever energy we're holding and emitting in that moment, create the circumstances of our next moment. This dynamic is what has generated the vibrational frequency that has created the life we're now living. The yum and the yuck. It's always simply been a matter of the energy we embody. And it doesn't stop at just how we perceive things, right? We've talked about how our perception of an event causes a thought, a thought causes a feeling, and what I want to *add* into this understanding now is that 95 percent of the time, our feelings are what determine our *actions*.

Beneath every behavior, there's a feeling. That's what causes behavior. It's been proven that our actions are born much more out of our subconscious feeling states, than out of any rational decisions we make. Anyone who's ever gone on a diet and rationally plotted out their meals and then found themselves inexplicably with a mouth full of potato chips knows what I'm talking about. We decide one thing; we do another thing. This is the lot of being human.

Scientists tell us the frontal orbital lobe of the brain is where our feelings come from. When researchers first came across someone with a malignancy in this part of the brain, they thought, *oh, okay, we can just cut it out because it's only about feelings. The guy won't have any feelings anymore, but he'll still have all his intelligence, and hey, maybe he'll be even more intelligent without all those feelings getting in the way.* So they removed his frontal orbital lobe, and it turned out the guy couldn't make even the simplest, most basic decisions. He couldn't decide what shoes to wear, which cereal to pour. He was immobilized, unable to decide anything at all. That's when brain science came to understand that our decisions are based on feelings, not rational thought. The reason we have feelings is so that we can decide which actions to take!

We think we make decisions with our objectively rational mind, but in reality, we make them based on emotions—which, as we all know by now, are often the result of faulty, unreliable, bucket-belief-derived thinking! Further, we know that many of our emotions that come up every day are the results of our compensating tendencies.

It's us looking for ways to relieve the tension caused by our bucket beliefs. See how it all ties together? This is how we keep creating the same kind of situations over and over again. Anyone can "prove" their beliefs are correct by pointing out that they keep seeing the evidence of them. "People are crooks. I can prove it because again and again I've been ripped off, cheated, and lied to." Why is that? Because it's what they created based on their lifelong belief that "people are crooks."

Beneath many of our feelings, there's a need. When we learn how to figure out what that need is, and how to meet it for ourselves, that's when we begin to address the cause rather than the symptom. That's when we truly take control of our lives. This is why you've been cultivating love and compassion for yourself and your needs! The more freely you love yourself and give yourself what you need, the less you'll look outside yourself to demand your needs be met, and the easier it becomes to embrace whatever arises in your experience.

Understanding that our actions are always motivated by our emotions makes it easy to see that learning to *embrace what is* will naturally, automatically lead you to take more positive, effective actions that will result in more positive outcomes!

Take out your journal and bring to mind a situation in your life right now that's difficult for you to embrace. Ask your Vertical Self, *What shifts in perception would I need to make in order to release my resistance to this issue and embrace it instead?* Record whatever comes to you. Next ask, *If I were embracing the full reality of this situation as it is now, what action steps would I be able to identify for moving it in a positive direction?*

You've worked with your Vertical Self enough by now that it will probably show you some actions steps that would result in improvements around this situation. Even if the impressions you get don't seem "doable" right now, or don't fully make sense to you, record them all in your journal. Don't discount anything your intuition shows you. Leave a page open so that you can add to this list of action steps as more occur to you. Remember that once you've posed a question to your higher knowing, the answer can come in myriad ways, sometimes through signs, and your job is to stay open to receiving them. Sometimes, like the chart in your journal demonstrates, the only "action" to be taken is to work toward a greater level of acceptance.

You can probably guess the rest of this second week of homeplay. Start taking the steps! Each day, look at your list and commit to taking some sort of action step(s) that will move this situation in the direction of you being able to embrace it more and more fully. My beautiful friend and bestselling author Paul Boynton built his tremendous *Begin with Yes* movement around the principle that taking action is what allows us to feel better, as opposed to waiting until we feel better to take action! According to Paul, "the secret to having a good life is not about having a positive attitude; it's about taking positive actions." I also love this bit of Chinese wisdom he shares: When is the best time to plant a tree? The answer is "20 years ago," but the next best time is right now!

HOMEPLAY FOR KEY 11, WEEK THREE

We've been focused on embracing your challenges, yet there's much value in recognizing and celebrating all the yum you've created too! For your third week of homeplay, ask your Vertical Self, *Where in my life am I already naturally embracing what is?* Identify the areas of your life where you feel in flow, where you're engaged in some activity that lets you lose all track of time, where you feel full-on embracing of the moment at hand. It's important to remember that the more time you spend in this state, the more high-vibration orders you're placing with the Universe!

Once you have a nice little list of these wonderful aspects of your existence, ask your Vertical Self, *How can I build more of this into my life? What are the action steps I could take to expand this in my experience?* Then, just like in the previous week, your homeplay is to take those steps! Open your calendar and fill it up with appointments with your precious self so you can deliberately block off time for cultivating and growing these things that bring you so much joy. Then keep those appointments! What kind of message are you sending your subconscious when you honor appointments you make with others, but easily cancel on you? Once you've made those appointments, give them the same respect and commitment you'd give to any other event on your calendar. This week's homeplay is a celebration and multiplication of the joy you've already created and attracted into your life. Make it a permanent celebration!

My joy-creating author-sister Summer McStravick calls this kind of self-care "stocking the pantry." It's up to you to make sure your pantry of ingredients for a joyful life stays well stocked.

HOMEPLAY FOR KEY 11, WEEK FOUR

For your fourth week of homeplay, you'll return to a practice of self-observation. Here's a classic metaphor I love that you may have heard: You're walking with a cup of coffee, and someone bumps into you. Coffee sloshes out all over the place. Why did coffee get spilt? The answer is *not* because someone bumped into you. The answer is because coffee was in the cup. If tea had been in the cup, tea would have gotten spilt. If lemonade, then lemonade, and so on. When life jostles us—when life gets lifey and bumps us around—whatever spills out of us is always going to be what's in our cup.

Many people are walking around with cups full of anger, frustration, blame, and that's what comes out of these people when life jostles them. Bringing your Vertical Self to the forefront of your existence is what lets you walk around with acceptance and compassion in your cup. Then, when life jostles you, what spills out of your cup is a high-vibration response that's always going to be more effective in bringing about a higher-vibration circumstance.

This week you're going to be the observer of what's in your cup. At various points throughout each day, you'll ask yourself, *What's in my cup right now?* Whatever the answer, you'll have compassion for you, because you know how to do that now. No judgment about what's in your cup—only observation and understanding. What's in your cup is the energy that's creating your reality. Are you creating primarily from an energy of love or an energy of fear?

Record your observations in your journal, and whatever you learn about you, *embrace that.* It is only by bringing this awareness into the light that we can shift it. Your journey continues, always! Observe your cup with compassion, and if you feel it needs an uplevel, use the tool of your attention, or any of your feel-to-heal tools, to create that.

We have an interesting phrase in our language. We say that we *pay* attention to this thing or that thing. We don't use that word "pay" in many other ways outside of exchanging currency, but it's a totally apt word for what we do with our attention. When we pay attention to something we're giving our most valuable asset to that thing. We only have a finite amount of attention available to us in any given second, hour, or day.

In every moment, we're spending our attention somewhere. And most humans go through life never having learned to manage this spending. So whatever glittery object out there is loudest, or shiniest, or scariest, that's where they give their indescribably valuable attention. If you look around, you'll see that most people on the planet today are driven primarily by their fears; that's just where we are, evolutionarily, so that's what's in their cups. And fears are loud, and ubiquitous, keeping us on high alert to threats that are mostly, today, imaginary. It's not typhoons and tigers anymore that we fear; it's more often threats to our egos, our positioning in society, or positioning with our loved ones. We fear losing what we've gained or not being able to realize our stated wishes and desires. But our bodies still treat these fears like we're about to be eaten by crocodiles, and that's not serving us. It's not serving us for all kinds of biological reasons, but also because it keeps so much of our valuable attention pointed in unbeneficial directions.

You've done incredible work to gain awareness of not only where you're spending your attention, but also what kind of attention it is. This is one of the most powerful steps you can take toward your elevated joy, and one that we'll expand on in the final key.

KEY 12

Live Vertically

"When you transform your mind, everything you experience is transformed."
—YONGEY MINGYUR RINPOCHE

Buddhists have a word for the skill you've no doubt acquired by this point in your journey. It's "piti." In Buddhism, cultivating piti means detaching from the learned idea that in order to be happy, something must be happening to make us happy. Buddhists understand that, thanks to impermanence, whatever is making us happy in one moment might not be there in the next. Same for whatever is making us unhappy. So, deepening our appreciation for this truth lets us loosen our grip on needing to control our experiences, needing to find that next happy-maker out there, and needing to cling desperately to whatever happy-makers we've managed to attract into our current situation.

A person who has cultivated the Buddhist quality of piti will still feel the effects of transitory emotions based on situations, but at the same time, they'll have a heightened recognition of the nature of impermanence, so that the perpetual grasping for wanted things and avoidance of unwanted things just becomes lighter. In Joy School lingo, it's remembering that we're just pushing pieces around the game board. Some rolls of the dice are going to move us ahead in the game, and some are going to set us back in the game, but we remember it's always just a game. Enjoying the playing of the game is how we win it.

What we think is a bad thing can be a good thing in the next moment, and vice versa. And even when things stay good or bad, they don't stay in our experience. Buddhists say, "The bad news is that nothing lasts. The good news is that nothing lasts." In Buddhist teachings, there's a caution around wanting to attain enlightenment in order to be happy because they know the equation is the other way around. Discovering the bliss of nonattachment, discovering how to be happy, is what then leads to enlightenment (and, ironically, more authentic happiness.)

A little story of Buddhist origin that I use in my trainings goes like this:

> A wise man (it always starts with a wise man in Buddhism!) lives in a village and one day a guest to the village comes to him and asks, "I'm thinking of moving here. What's it like here?"
>
> The wise man says, "Hmmm. Tell me. What's it like where you live now?"
>
> The guy says, "Oh, it's terrible. Nothing but crooks and jerks and nothing to do there."
>
> The wise man says, "Hmmm. I think you'll find it's the same here."
>
> The next day, another guest to the village comes to the

wise man and says, "I'm thinking of moving to your village. What's it like here?"

The wise man says, "Hmmm. Tell me. What's it like where you live now?"

The guest says, "Oh, it's lovely. Everyone is so kind and the town is so beautiful."

The wise man says, "Hmmm. I think you'll find it's the same here."

Ba-dum-bum.

It's all about what they've got in their cups. Or, as Anaïs Nin has famously put it, "We do not see things as they are. We see things as we are."

So again, the first step to becoming at choice about what's in our cups is to cultivate the habit of observing what's currently in the cup, and you have been practicing that skill to epic proportions, as well as the myriad skills for raising the overall vibration of your cup! All that's left for you to do is continue your progression upwards on the spiral. You've no doubt raised your Joy Setpoint dramatically in this past year, but the great news is that you can continue with these practices as long as you're wearing your human-suit. You've reached a new level of consciousness now, so once you wrap up this final month's practice, beginning again at Key 1 will afford you a whole new set of gifts and advancements the next time around!

HOMEPLAY, KEY 12, WEEK ONE

For your first week of homeplay this month, you'll repeat the self-observation practice you began your journey with. Go back to the eight pillars of a joyful inner landscape that you rated yourself on when we were at Key 1. Observe yourself this week and give yourself a new rating for each of these traits in your journal. Isn't it exciting to see how far you've come?

If there are some areas where you wish you'd made more progress, please understand that this work you've been doing is truly the work of a lifetime. We never get it done, yet the benefits and the joy are multiplied with each loop around the spiral. You'll continue to spot and redesign your bucket beliefs, becoming ever more efficient and skillful at that. You've undoubtedly created some meaningful changes in your *external* landscape as well. Look at the intentions you set when we started this journey together. Congratulate yourself for whatever manifestations your now-elevated vibration has attracted into your experience!

I interviewed my Hay House author-sister Barbara Carrellas on my radio show many years ago. She's a tantra coach and, among other things, she teaches men how to have better sex. She begins by asking the question, "What was going on when you had your first orgasm?" She's basically taking them back to a time when they formed their bucket beliefs around sexuality and orgasm. And for many, many, male humans (I'm sure many humans across the gender spectrum, but Barbara was focusing on males for this discussion), that meant shamefully hiding in the bathroom or their bedroom, alone, with the door locked, unsure what they were doing, just knowing they felt compelled to do it, hoping not to get caught, feeling super uneasy about the whole thing because someone somewhere along the way had given them the idea that this was *not* nice behavior they were engaging in. Likely a pretty common, scenario, right?

So, what do you do when you're trying not to get caught at something? You hold your breath. You make sure you're as quiet as you can be. You try to get it over with quickly so you can cover your tracks and go back to demonstrating *I'm not doing anything. Nothing to see here.* Right? So, Barbara, being a sexuality expert, would point out that the most natural expression of a male orgasm (or probably any orgasm, but again, she was talking to men) is one with plenty of full, deep breathing, and lots of noise and guttural expression, and the movement of energy through them in the way that their bodies are designed to express sexually. She taught them to slow their roll and *be* in that moment, which was usually the opposite of what was going on when they were orgasming, simply because they'd never recognized or questioned that subconscious bucket belief pattern they'd formed so long ago.

I share this example not because I want you to have better sex (though, of course, I want that for you, too, because I love you.) I share it because it's a nice, juicy, relatable metaphor for all our myriad unquestioned behaviors and limitations. These are the kinds of *aha* moments you'll continue to have now that you're trained in spotting your bucket beliefs! We've all been conditioned to behave or limit ourselves or follow certain rules that have no logical bearing on our current lives whatsoever, and now all of that is up for renegotiation! Until we bring all this conditioning up into the light of our present-day awareness, it continues to run under the radar of our conscious attention.

The guy Barbara was coaching in the above example was married for twenty years and rationally, in his brain, had no conceivable reason to feel guilty about sexual pleasure with his wife, no reason to go about sex in a way that reflected shame around the experience. Rationally, if you asked him about it, he'd say of course he didn't feel any shame around enjoying sex with his committed life partner. But since his earliest experience of orgasm took place in a certain energetic framework, that's how he continued to play out those scenarios, long after it didn't make rational sense anymore. Once he started using his new awareness to breathe during sex and let loose with all the noise and glorious sounds that wanted to come forth, it was whole new experience! Barbara made an incredibly successful career for herself around this kind of coaching.

This is what we do. Until we do the work to challenge our earliest perceptions, they run us. We don't see it, because it's become the water we swim in. We're blind to it. Until we're not. You've reached that superstar level now where you can get excited about the understanding that everything we experience is a Rorschach test! You know what I'm talking about, right? It's where you look at an ink blot and everyone who views it sees something different.

There's a flowering bush on the side of the road. The first human to walk by says, "Ah, the beauty of nature! I feel gratitude and inspiration at this lovely sign of spring!"

Next person to walk by says, "Ah, crap. All those blossoms mean pollen season is here. Allergies suck!"

Next to walk by says, "Those fragrant blossoms make me think of my mom who just passed. It smells just like her perfume. I bet this is a sign that she's with me. How special to get that communication from her today, just when I needed it."

Next one who walks by says, "That bush is blooming. Damn, that means tax season is here. Better get started as soon as I get back from this walk. Man, I hate tax season. I don't have time for this crap."

It's the *same* flowering bush! The flowering bush is a Rorschach test, just like *everything* else out there!

All these potentially limiting associations are happening automatically for almost everyone you encounter. But you, darling superstar—*you* have begun taking control of this dynamic. This is what it means to master your own consciousness. You are noticing your default settings and committing to cultivating new habits for how you spend your attention! This is how we sustainably raise our vibration to fly at that higher altitude!

HOMEPLAY FOR KEY 12, WEEK TWO

There's an expression that says, "If you ask the Universe to move a mountain, be prepared to wake up with a shovel in your hand." You're the co-creator. Now that you've kerklunked to this realization about how arbitrarily limited your life has been, you will be shown the steps to take to keep your vibration elevated, but then you'll still need to use the shovel. You must show up for you!

Take out your journal and ask your Vertical Self, *Right now, taking into consideration all of who I am at this moment, what is in my day-to-day life, soaking up my valuable attention, that no longer feels meaningful to me?*

We change. We grow. What's meaningful to us changes and grows. But our calendars and commitments and to-do lists don't always keep up. A simpler way to phrase it could just be, *what's still routinely pulling my vibration down?*

Trust that whatever comes up for you is perfect. Next, imagine that you gather back to you the attention, the energy, the prana, the chi that you've been spending in this area, or these areas, you've identified. Many of my gurus have talked about imagining there's a magnet at your heart center for pulling this energy back to you.

If it feels comfortable for you to use your arms to symbolically gather this energy back, do that. And if that feels silly, don't. Just pull it all back in however it feels right.

In case you're feeling resistance to pulling your energy back for yourself, I'll say now that I do understand that some things that drag your energy down are things you feel you should not withdraw that energy from. We'll talk about that in a second. For now, just imagine that you can gather back your attention from these things. It doesn't mean you're abandoning them.

And now you have this surplus—this budget of your most valuable commodity to spend in a new way. Next, you're going to ask your Vertical Self, *What is calling to be birthed that truly inspires, excites or delights me? What's a vibrational match to who I am right now? What would be an amazing, precious new seedling—or seedlings—for me to water and nurture and grow with my attention?* It could be a relationship—either attracting a new one or cultivating an existing one. It could be a living space or vacation, a creative project, a new hobby or skill you want to develop. It could be simply a new, even stronger commitment to your joy, your ease, your comfort in this journey. That's as worthy a goal as any!

Just see what your wise Vertical Self shows you, be it specific or non-specific. *What would be joyful for me to feed and grow right now?*

Once you've done that, and before we go any further, I just want to address the most common question that comes up about pulling our energy back from situations that we recognize as unwelcome thieves of our attention.

Let's say you have an unwell child, for example. Of course, that's going to be a draining situation that you would never want to pull your attention away from. But doing this kind of dialog with your Vertical Self can open up possibilities for bringing a *different* energy to it. It can show you where maybe something you've been doing isn't working. When we have a low-vibration circumstance that we want to elevate, we have to be very careful about the energy we're offering it. It's so natural to get pulled down to the level of the problem, but if you've jumped into the hole with the problem, there's no one up top to lower the rope.

When you pull your energy back from a situation that you've recognized to be vibration-lowering, it just means you're pulling back the *flavor* of energy you've been spending there. It doesn't mean you'll abandon the situation. It certainly *can* mean that, when appropriate. Many things in our lives *are* meant to be abandoned and left behind for our spiritual progress and growth; it just doesn't necessarily mean that. It's a case-by-case thing.

Okay, ready to resume your dialog with your wise Vertical Self? Bring to mind the new seedlings you identified that you'd be excited to joyfully nurture and grow. Holding these seedlings in your imagination, ask your inner wisdom, *What feelings will I experience as these seedlings come to fruition?* Remember—the things you want are always really about the feelings you believe these things will bring you, so strip away the details now to discover what kinds of feelings underlie these desires. What, in essence, are you wanting to experience? Will these seedlings bring you serenity? Passion? Excitement? Novelty? Contribution? You're basically asking, *Why do I want this?* Put pen to paper now and see what your Vertical Self tells you.

When you feel complete with that question, ask, *To effectively nurture and prioritize these seedlings, who would I have to be? What qualities would I possess? What kinds of traits would I have?* Vividly imagine yourself embodying these traits as you hold the vision of nurturing these seedlings. However your Vertical Self shows them to you, let these traits be recorded.

The truth you now understand about traits and characteristics is that we all have all of it within us. If you think about any trait you wish you had, or had more of, just the fact that you've identified that, means that this trait is in alignment with your truest nature. If you're judging yourself for lacking it, you know now that's just a misconception, a belief that got lodged in your filter somewhere along the way, and then caused you to create more evidence to support the belief. We all have the full spectrum of every human trait within us. It's just a matter of where we're currently resting on that spectrum. And we can always change that. However you imagined yourself to be just now, this is just a version of you that is closer to the truth of who you really are—who you'd be without all of those obstructions that got lodged in your filter long ago. This is just you, closer to your true nature.

Consider the feelings you identified wanting in that automatic writing you just did. Next, as you've done before, you're going to ask your Vertical Self, *Where do I already have these feelings in my life?* Just like last time, it might not be to the extent that you'd like, or the frequency that you'd like, but you do have something, or some *things,* in your life right now that are already providing this flavor of feeling for you. Let your wise inner knowing show you. And if you have to go back in time a bit to find examples, that's okay, too. If you've created it once, you can create it again.

Next, bring to mind the personal traits and characteristics you identified in that automatic writing session. Ask your Vertical Self, *Where do I already possess these traits? What's going on in my life where I'm already demonstrating this quality or ability or tendency?* Again, it's okay if you have to look into the past a bit. Just let your intuition show you. It might mean lining up your keyhole a little differently. Remember, we all have *all* of it within us. Allow yourself to bathe in the feelings you're conjuring in your imagination and the joy of feeling yourself with these traits. Putting your attention there is how you place the order with the Universe for more of that, please.

We're going to go on one of our little imaginative journeys now. If you'd like to sit back while I read it to you, go grab the audio at the Joy Kit at my website. Otherwise, read through and go on the journey on your own.

Be sure you're comfortable. Close your eyes, let your breathing be natural, and keep in mind that however you see, or feel, or experience this journey, it's just right.

You're in a little boat or raft—some simple little floating vessel of your design, however that looks to you—floating down a narrow stream. It's a stream of energy, and the energy of this particular stream is the energy of all the things in your life that are already bringing you the feelings you most want to have—all the things your Vertical Self just showed you in that last exercise. As you look from your boat into the stream around you, you see these things reflected in the surface of the stream, and from your heart you pour tremendous gratitude onto these things that are already in your life. Lucky you—already experiencing these wonderful, wonderful things! Put your hands on your heart and crank up the gratitude for these things.

If other, conflicting thoughts pop into your head, no big deal. Let them float through. Just keep turning your attention, again and again, to pouring gratitude, from your heart, into this stream all around you. See these things you appreciate so much as you gaze into the stream. And since time is fluid, and you already know you have the power to create such wonderful things, let some of those future seedlings you identified earlier start appearing in this stream now, too. It's all the same flavor of feeling, after all. Go ahead and shower these future circumstances with that same gratitude you've been pouring into the stream.

All this attention that you're giving to this feeling is causing the energy stream to rise now, and you notice that the shoreline on both sides of you has gotten much further from your boat. You've fed the energy of these high-vibration aspects of your life so well that you've actually expanded the stream. It's a wider stream now. Keep feeding this energy for a few more moments with your focused attention, and notice how the stream continues to get wider and wider.

Now you're in a big, wide stream. It's beautiful here. So tranquil. The weather's perfect. Next, I want you to bring to mind all the characteristics and traits that you already possess for creating beautiful things. These are the traits that you identified in your journaling earlier. Look into the stream and see examples of you being these things. Give huge gratitude and appreciation for *you*. Pour that gratitude attention right into the stream around you and these visions you're seeing. You might see examples of you being these things in the past, but I want you to also recognize the fluidity of time again, so that the visions that you see in this stream might also naturally extend into some future scenarios. You see you continuing to be this person—this person that you now recognize you already are—as you nurture the growing seedlings you planted today.

What's their full fruition going to look like? Really pay attention to what it looks and feels like to recognize yourself this way. This is *you*. This is all you. It's simply you living in closer alignment with your true core essence, your glow stick. If any conflicting versions of you pop into your awareness, that's just old, stale, habituated thought patterns. Let them float by. Don't try to push them out because that's just spending energy on them. Just use your deliberate focus to bring your attention back to the immense gratitude and love you feel for you—this truest version of you that's playing out in the energy stream you're floating in. You notice that the stream widens considerably more as you pour this valuable energy and attention into it. Spend a few moments with this imagining before going on.

With all the energy and attention you've been feeding into this body of water, it is just an immense river now. You can barely see the shorelines on either side. Up ahead, you see an island. The island has sprung up out of the energy you put into this waterway. Approach this island and let your little vessel bump up and rest comfortably on its sandy beach. This is the island where all the seedlings you've planted have come to full fruition, fed by the rich, nourished energy stream that surrounds it.

Go explore this island and immerse yourself in the feeling state, remembering the feeling state is what you're primarily after. The details of what's sprouted here may be a precise match to what you originally envisioned. Or, the seedlings might have matured in ways that are a surprise to you. Don't try to control the setting here so much as simply allow it to emerge. The important thing is that whatever has come from the seedlings, it absolutely brings you the feelings that you ordered up from the Universe. Stay here for a bit of exploring before you move on.

Whenever you feel complete, gently move your awareness back to the room you're in and spend some time journaling your thoughts, feelings, and impressions. I'll wait.

How does your energy feel right now? Do you notice a high-vibe frequency? Any amount of time that you can spend in this frequency is time spent placing *this* order with the Universe. You know how to do it now, so there's no reason for you not to be always creating all the beauty, joy, and magic you can stand—in both your internal and external worlds! Your homeplay for this second week of this final month is simple. Just return to this imagination tool as much as you possibly can. Bring it to mind as you drift off to sleep each night. Put yourself in your precious little boat on this scrumptious energy river. Visit your island. Go there in your imagination whenever you have a moment to yourself this week. It's a personalized tool you now own for elevating your vibration at will.

> I sometimes forget that
> I was created for joy
> My mind is too busy
> My heart is too heavy
> Heavy for me to remember
> that I have been
> called to dance
> the sacred dance for life
> I was created to smile
> to love
> to be lifted up
> and lift others up
> O sacred one
> Untangle my feet
> from all that ensnares
> Free my soul
> That we might
> Dance
> and that our dancing
> might be contagious.
>
> —HAFIZ

HOMEPLAY FOR KEY 12, WEEK THREE

You have set powerful forces in motion, darling reader. Your sub-conscious now understands that you are serious about your pursuit of higher consciousness and elevated vibration. Your intuition will now continue pointing you toward opportunities for letting go of energies that no longer serve you to make space for more of what does.

Here's a metaphor I use in Joy School for this continuing evolution of souls who have already done much work toward elevating con-sciousness. Imagine a clear glass, and at the bottom is mud, sludge. We'll let that represent all the stored away traumas—the biggies and the littles—all the feelings we didn't get to process at prior points in our lives, simply because we didn't have the emotional maturity, or the logic, or the personal bandwidth at that time. All of us humans have a glass like this because all of us, as kids, got some sort of mes-saging that it's better to shut down our feelings than allow them to move through us as they're meant to do. Even the most basic parental message of "Don't cry" points to the universality of this dynamic.

So, we all store away this muck that we're visualizing now as mud in the bottom portion of the glass. When we do the work that you've been doing this past year—the work of truly understanding and lov-ing ourselves with all our feelings and showing ourselves compas-sion—we're bringing in the light. Let's envision that light as pure, crystal clear, clean water being poured into the glass to the point of overflowing. What's going to happen? First, it will just thin out the mud, right? It won't be as gunky and thick because we've added this nice clear water to it. If we keep pouring more water into the glass (what you've been metaphorically doing) eventually much of the muck is going to be pushed up and out. It's going to get displaced by the clean, clear water, right?

This is what the spiritual journey is. And it can take years, or a whole lifetime, but we have to just keep pouring in the love and light—the clear, clean water—as more and more of the muck gets displaced! Rating yourself on the pillars of a joyful inner landscape (which are really the pillars of higher consciousness) showed you how much muck you've displaced from your glass this year! Good on you! You're now reaping the benefits of a mostly clear, gorgeous, sparkling glass of water. And . . . because you're human, you might still have a bit of old, hardened sludge down in the bottom of your glass.

Here's how it's likely to play out going forward. You might go through many days, weeks, or even months or years without anything seriously triggering you. Then, it happens. Some event or person does something that bumps into the glass. And when they do, the impact is just enough to dislodge some of the muck that had hardened and gotten stuck down in the bottom.

Since you're still doing the work of continuing to pour love and light into the glass, that bit of dislodged muck is going float up to the surface. You'll feel it as a discomfort, maybe a feeling of sadness, or anger, or frustration. You know that if you resist the feeling, deny it, you'd just be shoving it back down into the glass. So you stay aware of the process, and even celebrate it, welcome it maybe. Most importantly, you treat this discomfort with compassion and love. And then, that bit of muck gets to flow out of the glass. It's released and replaced by the light and love that you're now conditioned to continually pour in.

Our human minds like to understand what each bit of muck represents and how it got there, and there's nothing wrong with looking at that. But it's not necessary for the releasing. All that's necessary is that whatever feeling is coming up, we love ourselves right there. Or if we can't, we let others help us, or we come share it at Joy School and let our groupmates love us hard enough that we move into compassion for ourselves.

For everyone on this spiritual path, the un-gunking is a lifelong journey, but one that gets more joyful and blissful and rich as we travel it. Life is unlikely to ever stop throwing us curveballs, but the clearer our glass, the more we become a magnet for joy and peace and good things. That's the whole Law of Attraction aspect. If we're attracting anything into our experience that we don't like, it's just because some bit of muck is still in the glass being the magnet for that—maybe stuck way down at the bottom, buried in our subconscious. The only way to dislodge it is to keep bringing in the light, the love, represented in our little visual by the pure, clear water.

Let's see if we can get the glass a tad clearer now. Take out your journal and ask your Vertical Self, *What old, hardened bit of muck might still be stuck in the bottom of my glass?*

Sometimes it's the remnants of a very old wound that we believe we've addressed, yet it was painful enough that there's still healing left to do. One of my teachers used to say, "If the wound is deep, you will have to heal it many times." Let your intuition show you what bit of muck might be hardened in your glass now.

To continue with the example of my family-of-origin issue, I'd been clearing that desperate need for their approval and validation my whole life, but there was still an unhealthy chunk stuck down there apparently, so the Universe gifted me with an experience that bumped against the glass hard enough to dislodge it. It hurt coming up to the surface, so it was tempting to shove it back down, but I know better so I used the tools I've been sharing with you to release it. I was surprised to find I still carried that frequency since I'd done so much to heal it already. But I couldn't have attracted that experience if some remnant of the magnet hadn't been there, and often our family-of-origin wounds are the deepest and most in need of repeated healing. As we've discussed before, our negative experiences and feelings are always messengers that offer us opportunities to move in a positive direction. (In this case, it moved me in the direction of a long-overdue uplevel to my boundaries.)

Keep in mind that even though these painful experiences are messengers, it doesn't mean we need to decipher a detailed message. Chasing the message with our intellect can potentially just distract us from feeling the feeling. The whole intellectual picture might reveal itself to us, or the message might simply be that the feeling is here, and therefore requires our attention. Sometimes the feeling just needs to be welcomed and felt, with love and with no judgment. There could be hundreds of accumulated reasons we're triggered in this area, hundreds of times we've repressed that emotion. We don't need to review them all. We just need to give the feeling the space, attention, and compassion it deserves.

The feeling could also serve as a signal about a change you need to make or some action you need to take, but the more you allow and embrace the feeling, the more clarity you'll get around that directive. Without the usual defensiveness and reactivity, your intuition will be clearer, and you'll be much more effective in whatever action you're led to take.

Let's get you another powerful tool to use now. It's a two-part statement and the first part is "I love you." (That's you talking to you.) The second part of the statement is going to be unique to the muck bit you identified. This is your opportunity to validate yourself in the deepest sense. You want a statement that feels true and simple, nurturing and clearing. Ask your Vertical Self, *What phrase would best help me to show myself love and compassion around this particular issue?* It will be a statement that starts with "I love you" and ends with the best healing words for your unique healing around this muck. Invite that now.

Your homeplay this week will be to utilize this mantra-statement. Every day, look deeply into your own gorgeous eyes in a mirror and say, "I love you," followed by the specific healing statement your soul gave you. This is how you'll continue to pour the clean, clear water into the glass and displace whatever muck is lodged down there. Saying "I love you" to yourself in the mirror is a classic Louise Hay tool. At her eighty-fifth birthday party, she gave all of us party guests a small mirror with the words "I love you," on it. I cherish mine. I saved this powerful tool for last because many of my Joy Schoolers have found it too difficult to do before they'd laid the kind of groundwork you've now laid.

You now are more than ready to shower yourself with authentic love and adoration on a daily basis. As your glass gets bumped and new bits of muck get dislodged, change up the second phrase of your statement accordingly. That's how you'll digest each newest muck crumb in a gentle, compassionate way. If you fail to digest it, it will only be a matter of time until someone or something out there bumps into the glass again. Whatever happened to break this latest bit loose, be thankful it was dislodged for healing and clearing. There may be times when there's no muck ripe for healing and it feels right to leave off the second phrase. But I hope you never stop a daily practice of looking into your beautiful soul through the gateway of your precious eyes and saying, "I love you."

HOMEPLAY FOR KEY 12, WEEK FOUR

You've likely kerklunked by now on this most insanely powerful tool in your toolbox. It's love. Love is your most natural state, and the more you're able to relax into the love you are, the more authentic joy you'll experience. Your journey has been one of releasing the obstacles to love, moving those boulders out of the stream so that your love for you, for others, and for the world can flow unimpeded like it's meant to. You can feel the truth of that now, right?

Your final week of homeplay will be to wield this supercharged love tool as the manifestation ninja you've become. Whatever you want to call into your life, you're going to write a love letter to it. This is so much fun! If you want more money, take out your journal and write a gushy, extravagant, over-the-top love letter to money! Tell it how fabulous and handy and sexy it is and how you simply can't get enough of it! Make yourself laugh—the lightness of your energy will be irresistible to the Universe!

Write a love letter to the career you want to manifest. The home. The car. The puppy. The better-working knees. The shiny new saxophone if that's your jam. And, of course, it's a powerful tool for bringing people into your life. A romantic partner, a child you want to conceive, an employer you want to wow with your skills and talents, a new friend, a financial backer for the business you want to start. Writing a love letter as though this person is already in your life and you're showering them with your gratitude and adoration is a technique that has resulted in more miracles than I can count. It might have sounded silly to you if I'd suggested it a few months ago, but I know at this point you're ready to make lavish use of this practice!

Before I go, I want to remind you that I love you. Maybe that sounds like bullcrap. I would understand if that's how you receive it.

There was a time in my life when I definitely would have received it that way, too, from an author whose book I was reading. But maybe you've crossed the threshold where it doesn't feel like bullcrap at all. Maybe you feel where I'm coming from with that.

I've spent my whole life striving to evolve my consciousness, and I'll spend the whole rest of my life joyfully doing the same. Because all that means is that I'm committed to moving ever closer and closer to my true, core essence, which I know, inarguably, to be love itself. Yours, too. It's the essence of me and it's the essence of you and it's what connects us all in the oneness soup. Staying aware of that—that we're all just peas bobbing around together in this big old vat of oneness soup—that's everything to me.

If Malcolm Gladwell is correct in his assertion that it takes 10,000 hours of practice to master whatever it is you want to master, then you have no reason to doubt my love for you. I've certainly dedicated well over 10,000 hours to cultivating my connection with that true, Vertical me that is absolute love and joy, tirelessly teasing out and working to diminish those blocks we all have to experiencing ourselves that way. I'll never stop reaching for that next rung, and then the next, in my ability to live from that place. So, when I tell you I love you, it's for real. You're here joining me on this divine journey, and that alone is more than enough reason for me to genuinely adore you. You are loved. You are perfect. Wherever you are in this process, you are wildly, irrefutably, deserving of all the passion and joy and goodness there is. Right here, right now.

The truest *you* was never broken, and never needed fixing. I hope our time together has shown you that, and I look forward to our next lap around the spiral!

About the Author

● ● ●

Lisa McCourt is the author of many books about joy and love that have sold over 9 million copies, as well as host of the *Do Joy!* podcast and founder of Joy School. The thread that runs through each of these roles is her passionate commitment to unveiling and encouraging the love, joy, and compassion she trusts is inherent to the human condition.

When she's not teaching, leading her online joy groups, podcasting, or writing, she enjoys entertaining in her nature-enchanted backyard with her husband, two precious daughters, and friends, singing in the Agape Global Choir, and serving as President of her local PFLAG chapter. With open arms, she welcomes you to play with her at *LisaMcCourt.com.*